Praise for

ANYTHING IS POSSIBLE

"Insightful. Expectant. Illuminating. *Anything Is Possible* offers unshakeable hope for anyone who is walking in the midst of seemingly hopeless situations. Joby Martin reminds us that where our ability ends, God's infinite ability begins. This is a message full of foundational truth, life-giving hope, and sustaining encouragement for every believer."

—Louie Giglio, pastor of Passion City Church,
founder of Passion Conferences, author of
Don't Give the Enemy a Seat at Your Table

"I don't know of another way to say it: Joby's faith inspires me. Throughout the years, I've learned from his preaching, been entertained by his wit, benefited from his pastoral wisdom, and now, in *Anything Is Possible*, I am inspired by his faith. You can sense the closeness of the Jesus of the Gospels reverberating through these pages, ready to extend the same miracle-working power to all who will receive it. Joby is one of our generation's greatest communicators. Joby's preaching has changed the lives of thousands; you'll be changed as you read this book."

—J. D. Greear, pastor of Summit Church and author

"We all seem to be in need of a miracle, now more than ever. But when we ask for a miracle, do we actually believe? Not only that God can do it, but that He WILL do it…for us…today? With the skill of a master communicator and the heart of a devoted pastor, Joby passionately guides us back to the basics of our faith, that *Anything Is Possible*."

—Kadi Cole, executive leader, advocate,
and bestselling author of *Developing Female Leaders*

"Joby Martin's second book, *Anything Is Possible*, will challenge and encourage people from all walks of life. Joby shares nine powerful miracles of Jesus, as well as inspiring stories from his own life, to bring encouragement and hope. Joby is passionate about pointing people to Jesus and helping them find hope in the empty tomb and our God who is greater than our circumstances. This book is a must-read!"

—Phil Hopper, pastor of Abundant Life Church and author

"If the tomb is empty, then anything is possible… What if we really believed that? Joby Martin challenges us with this question in his second book, *Anything Is Possible*, and walks us through the scriptures to point us to the life-changing truth of Jesus on the cross."

—Tim Tebow, five-time *New York Times* best-selling author, founder of the Tim Tebow Foundation

"At a time when doubt seems to be looming, dreams are getting smaller, and hope seems to be fading, Joby and Charles Martin come and remind us in this power-packed, hope-filled book that anything is possible. So if you've been looking to get lifted, if you've been longing to hope again, and if your dreams can stand to get a little bigger, prepare your heart to be reminded that because the tomb is empty, anything is possible."

—Albert Tate, pastor of Fellowship Church and author of *How We Love Matters*

"If you're ready to take your faith to the next level, *Anything Is Possible* is a must-read. Pastor Joby Martin goes to the heart of the issue, exploring how Jesus' miracles have the power to change our lives today!"

—Dave Ferguson, lead pastor of Community Christian Church and author of *B.L.E.S.S.: 5 Everyday Ways to Love your Neighbor and Change the World*

"Joby Martin has a unique ability to make the deeper things of scripture simple and approachable. His biblical insights, practical applications, and real-life illustrations turn stained-glass concepts into everyday realities."

—Larry Osborne, pastor of North Coast Church and author

"Because I have spent my life serving children, I tend to view things through their eyes. So when I read Pastor Joby's book *Anything Is Possible*, I immediately thought: Children get that. But the older we get, the further we drift away from believing in possibility. Jesus never told a child to grow up, but He did tell grownups to 'grow down' when He said, 'Unless you change and become like little children, you will never enter the kingdom of heaven' (Matt. 18:3). Let this fresh and insightful walk through Jesus' miracles via the wit and wisdom of master storyteller Joby Martin rekindle your childlike faith in the Miracle Worker. Whatever your impossible is, give God the chance to change it to possible."

—Dr. Wess Stafford, president emeritus of Compassion
International, author of *Too Small to Ignore: Why the
Least of These Matter Most* and *Just a Minute: In the Heart of
a Child, One Moment... Can Last Forever*

"Do you (really) believe in miracles? In Joby Martin's gripping new book, *Anything Is Possible*, he challenges us with a clear and compelling picture, through nine miracles of Jesus, of how our lives can be changed for good!"

—Dan Reiland, executive pastor of 12Stone Church
and author of *Leadership Alone Isn't Enough*

"If you want your life to stay the same, do NOT read this book. But if you're ready for your mind to expand, dive into *Anything Is Possible*. In a world that seems to be becoming more and more linear and clinical, Joby gives readers a fresh look at just how much is supernaturally possible."

—William Vanderbloemen, founder and CEO of Vanderbloemen

"With the skill of an exegete and the travail of an expositor, Joby Martin gave us *If the Tomb Is Empty*. Now with the faith of a pilgrim and the heart of a pastor, he gives us insight into the certainty that with the power of Christ, anything is possible. Joby looks at the miracles of Jesus, not just to find something spectacular about which to write, but to point us to something much bigger than our issues. This must-read book captures the truth of the ages that with Christ, *Anything Is Possible*."

—Mac Brunson, pastor of Valleydale Church

"An astute reader must always be cautious about a book that deals with miracles. Many of them lead people to desire the miracles alone without giving any regard to the giver of said miracles. *Anything Is Possible* isn't just another fluffy book about miracles that depicts God as some sort of a cosmic genie. This is a blistering siren directing image bearers to the power of a just and merciful Father God. Apparently, *If the Tomb Is Empty* was just the appetizer. Now, it's time for the main course."

—Kyle Thompson, founder of Undaunted.Life and host of *Undaunted.Life: A Man's Podcast*

"Joby Martin writes like he preaches and that means that this book is all about Jesus…but there's a unique anointing in these pages that's surprising. Joby masterfully unpacks nine miracles Jesus performed when He walked the earth and then shows us how, because of the resurrection, anything is possible for us right now. I truly love this book and you will, too."

—Clayton King, pastor and overseer of Newspring Church and founder of Crossroads Camps and Conferences

"If you're feeling disappointed from putting your hope in things that have let you down, read this book. I found my own heart reorient toward the things that are most true, resulting in an inner strength and effervescent joy that increased with each turned page."

—Ryan Kwon, lead pastor of Resonate Church

"Joby possesses a theologian's mind, a comedian's timing, a preacher's fire, and a pastor's heart. I love that he has created a resource helping us see how the miracles of Jesus intersect our lives today."

—Ben Stuart, pastor of Passion City Church DC and author of *Single, Dating, Engaged, Married* and *Rest & War*

"Joby Martin has the gift of clarity and purpose. His teaching, and now his writing, cuts through the clutter to what matters most—and it pushes you to move. He is an inspiring teacher, a motivating leader, and a good man. I'm honored to call him a friend."

—Brian Tome, pastor of Crossroads Church and author

ANYTHING IS POSSIBLE

*How Nine Miracles of Jesus
Reveal God's Love for You*

JOBY MARTIN

with CHARLES MARTIN

Foreword by Matt Chandler

New York   Nashville

FaithWords
Hachette Book Group
1290 Avenue of the Americas, New York, NY 10104
faithwords.com
twitter.com/faithwords

Originally published in hardcover and ebook by FaithWords in March 2023.
First Trade Edition: March 2024

FaithWords is a division of Hachette Book Group, Inc. The FaithWords name and logo are trademarks of Hachette Book Group, Inc.

The publisher is not responsible for websites (or their content) that are not owned by the publisher.

The Hachette Speakers Bureau provides a wide range of authors for speaking events. To find out more, go to hachettespeakersbureau.com or email HachetteSpeakers@hbgusa.com.

Library of Congress Cataloging-in-Publication Data
Names: Martin, Joby, author. | Martin, Charles, author.
Title: Anything is possible : how nine miracles of Jesus reveal God's love
    for you / Joby Martin with Charles Martin.
Description: First edition. | New York, NY : Faith Words, 2023.
Identifiers: LCCN 2022047923 | ISBN 9781546001690 (hardcover) | ISBN
    9781546001713 (ebook)
Subjects: LCSH: Jesus Christ—Miracles. m | God
    (Christianity)—Love—Biblical teaching.
Classification: LCC BT366.3 .M276 2023 | DDC 232.9/55—dc23/eng/20230126
LC record available at https://lccn.loc.gov/2022047923

ISBNs: 9781546001706 (trade pbk.), 9781546001713 (ebook)

Printed in Canada

LSC-C

10 9 8 7 6 5 4 3 2 1

To God above
My family (G, JP, and RC) near me
Our church all around
Thank you for allowing me to make disciples...

CONTENTS

FOREWORD

In 2009 on Thanksgiving morning, moments after I put my six-month-old daughter down from her morning bottle, I suffered a grand mal seizure in front of my three young children and woke up in the hospital. The doctor in the emergency room informed me that they had found a golf ball–sized tumor in my right frontal lobe and I would need to go see a neurosurgeon as soon as possible. Five days later I sat in the office of a renowned neurosurgeon and heard that the tumor didn't look good and would need to be removed immediately. Forty-eight hours later I sat in my living room with my six-year-old daughter and four-year-old son on my lap and sang and wept and prayed surrounded by friends and family. The next morning I checked into the hospital and underwent an eight-hour resection of my right frontal lobe. I woke up in the ICU and progressed over the next couple of days to a normal room and then to neuro rehab. After a week there my wife and I sat in a room with my neurosurgeon and received the pathology report. Anaplastic Oligodendroglioma WHO grade III. At that moment the floor dropped out from under me. We were told this was terminal and that I would need to start radiation and chemotherapy as soon as I had recovered from surgery. Through tears we asked about the prognosis and were told two to three years. I did the math in my head real quick and realized that would put me at thirty-eight years old, Lauren at thirty-two, Audrey at eight, Reid at six, and sweet Norah at two. Although we needed to inform family, friends, and the church of what we had learned, for the next few hours neither of us could speak. We cried, felt power-less and lost, and quietly asked God for strength and healing.

For the next six weeks we did radiation and low-dose chemo, followed by eighteen months of high-dose chemotherapy. They did MRIs of my head every month and then every other month. Each MRI scheduled created an immense amount of anxiety and each clear scan an immense amount of relief. I was prayed over hundreds and hundreds of times and battled to believe that God would heal me while keeping my hands open knowing that my life was His. At the end of eighteen months there was no sign of any cancer, no resid-ual effects from surgery or radiation. Although the doctors would not use the word "healed," that was thirteen years ago now. The Holy Spirit healed me. It was a miracle.

Not long after I finished my chemo in 2011, I met Joby Martin at a conference in Orlando. I could sense in a real way the power and favor of God on him and was happy to pray over him as he approached planting the church he pastors to this day. He has been uniquely positioned to write this book on the miraculous. Not just because he knows his Bible and has marveled at the power of God to break through the natural order, but also because he has had a front-row seat to the continuing miracles God is doing in the people of The Church of Eleven22. I pray that your heart be encouraged and stirred as you read through the miraculous, beautiful power of Jesus in the pages that follow.

Christ Is All,
Matt Chandler

A NOTE ON THE TEXT

Almost all direct Scripture quotes in this book come from the English Standard Version. In some cases I've simply paraphrased instead of quoting directly from a published translation; in these cases, the Scripture will be set in italics.

"If Christ has not been raised, your faith is futile and you are still in your sins."

—Paul

"When I saw him I fell at his feet as though dead, but he laid his right hand on me saying, 'Fear not, I am the first and the last, and the living one. I died and behold I am alive forevermore, and I have the keys of Death and Hades.'"

—John

ANYTHING
IS POSSIBLE

Do You Believe in Miracles?

S o, there I was... (I told you that's how I start every good story.)
City of Jerusalem. A parking lot. A city bus lot, really. One of
the busiest places in all of Jerusalem. It's loud. People are shouting,
honking horns, and air brakes are doing that ear-piercing "phish"
thing they do when you least expect it. Diesel fumes, carbon mon-
oxide, cigarette smoke, and hot asphalt burn my nose. Nothing in
me wants to rest here and take it in. A few yards to my right, a rock
cliff looms. It's jagged and pocked with holes. Some large enough to
drive a car into. This is high ground, and from the time of Melchize-
dek and later the Jebusites, people once lived in those "caves." For
safety. Above us, on the hillside, what was once pasture or possibly
a vineyard, now spreads a Muslim cemetery. Its location has something to do with keeping the Gentiles out.

When I stare at the cliff wall and tilt my head slightly, three fea-
tures stand out. Two eyes. A mouth beneath. No kidding, it looks
like a twenty-foot skull. Older pictures confirm that erosion and
human use have chipped away at what was once much more defin-
itive. In the mid-1800s, Horatio Spafford—who penned the poem
that later became the hymn "It Is Well with My Soul"—was staying
in an upstairs apartment on the Western Wall of the Old City of

Jerusalem, when his house guest, General Charles Gordon, stared out his window at this same cliff and said, "That's Golgotha." The place of the skull. God preserved it. These men purchased the ground next to it. It contains an ancient garden. With a tomb carved out of rock.

This is where it happened.

Jesus, the only begotten Son of God, willingly shed His blood within a few feet of where I stand. And seriously, if it wouldn't burn my feet, I'd take off my shoes. This is holy ground. As buses and people swirl around me, the Scriptures echo. Speaking about the blood. The first is God to Moses: "For the life of the flesh is in the blood, and I have given it for you on the altar to make atonement for your souls, for it is the blood that makes atonement by the life" (Lev. 17:11). The next is Jesus Himself on the night He was betrayed: "This is my blood of the covenant, which is poured out for many for the forgiveness of sins" (Matt. 26:28). Historians record that when the Romans crucified a man, they hung him at eye level. Allowing passersby to spit in the condemned man's face served as more of a deterrent. You could see and hear the agony. I spin in a circle wondering where. Where did Jesus hang? Where did His blood splatter the earth?

Next is John's description of Jesus' Crucifixion, which he writes as an eyewitness: "But one of the soldiers pierced his side with a spear, and at once there came out blood and water" (John 19:34). The combination of the two—blood and water—confirms that Jesus was drowning in His own lung fluid, which also meant He'd tired of pushing up on His nail-pierced feet. Though He managed to do it at least seven times. Over my shoulder and across the Brook Kidron rises the Mount of Olives and the Garden of Gethsemane. It was there, on the last night of his life, that Jesus prayed and His blood vessels burst and He sweated blood. One of the more painful experiences in all of human history. The Son of Man felt the weight of the coming wrath of God and felt as if He would die. From there, they mocked Him, spit on Him, punched Him, plucked out His beard, beat Him with rods, drove three-inch acacia thorns into His skull, and flogged Him with a cat-o'-nine-tails, ripping chunks of flesh off his back and neck. Somewhere close to where I stand, they shoved a spear into His chest, and blood and water flowed.

Payment made in full. *"Tetelestai."*

Years later, Paul would bolster the Ephesians by reminding them of this same blood: "But now in Christ Jesus you who were once far off have been brought near by the blood of Christ" (Eph. 2:13). "Brought near." I've always loved that because left to ourselves we can't bring us anywhere. Later, Paul told the Romans, "we have now been justified by his blood" (Rom. 5:9). Justified. Just-as-if-I'd-never-sinned. An inconceivable notion. Made possible through what Peter called "the precious blood of Christ" (1 Pet. 1:19).

That happened right here.

Heat rises off the asphalt. Pigeons scurry. Women carry groceries. And yet John, an eyewitness, writes, "the blood of Jesus his Son cleanses us from all sin." (1 John 1:7). While the cleansing of our souls occurred right around here, this place is anything but clean. Which is just like Jesus.

Over and over in the gospels we read the words of Jesus saying, *My hour has not yet come.* But, in this parking lot, time expired. The hour came. This is where Jesus drained the Father's cup. Drinking every last drop. Justifying you and me, saving us from the wrath of God (Rom. 5:9). On this storied ground, Jesus walked down into the slave market, looked at all of us stacked up behind bars and shackled in chains, and told the slave owner, *"I'll buy them all."* And when the owner laughed and mocked, *"With what?"* Jesus climbed up on that cross and "poured out his soul to death" (Isa. 53:12). This is the spot where the will of God the Father "crushed" the Son and "put Him to grief" (Isa. 53:10). Where He made His soul "an offering for guilt" (Isa. 53:10). Where He, *Jesus, the founder and perfecter of our faith, who for the joy set before Him, endured the cross, despised the shame, and sat down at the right hand of the throne of God* (Heb. 12:2). Where He "delivered us from the domain of darkness and transferred us to the kingdom of his beloved Son" (Col. 1:13). Where He ransomed mankind. Sinners like you and me.

This is where.

To be honest, when I realized that the most sacred place on planet earth is now a busy bus stop, it bothered me at first. I thought it was sacrilegious. How could people just be walking over the place where the lamb was slain for the forgiveness of sin and not even be paying attention to where they were stepping? How could the place where the most important event in all eternity now be a place where people hurried to get where they were going? At first it seemed so out of place. Then it hit me. This is probably much closer to the reality that Jesus found himself in two thousand years ago than what I had in mind. A place where everyone could see Him on the cross, but few would pay the deserved attention.

Scripture tells us that the blood of Abel cries out from the ground. What's it saying? Well, in short, that we—all of us—are guilty. Condemned. But *the sprinkled blood of Jesus speaks a better word than the blood of Abel* (Heb. 12:24). What's it speaking? What does the blood of Jesus really say about you and me?

"*Tetelestai.*"

In Greek, "It is finished."

He said these words right here, just before He died.

As that reality settles in, I am overcome by the fact that this entire transaction is inconceivable. Why would the King of the universe leave His throne only to come here and die for me? Just being honest—I know me, and it's a bad trade. King for rebel. Makes no sense. And yet, this is where God so loved the world that He gave His only begotten Son.

As the afternoon sun falls, the shadows grow long and a cool breeze blankets Jerusalem, I can understand the dilemma of those who stood staring at Jesus' lifeless body. With sabbath approaching, they had maybe an hour to get His body in the ground. Matthew records that Joseph, a rich man from Arimathea, and a secret disciple of Jesus, went to Pilate and asked for the body (Matt. 27:57). This is always a reminder to me to make room for those who start out as secret disciples. God's not done with them. Pilate granted permission, and Joseph—along with some help—lifted Jesus' limp and bloodless body off the cross and carried Him to a tomb he'd had cut for himself. A new tomb. One in which no one had ever lain, thereby fulfilling Isaiah's prophecy: "They made his grave with the wicked and with a rich man in his death" (Isa. 53:9).

Somewhere beneath my feet, their tears mixed with his blood.

I walk across the parking lot, through a quiet gate, and into a garden. Tall trees create a canopy, and colorful flowers line the meticulously manicured stone walkways. Around me, people walk arm in arm and sing in hushed tones. I round a corner and the garden opens up. Steps to my left and right lead to a terrace below me. Two thousand years ago, an ancient stonemason carved a small stone pool into the center of the rock. About the size of a large hot tub. Cut into one corner is a groove in the stone. Vineyard workers would carry grapes in from the vineyard that surrounded us and barefooted women and children would crush the grapes. Making wine. The irony does not escape me. Jesus was arrested in a garden where they crushed the olives and oil flowed, and He was buried in a garden where they crushed the grapes and wine flowed. The Lord placed the very first image bearers in a garden to walk with Him. Satan deceived them in that garden and they suffered the results of their sin. Then the Lord became sin for His image bearers and dealt the death blow to satan, overcoming sin and death in a garden.

Oil and wine.

To my left is a stone wall. Rather plain. Nondescript. In the center is a hole large enough to walk through. Or carry a body through. At the base lies something akin to a track, or runner, like for a sliding glass door. Or large round stone. The wall is smooth from a century and a half of hands like mine rubbing against it. Touching it. Curiosity gets the better of me, and I "read" the stone with my fingertips, listening to what it might tell me. When Jesus paraded into Jerusalem on what we call Palm Sunday, His followers were shouting, "Blessed is the King who comes in the name of the Lord!" (Luke 19:38). Indignant, some of the Pharisees said to Him, "Teacher, rebuke your disciples" (Luke 19:39). Jesus stared out across the crowd and shook His head. "If these were silent, the very stones would cry out" (Luke 19:40). As my hand brushes the wall, I am struck by the knowledge that this is one of those stones.

At eye level, my fingers come across something not stone. Sharp, even. It's the remains of a rusted iron spike, about the size of my index finger, driven into the wall, to seal the stone by Roman decree so that it could not be rolled back by human hands.

I scratch my head. *Did they really think that could hold Him?*

Some say that this isn't truly the empty tomb; they believe the empty tomb can be found at the Church of the Holy Sepulcher. That's where Emperor Constantine's mother fell into a cave and decided that must be Jesus' final resting place. Soon after, religious devotees started building shrines around it and the building continues today. As does the infighting. I like this one better. Can I state with any certainty that this really is the burial site of Jesus? No, but the signs around me make a pretty good case.

I traveled here with two of my best pastor buddies, Ben Williams and Ryan Britt. All three of us are staring at the wall, and we're not saying much. Oddly, the other visitors have exited and we have the place to ourselves. Which is crazy. One of the most revered sites in all of Christendom, and we're basically alone. I'm about to walk into the tomb when Pastor Britt walks up alongside me, hands me his earbuds, pushes play, and suddenly Hillsong is singing in my ear: "They laid him down in Joseph's tomb."

That happened right here.

I am undone. Quickly.

Then the chorus: "O praise the name of the Lord, our God." Like those that carried the body, I too am crying. The older I get, the easier that happens.

I walk into the tomb, hit my knees, and find myself taking short, shallow breaths. This is the singular thing that changed everything, about everything, for everyone who would believe.

Because this was a rich man's tomb, the tomb had two areas. One was a foyer. A sitting room. The other had a preparation table and three carved-out flat areas, almost like bunks, where the family would lay the bodies. But, to this day, only one is finished. The other two remain raw cutouts. Suggesting the tomb was used exactly once.

Behind me, a tall man walks in. He's maybe six foot six and skinny as a rail. Like 150 pounds. As he unfolds a Nigerian flag, he looks at me and speaks in this deep, beautiful voice, "Hello, brother, my name is Musah."

We shake hands. "Joby."

"What do you do?"

"I'm a pastor."

"Me too."

He laughs an easy laugh, and points at the stone shelf. "We have the same Father. Same Savior. And He is our brother, therefore—" He points at me. "We are brothers."

If it were not true, it would almost be comical. A redneck from Dillon, South Carolina, and a pastor from Nigeria. Two guys from opposite ends of the planet, drawn by the same love, meet in an empty tomb outside Jerusalem. Brothers. Sinners. Saints. Children of God.

We pray for each other. Our families. Our churches.

Standing in that tomb, it struck me that Musah and I had something in common. We had answered the most important question ever asked, and our answer had us standing in that empty hole in the rock. The question has been phrased throughout history many ways but Pilate said it best: "What shall I do with Jesus who is called Christ?" (Matt. 27:22).

This is not just *a* question, this is *the* question.

One of my favorite writers and thinkers, C. S. Lewis, wrestled with this very question in *Mere Christianity*. And his answer is one of my favorites: "I am trying here to prevent anyone saying the really foolish thing that people often say about Him: I'm ready to accept Jesus as a great moral teacher, but I don't accept his claim to be God. That is the one thing we must not say. A man who was merely a man and said the sort of things Jesus said would not be a great moral teacher. He would either be a lunatic—on the level with the man who says he is a poached egg—or else he would be the devil of hell. You must make your choice. Either this man was, and is, the Son of God, or else a madman or something worse. You can shut him up for a fool, you can spit at him and kill him as a demon or you can fall at his feet and call him Lord and God, but let us not come with any patronizing nonsense about his being a great human teacher. He has not left that open to us. He did not intend to."

If Jesus really is the Son of God and He really rose again, and really walked out of the tomb—leaving it empty—then what does that mean for you and me? The choice is simple.

Spit or bow.

When Jesus rose again, he appeared to more than five hundred eyewitnesses over a period of forty days. History records many of those same people died as martyrs—for Him. Including all of His disciples, save Judas.* For what they saw. Put yourself in their sandals. What would cause you to be willing to die for another? Would you die for a corpse? A dead man? A lie? Me neither.

This is the anchor for me. This stone hole in the earth is the epicenter of everything I believe. I am by nature, and probably nurture, a skeptic. I really am. So when I meet the person in my church who tells me about their miracle, for whatever reason, there's this thing in me that's like, "Man, I don't know..." But, then I remember standing here. In this empty tomb. The greatest and most undeniable miracle of all time. Jesus was crucified. Dead. Buried. And on the third day He was raised from that tomb. The first disciples testify to it. The early Church testifies to it. The history books testify to it. I testify to it.

Which is why I wrote this book. A book about the miracles of Jesus. It's the epicenter of everything I believe.

If the Father, through the Spirit, raised the Son to life and Jesus walked out of this grave shining like the sun, then is there anything He can't do? And before you answer, remember, He just defeated death, hell, and the grave. The answer is no. There is absolutely nothing He can't do. That's what helps my skepticism. It's not the little miracles that point me to the empty tomb and help me believe He walked out. It's the empty tomb that points me to the lesser miracles and supports my belief that He's alive. Right now. And so when the next desperate need arises, and someone in my church stops me and asks me to pray for the healing the doctors have told them is impossible, the reason I go to Him praying for a miracle is simple.

Because this tomb is empty.

It couldn't hold Him.

---

* Tradition also holds that John the Evangelist did not die a martyr's death, although it wasn't from a lack of trying. They attempted to boil him alive but when that didn't work they exiled him to Patmos, where he saw the resurrected Jesus and wrote his Revelation.

Miracles are that intersection where the unexplainable meets the undeniable. Where the limited and finite ability of man ends and the unlimited and infinite will of God begins. Where "what is impossible with man is possible with God" (Luke 18:27).

Live long enough and you either have been, are, or will be in need of a miracle. Where we face something that we can't fix and run out of options. As a pastor, I see this weekly. I also see God continually do the undeniable. The unimaginable. The did-you-see-that stuff. I often feel like Peter and John must have when they were dragged before the religious rulers and commanded never to teach again in the name of Jesus (Acts 4:18). I love their response. The Joby translation sounds like this: *You do you, Scooter, but I'm going to keep speaking about what I've seen and heard.* Meaning, *I will not deny what I've witnessed.*

Right this second, you may be in the fight of your life. Where what you see is impossible. Where the scans are bad. Where your prodigal is not ever coming home. Where your marriage is beyond reconciliation. Where that mountain in your business is insurmountable. If that's you, don't fear and don't give up.

This tomb is empty.

And because it is, anything is possible. Anything.

This is not the new age gospel of "think good thoughts" or "I'm sending positive vibes your way." It's the age-old gospel of believe Jesus. And once again, "belief in," or *pisteuō*, stands at the center. That's why I spent so much time covering it in *If the Tomb Is Empty*. Belief is the bedrock because doubt is never more powerful and faith never more weak than when your circumstances are terrible and you can't see any light at the end of the tunnel.

And your enemy knows this.

Let me ask you this—what if the seemingly impossible thing you've been praying for is just on the other side of obedience? Would you act? Would you dig your heels in and choose to believe?

Take Him at His word? Despite your circumstances? I realize this has been abused and I am not a prosperity-name-it-and-claim-it preacher, but I am a Bible believer. The tension I often face as a preacher is convincing folks in my church that the abuse of the false prosperity gospel does not change the truth of the gospel as recorded in Scripture. God forbid we doubt the words of Jesus because of the abuse of the few.

Once again, "belief in"—or *pisteuō* in Greek—is the first step in obedience.

Jesus told the crippled man to rise and walk, and He told the man with the withered hand to stretch out his hand, and only when they did were they healed. What if there's a lesson in here for us? Before I get too far down this road, let me sum up this book in a nutshell—Jesus is alive, right now, ruling and reigning, and He's still doing today what He did when He walked the earth. The blind see, the lame walk, the dead are raised to life. How do I know this?

Because the tomb is empty.

Have I ever seen someone raised to life? No, but herein lies the rub. Just because I haven't seen it doesn't mean it's not possible and He's not still doing it. Don't think so? Okay, do you believe in nuclear bombs? Have you ever seen one explode? Then how do you know they're real?

See what I mean?

When I finished my first book, *If the Tomb Is Empty*, I knew I wanted to walk back up Calvary—also known as Mount Moriah and Golgotha—here to this acre or two of land. To that parking lot. To this tomb. And then walk you into and out of it. Why?

We find ourselves in a world that screams daily that God is a dead, indifferent tyrant content to watch us suffer. That's your enemy speaking and that is a lie from the pit of hell.

Jesus, God made man, is alive. He's undefeated and undefeatable. And He is deeply in love with you.

Anything Is Possible is part two of the story. In a sense, it's the action plan. Or the "what next" plan. Think about it—if the tomb is empty, then nothing is impossible. And anything is possible. This does not mean we control the timeline and the "when" or the "what" or the "how" of any miracle. We don't. He alone does. Jesus is not Aladdin, not a genie in a bottle, and calling yourself a Christian is not a magic wand to wave at your problems.

In the kingdom of God, Jesus heals "every disease and every affliction among the people" (Matt. 4:23). Luke says it this way: "Now when the sun was setting, all those who had any who were sick with various diseases brought them to him, and he laid his hands on every one of them and healed them. And demons also came out of many, crying, 'You are the Son of God!' " (Luke 4:40–41). The question I want to ask you is simple: Is Jesus still doing this?

My answer is "Yes. He is." I do not see an expiration date on the work of Jesus in my Bible.

Here's how I know this is true. When I was a sophomore in college, I got out of class, went to my fraternity house, walked into my room, and checked my answering machine. If you're in your twenties, an answering machine is like a machine that held your voice mail, usually on a cassette tape. And to make it even more crazy, it was attached to a landline. Anyway, I pushed "play," and my mom's voice erupted from the speaker. She was freaking out. "Joby, you have to pray. Your Mimi—" (Everybody needs a Mimi, right? She was my grandma on my mom's side.) "—Your Mimi was having a heart catheterization, and they've clipped her aorta, and she's bleeding out." Mimi was at Marion Memorial Hospital. I don't know why you call any hospital "Memorial"—that's a terrible idea. But anyway, Marion is like a suburb of Dillon, where I'm from. It's smaller than my church. My mom continued freaking out. "You need to pray, because she's bleeding out."

They life-flighted my Mimi to Charleston and the Medical School of South Carolina. I went to my room, I got my Bible, and I started praying. Multiple times in the Bible, Jesus says something like, *Ask whatever you will in my name, and it will be given to you* (John 15:7). Now, if you're new to Bible study, that doesn't mean cash, cars, and prizes. Jesus is not a vending machine. But it still means what it says.

And so I got on my knees. And, in a way that I have a hard time explaining, I felt the presence of God with much fear and trembling on my part. I was just begging God to save my Mimi. Just save her. All I could think was that she was bleeding out in this helicopter. So as boldly as I knew how, I asked God to stop the bleeding. He told me to ask in the name, in line with the character and nature of Jesus. So I did. I asked and asked and prayed and prayed.

When the helicopter landed in Charleston, we got a phone call saying that the bleeding had stopped. For no apparent reason. It was just gone. I got in my truck the next day, and I drove down to Marion from Richmond, and I opened the door in my grandma's house, and there was Mimi just vacuuming. "Oh, hey, sugar. Come on in." All right. Forty-eight hours after almost bleeding out, she was serving me sweet tea and fried chicken in the name of Jesus. How do you explain that? Simple.

Because the tomb is empty, then Mimi can vacuum.

I am writing to encourage you, to bolster your wall, to put all your faith and trust in Him. And stay there. Even when it's really hard. Now let me take you back to one of my favorite stories—which, by the way, was an actual event. This really happened. In the book of Daniel, King Nebuchadnezzar commanded everyone under the sound of his voice to bow down and worship the idols he'd made. Three Hebrews by the name of Shadrach, Meshach, and Abednego chose not to. Can you see the picture? There's a sea of people on their faces worshiping a golden idol save three guys standing in the middle. Nebuchadnezzar asks them, *"Guys, have you lost your mind? Is it true you don't serve my gods or the golden image I set up?"* Then he gives them a second chance, saying, *"If you don't worship, I'm throwing you into the furnace."* Then he mocks them with this: "And who is the god who will deliver you out of my hands?" (Dan. 3:15). Their lives are on the line. Bow or die. But look at their response, "O Nebuchadnezzar, we have no need to answer you in this matter. If this be so, our God whom we serve is able to deliver us from the burning fiery furnace, and he will deliver us out of your hand, O king. But if not, be it known to you, O king, that we will not serve your gods or worship the golden image that you have set up" (Dan. 3:16–18).

Now notice what happens. They obey God and are thrown in the furnace. They endure the fire. God allows it. But when Nebuchadnezzar opens the door again, he and all his leaders gather around and discover that "the fire had not had any power over the bodies of those men. The hair of their heads was not singed, their cloaks were not harmed, and no smell of fire had come upon them" (Dan. 3:27). *And there is another in the fire that is like the Son of God.* Think about it. The furnace was heated up seven times its normal temperature, and yet they didn't even smell like smoke.

I'm writing this hoping and praying that the Holy Spirit will do in you and me what He did in them. That we would believe despite what we can see. Paul spoke to this when he encouraged the Corinthians, "we walk by faith, not by sight" (2 Cor. 5:7).

Faith in what? The resurrection of Jesus. This empty tomb.

*   *   *

Walk with me back through these streets and alongside Jesus and those who followed Him and let's look with fresh eyes at the miracles of Jesus and what they tell us. How they encourage us. How they bolster us to doubt our doubts and believe our beliefs. Don't let that last sentence slide by you just because it's short.

The empty tomb should encourage you to doubt your doubts and believe your beliefs.

And notice, while I'm about to spend nearly three hundred pages encouraging you to believe and pray like crazy for miracles, we aren't simply chasing miracles. We're chasing the One who performs them.

Here's where we're headed. Because we can't cover all the miracles of Jesus, I've chosen a few of my favorites:

1. The wedding at Cana where Jesus turned water to wine.
   - Do you believe enough to obey, and will you do whatever he tells you to do?
2. The paralytic lowered through the roof by his four friends.
   - Do you believe Jesus will carry you?
3. The cripple at the pool of Bethesda who'd been lying there thirty-eight years.
   - Do you believe Jesus can heal you?
4. The feeding of the five thousand and Jesus walking on water.
   - Do you believe even when doubts creep in?
5. The raising of Lazarus.
   - Do you believe Jesus can raise the dead to life?
6. Mary anoints Jesus.
   - Do you believe Jesus is worthy of worship—no matter what?
7. The woman with the issue of blood.
   - Do you believe Jesus is who he says he is?
8. The resurrection.
   - Do you believe God raised His Son to life?
9. The helper—the gift of the Holy Spirit.
   - Do you want to know Christ and the power of His resurrection?

Jesus performed signs and wonders, not just because He had the power to do miracles, but because the miracles pointed to something else. An eternal reality. Restoring sight to the blind, bringing the dead to life, walking on water, all pointed to something greater. For example, if you're driving south on I-95 (or north, for that matter) and reach the Jacksonville city limits, you read a sign that says, WELCOME TO JACKSONVILLE. Well, that sign is not Jacksonville. It just points to something greater. Much greater. Each miracle of Jesus is a sign pointing to an eternal reality that is so much greater than just a demonstration of power here on Earth.

Jesus did this every time He performed signs and wonders. He was then and is now pointing to the Father's heart of God. This is not to suggest He didn't care about those He healed or raised from the dead. Nothing could be further from the truth. Remember He cried His face off at the sight of Lazarus' tomb. But in every miracle, He always had something bigger in mind. And that something bigger was pointing to the glory of your and my Father.

My first book, *If the Tomb Is Empty*, spent seven chapters looking forward to a risen Christ and an empty tomb. *Anything Is Possible* spends nine chapters walking with the risen Christ as He teaches why we can believe God for a miracle (and how to deal with it when we don't get that miracle).

Spoiler alert—I'm about to spend an entire book encouraging you that the reason we can believe God for the miraculous, the reason anything is possible, is because Christ is risen and the tomb is empty. It's the foundation of our faith.

*   *   *

Here, hold my hand. Come with me. Watch your step. Yeah, that's the groove where they rolled the stone. And feel that? That's what's left of the iron spike. Okay, now duck. Watch your head. Welcome to the tomb. There on the left is the little grieving foyer place and over there on the right is where they laid His body. Now just look around. Take it in.

Let me ask you something. Do you see anyone dead in here? Bones? Dust? Anything?

Me neither. And that puts us in good company. Two thousand years ago, when the disciples ran in here, they were met by two angels. I don't know if the angels were sitting or hovering, but when the disciples did what we've just done, they were met with these words: *Why do you seek the living among the dead? He is not here. He is risen.* This is why it's called the "empty" tomb.

*   *   *

Let me launch you into the rest of this book with a question. It's a bit of a gut check. And while the question is simple, the answer may not be.

Do you live this way? Every day? As if this thing is empty?

Turn the mirror. Look deep. Because over the next couple hundred pages, I am writing, hoping, and praying that you really wrestle with this: Do you live in a world where the Son of God still does the miraculous and, because the tomb is empty, anything is possible, even when we can't see a possibility? Or do you live as though God just stuck us here and told us to endure the suck-fest all for his twisted amusement?

Your answer matters. A lot. Maybe you should jot it over there in the margin along with today's date. Now circle it, twice, and darken the letters. Why? Because most of us live on a continuum somewhere between "He is risen and this thing is empty" and "No He's not, and it really doesn't matter," and our location on the swing is most often determined by our circumstances.

Throughout the miracles of Jesus, three things were routinely needed by those who asked for the miracle: belief, hope, and faith. And in most cases, they had very little of any. Like trace amounts. Which was and is entirely okay with Jesus. Every Sunday, I am reminded of this as I stand on a stage and preach to a sea of people who desperately need the same: belief in, hope that, and faith for. These three are the stuff that brings people like us pleading to the feet of Jesus.

Paul told the Philippians, *I want to know Christ and the power of His resurrection* (Phil. 3:10). And remember, he wrote this from prison, so his circumstances didn't really support the words coming out his mouth. But every time I read that I feel like raising my hand and jumping up and down: "Me too. Me too." So, what is that power? For us? Today? Well, for starters, it all starts right here. This empty tomb. This place should shake some stuff loose in us. Change how and what we see. Transform how we pray. How we live. How we love. Because in and through this man-sized hole in the rock, God did a thing, and continues to do a thing, which brings Him glory, reflects His nature, and which in turn reminds us who He is and who we are in Him. And, as we will see, it draws people to Him. In droves. It's a win-win-win-win-win all the way around.

This "Christ is risen" thing brings to mind a fundamental question, and we may as well wrestle with it right here. Because this is the peg upon which I'm hanging this book—and don't gloss over it or start skimming 'cause I'm quoting a block of Scripture. This matters. Paul is talking to the church in Ephesus. Folks like us:

"For this reason, because I have heard of your faith in the Lord Jesus and your love toward all the saints, I do not cease to give thanks for you, remembering you in my prayers, that the God of our Lord Jesus Christ, the Father of glory, may give you the Spirit of wisdom and of revelation in the knowledge of him, having the eyes of your hearts enlightened, that you may know what is the hope to which he has called you, what are the riches of his glorious inheritance in the saints, and what is the immeasurable greatness of his power toward us who believe, according to the working of his great might that he worked in Christ when he raised him from the dead and seated him at his right hand in the heavenly places, far above all rule and authority and power and dominion, and above every name that is named, not only in this age but also in the one to come. And he put all things under his feet and gave him as head over all things to the church, which is his body, the fullness of him who fills all in all" (Eph. 1:15–23).

See that part where it says, "when he raised him from the dead and…"? Don't skip over the *and*. It's really important. Because something happened after He walked out of the tomb. Jesus didn't just disappear into the ether. He's not taking a nap and He's not a disconnected clockmaker God who just wound us up, cast us off, and said, "Good luck. Don't get burnt."

He went somewhere. The question is where? Paul tells us, "And…seated Him at His right hand in the heavenly places." Okay, so He's seated next to God the Father but hooptie-doo. What good is that? Is He like in time-out or just taking a break? Paul answers that, too: "And put all things under His feet and gave Him as head over all things." The reason anything is possible is because Jesus is alive. Right this second. Seated next to God the Father. He has the Father's ear. On the cross, Jesus rendered an irrevocable defeat to the enemy, and now He is seated next to the Ancient of Days and He has all authority. There is no greater power, and no greater love. Nothing surprises Him, He's never caught off guard, and He has absolutely zero worries about you. I know it's corny, but He really does have the whole world in His hands, and that includes you. On this earth, Jesus spent thirty years in private life, three and a half years in public ministry, and over two thousand years in intercession for us. And He is interceding still.

Walk with me out of this tomb and back through the words and work and miracles of Jesus. From Galilee, to the desert, to Jerusalem, and finally, back here. Because the fact that He's not lying over there in a pile of bones and dust is still the greatest miracle in the history of miracles. Exhibit A before the jury that, with God, anything is possible.

Pray with Me

Our good and gracious heavenly Father, as we have been resurrected with Christ, may You continue to empower us to walk in a manner worthy of the gospel of Jesus Christ. Lord, it is for freedom that we have been set free. Father I lift up to You each and every man and woman who is beginning this journey of Anything Is Possible. *I pray that each of us would know deep down at the soul level that if the tomb is empty, then anything is possible. Father, I know that there are folks in desperate situations right now that are in need of a miracle. God, I thank You that when circumstances seem to be impossible, that is where You do Your best work. I pray for marriages to be healed. I ask that chains of addiction will be broken. I ask You that You would heal bodies and minds. I ask that You would restore relationships that have been broken for years. God, You are always faithful to Your promises, and I thank You and I praise You that all of Your promises are yes and amen in Jesus Christ. Lord, please let us be reminded as we walk through the pages of* YOUR WORD *and the pages of this book that You are the ultimate prize. Jesus, all we need is You. You are more than enough. I thank You for the promise in Your word that if we draw near to* YOU *then You would draw near to us. That's what we really need, to be near to You. We pray this in Jesus' name. Amen.*

CHAPTER 1

Water into Wine—Do You Believe Enough to Obey?

Have you ever wondered why Jesus' first miracle was turning water into wine? I know alcohol is a pretty hot topic down here in the Bible Belt, and talking about it really punches some people's buttons. More often than not, when I've heard preachers talk about this miracle, found in John 2, the passage has been used as a commentary on drinking. I just want to warn you—if you think that John 2 is a commentary on social drinking, then you've missed the point of the whole thing. In short, Jesus is pro-wine, and if you don't think so, just wait until He returns. I thought about giving you my thoughts on it here, but to do so seems a departure from the point. So, if you want my thoughts on what the Bible has to say about drinking, I've included a commentary in the back of this book. But whatever the reason for Jesus' first miracle, I sometimes wonder if it didn't have as much to do with Jesus' mom as anything else.

John, chapter 2. "On the third day there was a wedding at Cana in Galilee, and the mother of Jesus was there. Jesus also was invited to the wedding with his disciples. When the wine ran out, the mother of Jesus said to him, 'They have no wine.' And Jesus said to her, 'Woman…'" (vv. 1–4).

If it feels sharp or terse, that's because it is. The NLT translation doesn't do it justice. And the NLT translators even throw the word *dear* in there, but the Greek does not say, "dear woman," it just says, "Woman, what does this have to do with me?" (ESV) By the way, don't ever quote that because you think it's cool. This verse is to be read and meditated upon, not to be quoted to your mom or your wife! And you might say, "But, Jesus—"

Stop. You're not Jesus. Don't ever say it.

Jesus says to her, "Woman, what does this have to do with me? My hour has not yet come." Underline that. Bookmark it. We're coming back to it. In short, that hour is the hour when he pushes up on the cross and says, "*Tetelestai!*" It is finished.

In Jesus' culture, it was a huge embarrassment to run out of wine at a wedding. Especially for the groom. He's had a year to prepare for this week, and to run out so early in the celebration does not bode well for his marriage. Mary understands this, so she taps Jesus on the shoulder. But think about it. Why would she go and talk to Jesus?

Because she knows He can do something about it.

And even though He hasn't performed a miracle yet, she's not forgotten that very first miracle, when the angel showed up in her bedroom and said, "*Mary, you are with child and you are pregnant.*" And she said, "Hey, listen, I know I failed a health class, but there's a prerequisite to pregnancy that I have not participated in." And the angel essentially said, "Well, guess what? It's God's baby. And he's in there. Merry Christmas." Scripture says, *She hid these things in her heart.*

Mary knows full well that Jesus is the only begotten Son of God and He can do anything. Remember, that's what she told the angel: "*With God all things are possible.*" So she says, "*Hey, listen, they're out of wine.*" And then—don't miss this—here's the best advice in all of the Scriptures. She tells the servants, "*Do whatever He tells you to do.*"

Bam! Mic drop. How different would all of our lives be if we just did that?

Recently I was having a pretty intense conversation with one of my children based on some unwise decisions they had made. To make my point that their obedience to me would lead only to freedom, these words came out of my mouth: "If you would just do what I say, your life would be so amazing." And the Spirit of God nudged me. It felt like He said, "Say that again." Does the Spirit of God ever sound a little sarcastic to you? And as I repeated the words I thought, "Okay, God. I got it. If I would just do what YOU say to do, my life would be amazing." Point taken.

John 2:6 says, "Now there were six stone water jars there for the Jewish rites of purification." In the first century, there were ceremonial washings all over the place. I don't know if you've seen the Jesus movies on TV, but there's a whole lot of beach and not a lot of ocean. It's really sandy. Everybody's dirty all the time. When you arrived anywhere you wouldn't have time to shower like we do today. You'd wash your hands, and you would do it ceremonially by sticking your hands all the way up to your elbows into these big stone jars, washing all the dirt off your hands, and then shaking them dry.

Also, first-century weddings would last for a week. Meaning, people had been washing their hands in these jars over and over and over. Each jar held twenty or thirty gallons. Jesus turns to the servants and says, "Fill the jars with water," and they fill them to the brim. And when they had, He said, "Now draw some out and take it to the master of the feast."

Think about the servants. Put yourself in their shoes. They think they're about to prank the master of the feast. I know he's had some wine. You think he'll notice if we slip him some nasty, dirty water? Do you know where their hands have been? Now imagine their surprise when the master of the feast tasted the water, now wine.

Then the master of the feast called the bridegroom and said, *"Hey, bridegroom come here. Everyone serves the good wine first. And when people have drunk freely, you bring out the poor wine."* You know what I'm talking about. It means you start your evening off with a nice local craft beer, but by the end it's nothing but Natty Light. From high-end stuff with a cork to a box. From Caymus to cardboard. That's just what it is, okay? I'm just reading the Bible.

The master says, *"You've kept the good wine until now."* This is the first of His signs. Notice that. It's a big deal. This is the first of the signs that Jesus did at Cana, in Galilee, and manifested His glory, and His disciples believed in Him and trusted Him. Miracles, particularly in the Gospel of John, are called signs because they point to something greater.

They manifest His glory, and that leads to belief. These are not fables or parables. They're actual historical events. I once heard somebody explain miracles in regard to dimensions. Like this— imagine you lived in a two-dimensional world. All you had was length and width, so you lived on this piece of paper, and you're a stick figure. And if there was a line across the piece of paper, when you got to it, it would be impossible and impassable. But if you were a three-dimensional person, you're like, "It's not even hard. Watch this, you just step over it." And in the two-dimensional world, you would see the three-dimensional person step over and be like, "It's a miracle." So what if the creator of all things just has more dimensions than we do? And all we can do is our five senses and the laws of nature? And so He's like, *"Look, this isn't even hard to do…If I spoke water into existence, I can switch it to wine, or walk on it, or make it stop, or whatever I want."* You know what I mean?

Yale physicist Robert Adair proved mathematically and scientifically that it's impossible to hit a ninety-mile-an-hour fastball. He measured all the things, like how long it takes your eyes to perceive the ball and tell your brain, That's a strike, and tell your hands, Throw the bat at the ball. It's close to 0.5 seconds for that to happen, but it takes only 0.4 seconds for the ball to get from the pitcher's hand to the catcher's mitt. So it's statistically impossible to hit a ninety-mile-an-hour fastball. But it's undeniable that people do it all the time. It's not even that hard for those guys. A third of them do it every time and get on base. Just because you can't explain it, or account for it scientifically or mathematically or medically or whatever, doesn't mean it didn't or can't happen.

So how difficult do you think it was for Jesus, the creator of everything in the known universe, who just spoke it into existence, to take some dirty water and turn it into wine? Because He is before all things and in Him all things hold together, and through Him all things were created by Him and for Him and through Him and to Him. So what we see as miraculous is just like another day at the beach for Jesus.

So Jesus told the servants, *"Take the jars. Fill them. Dip out some dirty water. Take it to the host."* What? You kidding me? That doesn't make any sense. It's dirty water. Or is it? What if God's great miracle in your life is just on the other side of a step of obedience? Because—look closely—what came first? His miracle or their obedience to His word?

When was the last time you acted upon what "He told you to do" even when it made no sense to you whatsoever? If you can't remember, then you may not be in step with the sovereign savior. Here's why this matters: Faith does stuff. Faith acts. Faith fills the jars and takes some dirty water to the host. So, where are you in your faith walk? Dipping your toe or diving in? According to Scripture, *we walk by faith and not by sight* (2 Cor. 5:7), and *without faith, it's impossible to please Him* (Heb. 11:6). I'm trying to get us to the place where we dive in and please Him.

Back to Cana: Here's why Jesus turns water into wine. It's really found in two verses in John 2, verses 4 and 11. In verse four, it says: "And Jesus said to her, 'Woman, what does this have to do with me? My hour has not yet come.'" What does He mean here when He says, "My hour has not yet come"? Good question. He's talking about that moment He goes to the cross, pushes up on his nail-pierced feet, and says: "It is finished."

That's the moment.

Because in that moment He will become sin and endure the full wrath of God. But this moment is not that hour. In verse 11, it says: "This, the first of his signs, Jesus did at Cana in Galilee, and manifested his glory. And his disciples believed in him." Said another way, His disciples trusted him. Here's the thing about a sign—a sign isn't really anything in and of itself. A sign is not the thing; a sign points to something greater than itself. If you're driving down I-95 and you see a sign for Jacksonville, that sign is not Jacksonville. That sign points you to something greater than that sign: Jacksonville.

Signs point to the real thing. Jesus didn't just turn water to wine so that the party could go on. That's not the point. The purpose of Jesus' miracles isn't necessarily to show his raw power. He wasn't just flexing for the sake of flexing. He could have walked around and just levitated everybody. "Hey, you don't believe in God? Watch this." Although He could, He didn't do that. He's not demonstrating his raw power so you think He's all that. The fact that He turned water into wine points to something. And that something is His redemptive purpose.

The reality is that we are the dirty water that has been transformed into the good wine.

Now here's what I think, and I admit I'm making a bit of a guess, but give me a little hermeneutical license, all right? Note: I'm not saying I'm right. This is an opinion. Said another way, the Bible's over there. I'm over here. What if Jesus is doing what every single person at a wedding does? And I don't mean every single person. I mean every unmarried person. Every time an unmarried person goes to a wedding, they think about their wedding. If you're a girl anywhere between ages of like four and 114, that's what you're thinking about. At every wedding, all the single ladies get back here and judge, chirp, and critique. It's just what they do. "Her dress was all right, but I don't think I'd wear that in white...And those over there, they looked like Easter eggs." You know that's what you do.

It's the feminine experience—this weird mix of competitiveness and hope. And if you brought a date, you're dropping hints. And if you're a guy, you're no different. You're standing there watching all this around you and you're imagining yourself in the middle. That moment she walks down the aisle. We all do. What if Jesus, a single man, about thirty years old, is thinking about his own wedding?

And some of you that just read that are like: "Whoa! Hey, wait a minute now. Jesus never got married."

True. At least not here on earth. But weddings matter to Jesus. In fact, the Bible begins (Genesis 2) and ends with a wedding, and the first sign occurs at a wedding, so I think it's safe to say that Jesus is into weddings. Go with me to the book of Revelation. Chapters 19 and 21. It's a description of Jesus' wedding day.

"Then I saw a new heaven and a new earth, for the first heaven and the first earth had passed away, and the sea was no more. And I saw the holy city, new Jerusalem, coming down out of heaven from God, prepared as a bride adorned for her husband. And I heard a loud voice from the throne saying, 'Behold, the dwelling place of God is with man. He will dwell with them, and they will be his people, and God himself will be with them as their God. He will wipe away every tear from their eyes, and death shall be no more, neither shall there be mourning, nor crying, nor pain anymore, for the former things have passed away.' And he who was seated on the throne said, 'Behold, I am making all things new.' Also he said, 'Write this down, for these words are trustworthy and true.' And he said to me, 'It is done! I am the Alpha and the Omega, the beginning and the end. To the thirsty I will give from the spring of the water of life without payment' " (Rev. 21:1–6).

"Then I heard what seemed to be the voice of a great multitude, like the roar of many waters and like the sound of mighty peals of thunder, crying out, 'Hallelujah! For the Lord our God the Almighty reigns. Let us rejoice and exult and give him the glory, for the marriage of the Lamb has come, and his Bride has made herself ready; it was granted her to clothe herself with fine linen, bright and pure'—for the fine linen is the righteous deeds of the saints. And the angel said to me, 'Write this: Blessed are those who are invited to the marriage supper of the Lamb' " (Rev. 19:6–9).

To all of us surrendered to the Lordship of Jesus Christ, this is where we're headed. The most epic party in the history of parties. When Jesus said, "*I am the way, the truth, and the life, and no one comes to the Father but by me*" ... this is what He's talking about. His wedding. To all the rest of you not yet surrendered, I've got great news. You too are invited. He doesn't want anyone left out. He wants all to come to repentance and that none should perish. But there's a catch—you have to RSVP before either the event or your death. Whichever comes first.

When I read about the miracle at Cana, I think Jesus is staring at that dirty water turned wine and He's looking at His mom, His friends, the servants, and the wedding attendees, and He's thinking to Himself, "*I know this is going to blow your mind but stick around. I'm just getting warmed up.*"

While that feast is somewhere in the future for all of us, Jesus also knows that in the much more immediate or short term, He, like the guy who threw the weeklong party for the wedding, is going to have to pay a price. Now I have to be careful here because we're dealing with two cultures separated by about two thousand years, but in that culture in that day and age, a price was paid for the bride. The more beautiful the bride, the greater the price. I think Jesus is staring at that water, looking at you and me in the future—the spotless bride of incomparable beauty—and He knows the purchase price.

His very own blood.

If you're new to Bible study you may be wondering, "How am I getting this wine-equals-blood thing?" I'm glad you asked. On the night Jesus was betrayed, He gathered His disciples in the upper room, and they thought they were going to celebrate the Passover. A yearly feast celebrating the liberation of God's people out of slavery in Egypt.

On that night, Jesus took the bread and was supposed to say Jewish Rabbinical stuff about Moses and Pharaoh and, "Let my people go." But instead of doing that, He personalizes it, breaks the bread, and says, "This is my body."

For them, this was like driving down the interstate at 80 mph and throwing the gear shift into reverse. They had no idea what He was talking about.

After the meal, He held up this cup filled with wine. And said, *"This is my blood. Poured out for the forgiveness of sin."* Then He goes on to say, *"This cup is a cup of the new covenant."*

Covenant and *testament* mean the same thing. And the old covenant is a covenant of law. Like those stone jars of purification, they represented the rites and rituals—or the work—you have to go through in order to be made right. He says, *"That has been fulfilled in me. And this is a new cup, a cup of my grace. And as often as you drink of this, as you take my body and blood into you, you do this in remembrance of me."*

Later that night, after they had finished the Last Supper, they go to the Garden of Gethsemane. Gethsemane was (and still is) an olive grove. It means "the place of crushing." As the weight of that presses down on Him, He looks at His disciples and says, *"Peter, James,*

John, come with me. I need you to pray for me." And as they pray, His blood vessels burst, He sweats blood and cries out, *"Father, if there be any other way, let this cup pass from me."*

The disciples are clueless. Until the next day when they see Him hanging on the cross.

You ever wonder if Jesus is the only way to God? Jesus asked the same question in the Garden of Gethsemane. That's what he's saying: *"Father, if they can just obey the commandments, if they could just be good enough, if there's some truth claim in another world religion that leads them to you, can we just go with that way? 'Cause it seems like an awful waste of my blood on Calvary tomorrow if there's any other way."*

Despite the crushing weight, Jesus said, "Not my will, but yours be done." And when God judged sin on the cross, He poured out the cup of wrath on Jesus. In exchange, Jesus poured (and pours) out on us the cup of grace by his blood.

In Matthew, chapter 26, before Jesus is crucified, dead, buried, and resurrected, He says to His disciples, *"The next time I drink out of this cup, I'm going to drink it with you in paradise."* At the marriage supper of the Lamb.

I can't prove it, but I wonder if Jesus is standing in Cana thinking about what He will later reveal, and John will attempt to describe in Revelation, chapter 21, verses 1 through 6: "Then I saw a new heaven and a new earth, for the first heaven and the first earth had passed away, and the sea was no more. And I saw the holy city, new Jerusalem, coming down out of heaven from God, prepared as a bride adorned for her husband."

One of the primary illustrations used in the Bible to describe the relationship between God and His church—and not the local organization, but the group of people who love the triune God: Father, Son, and Spirit—is a covenant. Not a contract. Most people who grew up in church think of their relationship with God as a contract.

If I do these things, then God would love me. And the gospel says, no, no, no, no, no, no. This is not a business transaction with AT&T. This is an intimate relationship with your heavenly Father. And the closest picture that we can find to that is covenant, where two people who don't know anything about the future know this: No matter what happens or what we experience or what comes our way, I promise, with all that I am and all that I'll ever be, for better or for worse, for richer, for poorer, in sickness or in health, that I'm going to love you and lay down my life for you.

Can you imagine being at a wedding where the bride and groom signed contracts? When the preacher said, "for better or worse," the guy could respond, "Hold it there, Padre, I'll take better, because I'm really not into worse"? And then looked at his bride and said, "Okay. I'll love you as long as you cook this much, sleep with me this much, and you can only gain like ten pounds and one size"? Her response might sound something like, "Only if you earn a high six-figure income, maintain two club memberships, provide bimonthly spa treatments, a new car every two years, and three girls' weekends a year. Oh, and I've already picked out the house. Here's my Zillow account. We good?"

If you were watching that, you'd be like: "Ooh, this is never going to work."

This may be tough to hear, but a marriage works only when both parties have surrendered to the Lordship of Jesus and then enter into a covenant with each other.

John is seeing something that's tough to describe. He says, "I saw the holy city, new Jerusalem, coming down out of heaven from God, prepared as a bride adorned for her husband." And then here's the relationship part: "And I heard a loud voice from the throne saying 'Behold, the dwelling place of God is with man. He will dwell with them, and they will be his people, and God himself will be with them as their God. He will wipe away every tear from their eyes, and death shall be no more, neither shall there be mourning, nor crying, nor pain anymore, for the former things that passed away.' And he who was seated on the throne said, 'Behold, I am making all things new' " (Rev. 21:2–5).

Jesus did not just clean up the water. Reverse osmosis with a double filter. He transformed it into something new. Jesus doesn't say: "*I'm just trying to make things better.*" He said, "I am making all things new."

Big, big difference.

If you back up to Revelation chapter 19, John describes a wedding party. In Revelation 19:6, he says: "Then I heard what seemed to be the voice of a great multitude, like the roar of many waters and like the sound of mighty peals of thunder, crying out, 'Hallelujah for the Lord our God the almighty reigns.' " Now listen to this description of a party: " 'Let us rejoice and exult and give him the glory.' " And here's why—" 'for the marriage of the Lamb has come, and his Bride has made herself ready; it was granted her to clothe herself with fine linen, bright and pure'—for the fine linen is the righteous deeds of the saints. And the angel said to me, 'Write this: "Blessed are those who are invited to the marriage supper of the Lamb." ' "

What if that's what Jesus is thinking? What if He wants to show throughout all human history a picture of what it looks like to be invited to the great wedding supper in heaven where every single person, no matter what you believe yet, no matter what you've done, no matter how you grew up, is invited?

And don't think some get preferential treatment while others stand out in the cold. There's only one way into this party and it's through the life, death, and resurrection of Jesus. And further, the price for your ticket has already been paid in full.

What did he mean when he said this was a sign? Notice what He did not tell the servants to do. "*Hey servants, see those six stone jars? Here's some Clorox wipes. Why don't you go over there and scrub the dirt off the outside?"* That would have been the response of religion. Because here's the truth: If they clean the outside with a little wax on, wax off, until their arms fall off, the water is still dirty. Nasty. That's religion.

This dirty water is a picture of you and me. Our spiritual condition. On the inside, we're a mess. Even if you don't believe in Jesus, you can agree we're pretty much all a mess. The Christian life is not sin management. It's not trying to strain bad stuff out of your life. That's just remorse and resolution. The Christian life is repentance.

The servants dip out the water and take it to the master, and somewhere in there it is transformed. Completely. The old is gone. The new has come. A new creation.

Here's the point—you are the dirty water. And you have been invited into a covenant relationship with God! That will be celebrated in heaven with the marriage supper of the Lamb. And you are invited.

Right now, on behalf of Jesus, I would like to invite you. You're thinking, *Okay, well, what do I do?* Actually, all you do is RSVP. You say, "I'll come. How do I do that?" You believe. You admit, "I need a Savior, and it is not me." You believe that when Jesus Christ died on the cross, His death counted as payment for your sin. Even if you don't fully understand, you can fully believe that when Jesus died on the cross, it counted for you. It's pretty simple too. The Bible says, *Believe in your heart that Jesus Christ raised from the dead and confess Him as Lord.* Then go to the party.

Notice I said it was simple. I didn't say it was easy.

If you've been a Christian for a while, then let's just thank Him for what He did to our nasty water. And let's keep one eye on the wedding feast of the Lamb. I think it'll be here sooner rather than later. And if you would say for the very first time that you are ready to receive the invitation of Jesus, to have your sins forgiven, to be in a covenant relationship with the Almighty God, to be invited to that eternal wedding feast, then just tell Him.

I don't have magic words. And you don't have to repeat after me. Just hit your knees, admit you need a Savior, believe that when Jesus died on the cross it counted for you, and confess Him as Lord of all. The Bible says when you do this you are saved. Born again. Made new. And if you surrender your life to Christ, would you please let me know so that I can help you with your next steps? Email me: joby.martin@coe22.com.

Communion

I've never heard of a book beginning with communion, but whatever. We've always been a little unorthodox at my church. Gather some bread and wine. And I would encourage you to actually do this. I know that you are busy and that it will be inconvenient to actually stop what you are doing and go grab the elements. But trust me, it matters. If you're a grape juice person, no problem. You do you. If you're in prison, or on a plane, or too young or whatever and don't have access to either, no problem. Use what you've got. The important thing is the remembrance. If you can, do this with brothers and sisters in the faith. If not, remember that Jesus promised that He would always be with us. You are not alone.

At their last meal together, Jesus looked at His disciples and said, *"As often as you eat of this, do so in remembrance of me."*

When Jesus led others in communion, while He had a lot going on—like redeeming the world—He wasn't in a hurry. Often when I lead a communion service at church I feel so rushed. Jesus was never rushed. Worry and hurry were never a part of Jesus' MO.

First, He took the bread, which reminds us of Jesus' body broken for us and brings us to confession. "Jesus, I repent of all my sin.

Known, unknown. In thought, word, and deed. I'm so sorry. Please forgive me." Gospel confession is not confessing your sin so that you may be forgiven. Confession is confessing your sin because at the cross you already have been forgiven. It is finished.

So, let's do that together. Take the bread, break it, and eat. This is the body of Jesus broken for you.

When our Lord Jesus held up the cup, He was fulfilling the old covenant and also cutting a new covenant with all mankind. In the old covenant, salvation was based on law, but in the new covenant salvation would be granted by grace, through faith. The question was no longer "Can you obey all the law all the time?" but "Do you believe that when Christ died for you, His death counted in your place?" This is why belief—or *pisteuō*—matters so much. This shift from law to grace was a mind-shattering paradigm shift. Under the new covenant, the wine represents Jesus' blood—shed on Calvary—that cleanses us from all unrighteousness. And because of the empty tomb we are credited with his perfect life.

Paul in First Corinthians says that before we take the cup of the new covenant, we should be grateful and thankful toward God. If the broken bread reminds us of the broken body of Jesus, then the shed blood in the cup points us to the empty tomb and the resurrection.

So take a minute and bow your head and close your eyes and praise God for the forgiveness of your sin. Praise God that He has paid the price. Praise God that He calls you friend. Praise God that the same power that brought Jesus out of the tomb now resides in you. Just tell him how grateful you are because He drank the cup of wrath so that we might drink the cup of grace.

Now, take the cup and drink. This is the blood of Jesus, shed for you.

We started this chapter with the words of Mary: *"Do whatever He tells you to do."* Still the best advice ever given. Imagine how different our lives would be if we just did that. From the servants' obedience, Jesus turned something nasty and dirty into something entirely new. And perfect. Chances are good it was the best wine this earth has ever known. Could He have performed that miracle without the servants' help? Sure. But He didn't. He chose to use them for His good and to accomplish His purposes. And, if you think about it, He allowed them the joy of seeing it happen. The did-you-see-that moment. But remember what was required for them to see it. That makes me wonder—what if the miracle you've been praying for, crying out to God for, is just on the other side of that small step of obedience? Will you obey? Will you do what He tells you to do?

Pray with Me

Dear Father, we love You because You first loved us. God, we know that You love us because You demonstrated it. When we were yet still sinners, You died for us. You shed Your blood for us, and God, we remember it. We reparticipate in that gory and glorious event on that day. It started with You nailed to a tree on a hill, but it did not end there. It ended with an empty tomb, a resurrection, a Great Commission, and an ascension. And we long for the day when You rip the sky open and You come back and get Yours. Jesus, You said, "As often as you eat of this bread and drink of this cup, you do so in remembrance of me." And so we do. Lord, I pray for the man, woman, and student that You are calling to step out in faith. I pray that we would, by the power of the Holy Spirit, heed Mary's advice. Lord, I pray that we would do whatever You tell us to do. God, would You give us eyes to see and a faith to believe that often the miracle we are looking for is just on the other side of a step of obedience? Please help us to remember above all else what we need is You. Please never let us lose sight of the only eternal miracle: That You have taken what was gross and discarded, us, and transformed us into something beautiful and valuable. Sons and daughters of the most high God. Amen.

CHAPTER 2

The Paralytic—Do You Believe Jesus Will Carry You?

Have you ever been desperate? Completely without hope? With no chance of anything ever getting better? If you're a parent, imagine one of your children is sick. And not just a sinus infection, but something that would debilitate them for the rest of their days. Or maybe it's your boyfriend or girlfriend or your parents or somebody you love like crazy, and they're sick and no hospital or doctor in the world could help them. What would you do to help them? Let me say it another way—what would you *not* do?

Years ago when I was a youth pastor, the Jacksonville Beach Police Department called me and said, "How would you like to be the chaplain for Jax Beach PD?" I was pumped. "All right, what do I do?" Turns out, I had to pastor the cops and give bad news to people. That was not that awesome. But when they said, "But...you get a uniform and a badge," I was all in. "Well sign me up for that, Scooter."

The uniform was awesome. But the badge was the real deal. Or, at least it looked real to me, and I convinced everyone else that it was. It came with a badge number and my name stamped on it. "Officer Joby Martin." Best yet, they gave me this little flip wallet. Like *Starsky and Hutch*. (For you Gen Zers...google it.)

A few months later, I was in the hunting section at Dick's Sporting Goods, talking to the guy at the counter. My son, JP, was with me. At the time, he was four years old, and about three feet tall. Give or take. I told him, "Hey, listen, you stay right here. Okay? Daddy's going to talk to this guy. And you need to stay right here." Then I looked away for a second and when I looked back, he—like every other kid in that situation—had moved. I grabbed him by the shoulder and moved him back. "No. Right here. Don't move. You understand?" "Yes sir, Daddy, I understand."

I talked to the guy for probably a few seconds. Or, at least that was what I reported to my wife, Gretchen, after the incident in question. Whatever. It was a long second. But when I looked down, JP was gone. As in adios'd. Not there anymore. Nothing but air vapor where his body once stood. And I thought, *Oh, my goodness, I'm going to string him up by his toes.* And so I told the attendant, "Look dude, I'll be back in a second." And I thought, *Boy, when I find this defiant child, I'm not going to put him in the corner to think about the error of his ways.* We don't "think about it" in my house. You understand? We get after it. I was pretty much going full Pentecostal and planning to lay my hands on him, if you know what I mean. And so I was looking around. But I wasn't seeing him. And then—if you're a parent you understand completely—what began to happen was that bubbling anger began to turn to a little bit of *I can't find him. Uh-oh . . .*

At the time, JP was shy of the height of a clothes rack. Meaning, he could fit inside them, and because we're Lewis fans in our house and we'd read *The Chronicles of Narnia*, everything was a wardrobe to him. Which meant I was pulling back racks of clothes to stare into the hollow part in the middle, and yet I didn't see his little blonde head bopping around.

From there, I went to the fishing section, because he's a Martin. Fishing is what we do when we're not hunting. But he wasn't there either. Now my anxiety was ramping up because he's a cute kid, and in my head I was hearing a voice whispering that somebody would steal that joker and sell him on the internet or whatever you do with them.

By now I was running. Basically cruising the racks of clothes just looking for feet at the base. But I didn't see feet. And at this point, I was at panic level. Mom panic. Not that Mom is panicking, but what am I going to tell Gretchen when she finds out that I've lost our son?

My mind went to a bad place quick—I saw him duct-taped in the back of a van. I didn't know what to do. So, I did what every parent would. Whatever it took. I flipped out my badge and told the manager in a loud, authoritative voice, "Jacksonville Beach PD. We've got a missing child. Code Red. We need to find him. Shut her down."

Turns out they have a protocol for this sort of thing. The manager got on the little speakerphone, and his voice was shaky. "We got a Code Blue Purple! Code Blue Purple!" All around me, people stepped into action. Somebody threw a switch and the escalator stopped. The elevators shut down. Associates blocked all the doors. People were piling up at exits. No one was getting in or out.

I was standing on the second floor, staring down on the crowd, about to paratrooper down and arrest some pervert with my son stuffed beneath his jacket. I didn't know if you could arrest people with a chaplain's badge, but I really didn't care. I was close to losing my mind. If you've seen my picture or seen me preach, you've no doubt noticed I don't have any hair. Not since I lost it all that day in Dick's Sporting Goods.

Studying the crowd, I rushed around a corner, which brought me to the top of the escalator, and who did I find staring back at me? My little Rick Flair lookalike blond son. Maybe a little sheepish. Just a curious kid, wanting to know where the escalator steps went when they disappeared into the floor. I'd found him unharmed and unstolen. Now we had another problem, and it started with all the laws I just broke using my badge to shut down Dick's Sporting Goods. So I picked him up by the neck, carried him to the exit, and flashed my badge at the manager. "Got him. Carry on. Nice job on your Code Purple. Good job, boys. I'll make sure to recognize you in my report."

Later that night, when I told Gretchen some version of this story, she grew very anxious, wondering if our phone was about to ring with actual police on the other end. Gretchen is a rule follower and a law abider. She asked me, "Was that legal?"

Legal? What has that got to do with anything?

Honestly, I don't care. Didn't then. Don't now. Because when I thought something was wrong with JP, when I thought someone had stuffed him in a bag in the back of a van down by the river, I was willing to do whatever was in my authority, or maybe even a little bit beyond it, to get him back.

That's desperation.

And that's the kind of desperation you have to read into this account of the paralytic whom we find in Mark 2. This is not just a Sunday school story about a man lowered through a roof. This was a real man. Really paralyzed. Really unable to go to the bathroom by himself. Really without hope. Really at the end of his rope himself.

So here we go.

Mark 2:1–2 says, "And when he—" the *He* is Jesus "—when [Jesus] returned to Capernaum after some days, it was reported that he was at home. And many were gathered together, so that there was no more room, not even at the door." Turn back to Mark 1, and Jesus' ministry is in full effect. He's called the disciples, cast out demons, healed all kinds of people—even a leper. If you're going to go into ministry, you may want to write this down—heal a leper and buckle up, buddy, because people are going to show up.

Given signs and miracles and wonders, Jesus can't go anywhere without recognition. Anonymity is out the window. People just want a glimpse. To touch the hem of His garment. In Mark 2, Jesus is teaching at a home and the place is packed out. There's no more room in the house. And it says, "And [Jesus] was preaching the word to them" (v. 2). Again, Jesus performed miracles not just to demonstrate His real power, but to demonstrate His redemptive purpose. The miracles pointed to the mission—to seek and to save the lost.

Verse 3 says, "And they—" these are the friends "—and they came, bringing to [Jesus] a paralytic carried by four men. And when they could not get near him because of the crowd..." This house is standing room only, so these four friends have a problem—they can't get anywhere near Jesus.

But these friends are willing to do whatever it takes, so they climb up on the roof and start digging a hole. Tearing away the thatch, rifling through layers of reeds and palm branches and mud and clay. In short, this took a minute, it made a mess, and everyone inside knew they were coming. Including Jesus.

Imagine your disciple group. Word has spread. You're packed out. But somebody you've never met really wants to join but can't get through the door. And while you're teaching, you hear this strange knocking and scratching and sawing, and when you look up someone has bored a hole in your roof.

I don't know if you've ever replaced a roof, but it's not cheap. And not only that, but everyone sitting beneath all that chaos is now covered in sawdust and specks of shingle, and running water hasn't been invented yet, so everybody can't just run home and take a shower. This experience was messy for those closest to Jesus. Not to mention expensive for the homeowner. But this did not deter the four friends, and they didn't care if it ticked off all the people who got there early and on time and had seats for themselves. They were willing to make everybody on the inside uncomfortable so that they could get their friend to Jesus. It says they removed the roof above him, and when they made an opening, they let down the bed on which the paralytic lay. Put yourself in the room. Can you see the four ropes and the cot, and hear the grunts of the four guys holding the rope?

I love this picture. One sick man carried by four good friends. It begs the question: Do you have friends like that? Friends you can count on to carry you to Jesus? Now for the majority of this chapter, I'm going to ask you, "Are you that kind of friend?" But right now, I want to flip the mirror. Take a second and answer that question. Yes or no? Write your answer in the margin. Better yet, write their names.

There will come a day where you cannot make it on your own. Where you find yourself paralyzed. Either by fear or doubt or a financial situation. Or a relational situation. Or in raising your children or a health crisis. The day is coming. Do you have four friends who will carry you to Jesus when the fertilizer hits the ventilator? What are their names? Write them, over there in the margin. If you can't write four names, then Houston, we have a problem. Because you and I were created for relationships. And you need those kinds of friends before you need those kinds of friends. It's like a retirement account. If you wait until you need it to start investing in it, it's way too late.

And let me tell you who's the worst at this. Married men. We've got that one relationship and we're "All right, I'm done." But in truth, you don't have lower-you-through-the-roof friends. You have buddies. And buddies are all right. You got golfing buddies and hunting buddies and drinking buddies and surfing buddies. But buddies are usually just a distraction from what you actually need. When's the last time you had a spiritually significant conversation with one of your buddies? When you confessed your sin and asked him to pray for you? If you can't answer, you've got a problem, brother. What you need is a band of brothers who would be willing to rally around you when you are in your time of greatest need. Or get in your junk if you're a train wreck waiting to happen. If by this point you haven't written four names in the margin, then how do you plan to get to Jesus when you're paralyzed?

Women, this is true for you too. Not only that, but let me ask you: Who's praying for you? If you've got something going on in your life right now, who is praying for you? Do you have four people that you could text and say, "Please pray"? And you would give them the real deal. Not that little silly Bible-bookstore "I just have an unspoken." And not the edited stuff you want us to see on Instagram and Facebook.

Sometimes we may even need someone to lay hands on us and anoint us with oil. If that makes you uncomfortable, then write this down: Get over it. Scripture says to do it (James 5:14–15). So, we do. I hope and pray that you are at the kind of church that fosters such close relationships that they even make you a little uncomfortable sometimes. I hope that you have brothers or sisters in Christ who get so involved in your life that it stretches you. The kind of people that are more concerned about you than what you think about them. Do you have real friends like that?

Several years ago, I was preaching on fatherhood. Near the front was a dad who'd brought his whole family to church. His oldest daughter was home from college on fall break. At the end of our services, I encourage everyone to respond to the gospel. Don't just sit there. Do something. Moved by the message, his daughter headed to the altar, knelt, and prayed. The dad, moved by his daughter's heart, thought to himself, *I need to go pray for my daughter.*

So he walked down, put his hands on her shoulders, and whispered Psalm 139 in her ear. "Dear God, I praise you because *I am fearfully and wonderfully made. Your works are wonderful, I know that full well.*" He was just telling her how proud he was of her.

If you're a college-aged daughter, wouldn't you love to have your dad praying over you like that? When he finished, he kissed her on the head, walked back to his seat, and who did he find there?

His daughter.

"Whoa!" He pointed to the altar, then at her seat. "What are you doing here?"

"Sitting with you."

"But . . . you went to the altar to pray?"

She shook her head. "No. I went to the bathroom."

He turned slowly toward the altar. "Oh boy."

At the end of the service, he pulled me aside, "I need to tell you something."

Imagine that girl, she's eighteen, nineteen years old. Down there praying for a date. Right? "Dear God . . ." Then some old guy starts whispering in her ear. "This is creepy." Or maybe she's thinking, "This is the friendliest church I've ever been to in my life." The Lord does work in mysterious ways. Later on, we found her and had a good laugh, proving once again that church life is both fun and messy.

But back to my question . . . straight up—do you have friends praying for you? If you go to the altar, does someone walk with you? The paralytic's life is not good. In fact, it can't get much worse. But he's got friends who do whatever it takes to get him to Jesus. Mark 2:5: *And after they'd torn a hole in the roof, they lowered him down. And when Jesus saw their faith* . . . Pause. Faith is not a feeling. Faith is not mustering up this fuzzy feeling every week and pushing away doubts. Faith is believing that God is who He says He is. It's a choice. A decision of your will. Your gut. The Bible says, *Without faith, it's impossible to please God* (Heb. 11:6). And He always keeps His promises to the point where it produces action.

Faith is something that Jesus can see because it produces fruit we call works. One of which is belief. *Pisteuō.* And when he saw their faith, He said to the paralytic, "Son." That's what he starts out with.

Son. Why? Because there was a group of first-century religious people who believed a physical ailment was inflicted by God as spiritual punishment for sin. We find this out in John 9. The disciples see a blind man and asked Jesus, "*Who sinned? This man or his parents, that he would be born blind?*" And Jesus says, "*No, boys. This is not how it works*" (vv. 2–3). The physical ailment is not punitive. It's to put God's splendor on display.

Put yourself on the mat. Imagine what he's been told his entire life. And based on the words of Jesus, I imagine he needed to hear the word *Son*. Something in his heart needed that. Because evidently his identity was tied to his disease. But not with Jesus. Jesus is the only one who gets to tell him who he is. And of all the labels, Jesus starts with *son*. "Son, your sins are forgiven" (Mark 2:5).

Immediately, the religious elite are in an uproar. "*That's not what we came here for. We did not come to see sins forgiven. We want to see a miracle.*" Verses 6–7: "Now some of the scribes—" Those were the religious people. "Some of the scribes were sitting there, questioning in their hearts, 'Why does this man speak like that? He is blaspheming! Who can forgive sins but God alone?'" Actually, they're right. Who does this man Jesus think He is that He forgives their sin?

Every single time we sin, we sin against the Almighty God. And only the Almighty God would have the authority to forgive sin. And so when they are questioning who can forgive sins but God alone, Jesus is saying essentially, *You're absolutely right.* In truth, He's foreshadowing how He is going to forgive sin because to forgive sin, you've got to have the authority to do so, and that authority is either earned or given. Jesus has both. He earns it on the cross. And it is given to Him by God the Father.

Verses 8–9: "And immediately Jesus, perceiving in his spirit that they thus questioned within themselves." Notice they did not say this out loud, just in their hearts. Meaning, Jesus knows the thought of every man before it becomes a word. So He says, "Why do you question these things in your hearts? Which is easier, to say to the paralytic, 'Your sins are forgiven,' or to say, 'Rise, take up your bed and walk'?" Well, it's a tricky question.

On the surface, it's easier to say your sins are forgiven. Anyone can do that and no one standing around would expect any outward or physical change. But to say, "*Get up and walk in three, two, one,*" and have the man do it, that's next-level. I'm not saying forgiving sin is easy, it's not. But healing a paralytic takes right-now power. Not physical therapy over six months. He told the man, "*Get up and walk,*" and folks watched it happen. Right that moment. But, in actuality, it's infinitely harder to forgive sin than it is to heal that man.

First, He had to live a perfect, sinless life. Then He was crushed. Flogged. Made unrecognizable as a man. Then He walked to the cross where all the wrath of God was heaped upon Him, and He shed every ounce of His precious blood.

So what's easier?

It's much easier for the creator of the universe to heal a man than to forgive sin. But in saying, "Your sins are forgiven," Jesus is making a point. And it's the same point that will eventually get Him killed. He's claiming to be the Son of God—which He is. In verse 10, He says, "But that you may know that the Son of Man has authority on earth to forgive sins…" If it weren't true, this would be ludicrous, but He says this to set up the fact that the miracle He's about to perform will confirm the truth that He alone is able to forgive sin. In the first century, Jewish rabbis recorded their traditions and their commentary on the Torah in what is called the Talmud. One such tradition was that God could not and would not bless or help a liar. With that as the backdrop, look at Jesus through their eyes as He heals the paralytic. If God won't help a liar and this man gets up and walks, then, logically, it must be true that this man has the power to forgive sin. Which means He's the Son of God.

Those rabbis have no box for this.

As the now-forgiven paralytic stares at Jesus, Jesus says, "I say to you, rise, pick up your bed, and go home" (Mark 2:11). This too could be ridiculous if you don't understand what Jesus is doing. The paralytic has been lying on that thing a long time and, for starters, he can't get himself to the bathroom. Fact—that's a nasty mat. But Jesus instructs the man to roll it up and tuck it under his arm not because it has anything to do with his current condition, and not because he might need it again, but because it establishes the record of who he was and who he is now—in Christ Jesus.

Verse 12: "And [the man] rose and immediately picked up his bed." Again, this isn't physical therapy. Not a slow miracle. It's boom. Jesus said, "*Get up*," and the man got up, picked up his bed, and walked. And he went out before them all so that they were all amazed and they glorified God. That's worship. When you see God for who He really is. And what He has done. Not only in you, but in those around you. And when they saw the miracle, they said, "We never saw anything like this."

In Mark 2, the paralytic had four friends, and each held a rope. These men were rope holders. What were their ropes attached to? The four corners of his mat. What if there are four corners to you and me helping people come to Jesus?

Corner Number One

The first corner is sharing your faith. Do you personally share your faith? Do you tell the story of what Jesus has done in you and through you to people who need Jesus? Jesus says it this way in Acts 1:8: "But you will receive power when the Holy Spirit has come upon you, and you will be my witnesses in Jerusalem and in all Judea and Samaria, and to the end of the earth." The word Jesus says three times in this sentence is *you*. You are the witness. It doesn't say "the preacher" will receive power when the preacher has the Holy Spirit. It says *you*. Just everyday disciples like me and you. If Jesus is your Lord, we are called to share our faith. And why wouldn't we? He has saved us from eternal damnation and is taking us to the Father. Why wouldn't we want to tell others that?

Jesus calls the ordinary, average, everyday, fully devoted follower of Jesus to be His witness everywhere we go. To share our faith as the Holy Spirit leads you to. And if you're a Christian, the same Holy Spirit that resurrected Jesus from the grave lives in you and wants to lead, guide, and direct you to share your faith.

Sometimes it's the whole ball of wax. The gospel, beginning, middle, and end. And it's not rocket science. It's actually pretty simple. Just diagnose the problem and make it easy. We all have the same problem. "Hey, listen, you're not a bad person who needs to be better. You're a dead person who needs life. And life is found only in Jesus." Sometimes the Spirit leads you to just share your story. "Hey, I don't know how to answer all of your theological questions, but here's what I know: My life used to be like this, then I met Jesus. And this is what it's been like since then." Everyone can do this 'cause we all have a story and nobody knows our story better than us.

Sometimes, the Holy Spirit leads you to share an invitation. Somebody new moves into your neighborhood. "Hey buddy, welcome to the neighborhood. You found a church? How 'bout I take you to breakfast and then we'll go to my church?"

Sometimes you need to share a burden with someone going through a rough time. And sometimes the simplest, least offensive way to do this is to say, "Hey, can I be praying for you about something?" Or maybe, "Hey, listen, I'm a praying person. And I believe that God hears my prayers. Not because I'm special. But because He's a Father. And He's a good Dad. That's just who He is. So can I just be praying?" Maybe it's to share in an act of kindness because your neighbor or somebody, your friend, is going through something and so you take them a meal, cut the grass, or write them a handwritten note.

Sometimes the Spirit just leads us to share one more cup of coffee. Just continue building that relationship so that our friends know, I'm not trying to do anything to you. I'm just trying to share something with you that's really important. We talk about good movies. We talk about good restaurants. We talk about good sports teams. Doesn't it seem crazy that we wouldn't talk about the Good Shepherd?

Two years ago, I was leading a tour in Israel. People often ask, "What was the most impactful site you saw?" I think as a rule you have to say the empty tomb. It is, as we have discussed, the foundation of our faith. But for me a close second was Caesarea Philippi. This is where Jesus takes the disciples on a camping trip in Matthew 16. Jesus, while overlooking this city that was defined by debauchery and sexual immorality, asks this question: "*Who do people say that I am?*" He then asks them, "Who do you say that I am?"

Peter says, "You are the Christ, the Son of the living God." Jesus famously says, "Blessed are you, Simon Bar-Jonah! For flesh and blood has not revealed this to you, but my Father who is in heaven. And I tell you, you are Peter, and on this rock I will build my church, and the gates of hell shall not prevail against it" (Matt. 16:13–18). This is the first time "church," or "*ecclesia*," has ever been mentioned in all of human history.

When I arrived at this site for the first time, I was overwhelmed. I lay on a rock and simply asked God the question: "Lord, is the thing that we are doing in Jacksonville each weekend what you were talking about when you mentioned 'church' here? If not, I need you to tell me." For the next four hours I lay on a rock and listened. It felt like God affirmed what we are doing because we are simply trying to do what Peter did that day. We proclaim the gospel, that Jesus is the Christ, the Son of the living God.

The next day I felt like God confirmed what we were doing as a church. We were inside the city of Jerusalem at Caiaphas' house. Caiaphas was the high priest during the time of Jesus. He's the one responsible for arresting Jesus in the Garden of Gethsemane. After He was arrested, the soldiers brought Him to Caiaphas' house, where He was held in the basement—in a type of holding cell where Jesus spent His last night on earth before His trial and Crucifixion. From the cell, I climbed the steps to the porch. The thing is huge, with maybe the best view in all of Jerusalem. From Caiaphas' house, you can look onto the Old City, or where the temple would have stood during his day, you can look south to the City of David, and you can look east across the Brook Kidron and onto the Garden of Gethsemane and the Mount of Olives.

As I stood on the porch admiring the view, I heard, "Pastor Joby?" And I thought, *You have got to be kidding me.* It's one thing when I'm in my neighborhood Walmart. It's another thing halfway around the world. Our guide looked at me and said, "Who are you?"

"I'm a redneck from Dillon."

When I turned around, I met these kids. Half my age. College students. Never met them before. "What are you doing here?"

"Well, we go to your church."

"Time-out," I said. "It's not my church. If you're there and I'm there, we're there. It's our church. That means we go to church together."

Then they told me, "We're here with YWAM." YWAM—Youth with a Mission—is an incredible ministry with a worldwide reach yet a simple mission: to know God and make Him known. Which they've been doing for more than sixty years. In short, they've been doing exactly what Jesus said to do all around the world. The kids—young adults, I guess—said, "We've been on mission in Jordan for the last month." I love that: "On mission." It really is that simple. It's about here that I clued into the fact that they weren't talking about the Jordan River. They were talking about the country, sharing the gospel with Muslims.

And because they were all broke college kids, they were doing Israel on the cheap, staying in hostels, eating nothing but pita bread and hummus. So we emptied our pockets and gave them all the money we had. "Here, seriously, get a hamburger or something." And then I said, "Can we just pray for you?" Here's the thing: This is family. Halfway around the world. Doing Acts 1:8—witnessing "in Jerusalem and in all Judea and Samaria, and to the end of the earth."

And so we gathered up and I was praying. And I was not saying a little dinner prayer. We were laying-hands-on praying. Maybe it's because I read the Bible a lot, but when I start praying, Bible verses come into my mind. That's just how it works. "Our good and gracious heavenly Father, thank you for this part of our family..." And in my mind I heard Jesus speaking the Great Commission— in which they are currently participating. "Thank you so much for these young men and women who are actually living out the Great Commission."

Then, BAM! Booyah! Over my right shoulder stands the Kidron Valley, and just on the other side is a little town called Bethany. Sitting smack in the middle of the two is the Mount of Olives, where Jesus ascended to the right hand of God the Father. But not before He gave the Great Commission that said, "Go therefore and make disciples of all nations, baptizing them in the name of the Father and of the Son and of the Holy Spirit" (Matt. 28:19). And I began to think, *Holy moly. I've read that forever. And now I can see it. I'm touching it. Jesus, what You said two thousand years ago, right over there, is boomeranging. Acts 1:8 is literally boomeranging from Jerusalem, Judea, Samaria, and to the far corners of the earth, including Dillon and Jacksonville, only to find its way back here. And now that sucker is right back here in Jerusalem.* I'm all freaked out. Starting to get all Pentecostal. "Lord, just fill them with Your Spirit, which fell on the southern steps right over there when Peter preached on the day of Pentecost and the Spirit fell on three thousand believers. And from that day to this day the Word spread."

As I finished my prayer I feel like the Lord answered in me the question that I was asking at Caesarea Philippi. The church that I had given my life to was founded upon the rock of the gospel of Jesus Christ, and the gates of hell would never prevail against it.

For twenty years, I've been teaching people the Bible. And for the last ten, I've taught the Bible to a group of people every four days. Once on Thursday night, twice or three times on Sunday, depending on the season, then again Thursday. Wash, rinse, repeat. Teaching requires that we know that material at a level deeper than if we're consuming it for our own benefit. And what we're teaching matters. It's life and death. Literally. I'm praying to deliver the Word in such a way that unbelievers walk out of unbelief and into belief and faith. Standing in Jerusalem, I saw this happen.

That's corner number one.

Corner Number Two

The second corner of the mat is serving in your local church. The book of Ephesians is all about the gospel. The first half is the declaration of the gospel; the second half is the demonstration of the gospel in the church, the family, our work, et cetera. In Ephesians 4:11, it says, "And he gave"—that's God—"and he gave the apostles, the prophets, the evangelists, the shepherds, the teachers…" In our context, more often than not, those folks are church staff. Pastors, ministers, people who work here at the local church. And He gave those positions and here's why. Verse 12: "to equip the saints for the work of ministry, for building up the body of Christ."

Guess who the saints are? You. That's right. You with this book in your hand. Provided you've surrendered to the Lordship of Jesus Christ. If that's you and you have, then according to Scripture, you're a saint. Our job in the church is to equip you. And one way we do that is to create an environment where you can bring a friend into this place and they are never hindered getting to Jesus because of the crowds. Our hope is that when people pull up in our parking lot, they are met by and loved on by saints equipped for the work of the ministry. And, just being honest, we need saints in the parking lot because some of us drive like the devil. And we need saints at the front doors greeting folks. Making them feel welcome in this house regardless of their condition. And we need saints in our kids' rooms because in there we have parents handing over to us the most precious thing they have. And we're not babysitting their children. We are demonstrating the gospel, declaring the gospel in age-appropriate ways, and praying over them like crazy.

In Matthew 16, when Jesus says to Peter, "On this rock, I will build my church," he actually says, "I will build my *ecclesia.*" *Ecclesia* is a Greek word that means "a group of people called out on purpose." When used by Jesus, it was not a religious word at all. For instance, people picketing would be an *Ecclesia.* Jesus is saying, *"I'm calling out this group of people. And their purpose is the declaration of the gospel."*

Between 300 and 400 AD they began to use the German word *Kirche* instead of the Greek word *Ecclesia* to mean "church." *Kirche* means "the Lord's house." So what began as a movement stopped in a building. Which is really a shame. This is why I teach that our church is not defined by the place in which we find ourselves, which is good because we're not really into fancy buildings. The different campuses of our church meet in a Walmart, in a sports bar, in two prisons, in an old Lutheran church, in an hhgregg store, in an old Baptist Church, in an Ace Hardware, in a high school, and on some dirt in Saint Johns County. We are happy to gather in any place that is available. It's not the pews or the steeple that makes it a church but the people of God gathered in His name. Our focus is not our buildings. Buildings come and go. We are focused on discovering and deepening our relationship with Jesus.

The local church mattered to Jesus, so it matters to us. Jesus said, "The Son of Man came not to be served but to serve, and to give his life as a ransom for many" (Mark 10:45). If you're not serving His bride, you should be. That's corner number two.

Corner Number Three

The third corner is bearing the stretcher. Putting your shoulder under the load. Being willing to tear a hole in the roof if that's what it takes. Bringing our friends in need to Jesus. And to do so, the question we need to ask is this: "Are you willing to make a mess and disrupt the comfortable who already have a seat in order to make room for one more?" Are you willing to do whatever it takes to make room for everybody? Because everybody's invited. Every tribe, tongue, and color. Whether you're the paralytic with a nasty mat, or a scribe and a Pharisee who reads Greek and Hebrew, our doors are open. One of my difficulties with contemporary churches in America is this idea that you have to be one of us before you can belong. You have to look like us, dress like us, talk like us, and don't do the stuff we don't do like us.

If you read *If the Tomb Is Empty* then you know that one of the most formative experiences of my early pastoral life was meeting a stripper named Sunshine and inviting her to church. To her credit, she accepted the invitation. But to the great discredit of the men in my church, they told me, "One of the reasons we have this church is to protect our children from people like that." Shame on you.

I promised myself then I would never build or work for a church like that because that's not the church Jesus started. It was and is His desire that all would come to repentance and that none should perish. So let's build a church like that. And the way you build it is to build people who build one another. Who carry stretchers. Rip roofs off. In the economy of God, God is entirely okay with you hanging out with Him before you believe that He is who He says He is. In fact, it was the hanging out that brought unbelievers to belief. Scripture is full of people who hung out with Jesus before they believed in Him. And remember, before they started hanging out with Him, their lives looked nothing like His. But turn the page and their lives looked a whole lot like His after they'd been hanging out with Him.

At our church, we are not satisfied with full rooms. We will do whatever it takes to rip the roof off, even though we know it's messy. And I know it bothers people who already have a seat, but tough. We don't write our names on the pew because we are all guests in God's house and they don't belong to us. We need to scoot over and make room. We're talking about eternity. It's also pretty expensive, but what's a single life worth? Just one? We want to do everything short of sin to take the gospel to as many people as possible.

Let me tell you who loves this kind of church. The person who has a prodigal son or a daughter who is far from God. I know, because they tell us. That's why we don't have a dress code. Why I don't wear a suit—not that I want to. Our bottom line is that you don't have to get cleaned up to take a bath. You can walk in church dirty because once you sit in His presence and He bathes you in the gospel, He will do the work only He can, and He knows exactly what you need. Our job is to help arrange the meeting.

Other pastors and church plant people have often asked me, "What's the secret to your church's growth? What're you doing?" The secret is, *If I am lifted up I will draw all people unto Myself* (John

12:32). So, we lift Him up, make much of Jesus, don't shy away from the stuff in the gospel that is difficult or unpopular, and make sure everyone is invited and that we make room for everyone. I'm not standing up there trying to win a popularity contest. I've said this before: I'm nobody, trying to tell anybody about the somebody who died for everybody. And, just being honest, the message is moderately delivered and exceptionally received.

We have never focused on being a big church. We have always just tried to make room for ONE MORE. Because Jesus is the kind of shepherd who will leave the ninety-nine for the one.

Our heart—and, I believe, the heart of Jesus—is to create a triage of sorts where, by the power of the Holy Spirit, people in need of life support are carried in on stretchers and they surrender their lives to the Great Physician. Come one. Come all. If you're banged up, broken, nothing but a wretched, black-hearted sinner in need of life support, you'll fit right in. I've said it often: "Welcome to the island of misfit toys." Because we are. And thank God we don't have to rip the roof off because we've already made enough room beneath it. We have a seat for you. Right down front. Thinking that you have to clean yourself up and get your act together before you come to church is like thinking you have to wait for the bleeding to stop to go to the ER.

As pastor, one of the things I love to watch most is the transformation from wounded on the stretcher to carrier of the stretcher. How does this happen? Jesus, Jehovah Raphah, Our Healer, met them in their pain. Healed them. Filled the hopeless with hope. Then those same people, grateful for what He has done in, to, and through them, pick up a stretcher and venture back out across the battlefield, loading up the wounded. It's just what we do. Rescuing the wounded should be as normal as walking through the front door. That's corner number three.

Corner Number Four

Last, corner number four. And if the fourth corner doesn't happen, then this is all just an exercise in futility. The fourth corner is for God to do what God does. In Ezekiel 36, God says, "And I will give you a new heart, and a new spirit I will put within you. And I will remove the heart of stone from your flesh and give you a heart of flesh" (v. 26). Simply put, you can pray your face off, you can put yourself in great environments, and you can invite people, but until God causes the heart in us to change, nothing will ever change. In John 15, Jesus says it this way: "Greater love has no one than this, that someone lay down his life for his friends" (v. 13). Read that closely and you'll find that Jesus is the only religious leader to ever offer friendship.

Religious leaders throughout history have offered teaching, a way to live, and a philosophy of life, but Jesus offers Himself. Friendship. Jesus says, "Greater love has no one than this, that someone lay down his life for his friends. You are my friends if you do what I command you. No longer do I call you servants, for the servant does not know what his master is doing; but I have called you friends, for all that I have heard from my Father I have made known to you. You did not choose me, but I chose you" (John 15:13–16).

Imagine living in the first century with a need. Something no amount of money can fix, and one you've tried to meet over and over in any number of ways and nothing worked. Suppose you were paralyzed, and four of your friends each picked up a corner of your mat and lowered you to Jesus. Imagine the fear and trepidation as they lowered you into a church service that was disrupted by the aforementioned friends, and you lock eyes with the Almighty Son of God. In the flesh. Bam!

Now come back to this century. To this moment. And to the chair you are sitting in right now. Because time doesn't constrain

Jesus. He was on the throne yesterday, is on it today, and will be on it tomorrow. And the reason He's on that throne is because that tomb is empty. And if that tomb is empty, then anything is possible and we get to bring our needs, pains, hurts, and deepest desires to the King of Kings and Lord of Lords, who happens to be our "friend." His words.

Are you in need? Right now? Are you paralyzed with fear? Are your finances wrecked beyond repair? You got a health problem? A terrible diagnosis? A bad scan? Do you live with a secret sin that you've held on to for years or even decades and shame is paralyzing you? You feel ten million miles away from God?

If this is you, then maybe it's time to reach out to one of your four friends. And if you don't have four, then reach out to one. And not just in a text. Call them. Invite them to your home, open your closet door where you keep the skeletons, and get real. Risk the truth. And then bring all that to the feet of Jesus. He said to come boldly before His throne of grace, and ask to receive grace and find mercy in our time of need. Is this your time? And we don't come boldly because there's anything in us about which we should be bold, but we do so in obedience. Because He commands it.

When Jesus said, "It is finished," an earthquake cracked through the middle of the temple and tore the curtain that separated the presence of God from the people of God. In the Old Testament temple system, the Holy of Holies contained the presence of God and the people were not allowed in. They had to stay outside in one of the designated temple courts and worship from afar. But when Jesus made the payment that satisfies the law and justice of God on the cross, the chasm was bridged, and that curtain of separation was torn. And when it tore, it did so from top to bottom. God coming to man. Not bottom to top—man making his way to God. Top to bottom is a reminder that in the temple, once a year, the high priest had to cleanse himself and walk into the Holy of Holies with a belt tied around his ankle in case he got it wrong and God zapped him from on high. Top to bottom means that sons and daughters like you and me get to climb up into the lap of our heavenly Father.

This is corner number four. God doing in us what only He can. Our job is to come, make room, be obedient, and invite Him without reservation.

The four corners are: share your faith, serve the bride, carry a stretcher, and leave room for God to do what God does. Doing this will wrap arms around the broken and help bring them into the kingdom of God.

Let's go back to the question I asked you at the beginning. How desperate are you? Let me speak to those of you lying paralyzed on the mat—if you're in need, reach up, reach out, grab four friends, and then fall flat on your face at the feet of Jesus. And pray like crazy. For everyone else, maybe things are going good right now. Praise God for that. James says, *Is anyone among you cheerful? Then you should sing. Praise God for your life* (James 5:13). My question to you is this: Do you have a friend lying flat on the mat? Is the Lord nudging you to reach out? To make the phone call? Why don't you call two or three other friends and go to that person? Why don't the four of you become the hands and feet of Jesus, pick up the corners, and bring that paralyzed person to the Father. This is way beyond just inviting somebody to church. This is being the *ecclesia*. The body. This is doing what Jesus did and is doing. When was the water turned to wine? After the servants did what Jesus said and took some to the master of the feast. And when was the paralytic healed? After his friends carried him to Jesus, ripped the roof off, and lowered him down. And when they did, Scripture says an amazing thing: "When Jesus saw their faith"—that's the faith of the four friends—"he said to the paralytic, 'Son, your sins are forgiven'... 'I say to you, rise, pick up your bed, and go home'" (Mark 2:5, 11).

When was the paralytic healed? After Jesus marveled at the faith of the four friends. All of us are praying for, hoping for, and waiting for a miracle. My question while you are praying and hoping is this: What has Jesus told you to do, and will you obey Him?

Pray with Me

Our good and gracious heavenly Father, we come to You by the name and invitation of Your Son Jesus Christ. God, I need help! I come to You with a need that I cannot fix on my own. Lord, would You please do for me what I cannot do for myself? God, would you please heal me? Or God, would you please heal my friend? Lord God, would you start with my soul? Just as You did with the paralytic, would You start by forgiving my sins? It costs You way more to forgive my sins than it does to heal my body. Lord, You know me. You know every hair on my head and the intentions in my heart. God, I need Your help. Lord, I need freedom. Would You please grant me that? Lord, I need to know that I am Your son and that You are my Father. Would you please protect me from the lies of the enemy? He wants me to believe that I am defined by my past, by my mistakes, by my scars. Would You please seal it upon my heart that I am defined by Your scars? Father, I pray for my relationships. I ask that by Your grace I would always be surrounded by at least four friends who at great expense to themselves would be willing to bring me to You. And I pray that I would be that kind of friend in someone's life. Lord, I thank You that because of the cross the pretending game and the performance game are over. Thank You for looking into our eyes and calling us Your own. We pray this in the name of the only one who matters when we pray. We pray this in Jesus' name. Amen.

CHAPTER 3

Healing at the Pool of Bethesda—Do You Believe Jesus Can Heal You?

Before we dive in, let me ask you a simple question that may have a difficult answer: Do you want to be healed? Is your body sick? Your heart broken? Even your memories? Jesus often asked this question, so let me ask you: Do you want to be completely healed? You know the answer better than anyone, but before we dive in we should wrestle with the question. Now write your answer over there in the margin. And if you're really brave, write the name of the thing from which you want to be healed.

Now bookmark it. We're coming back to it.

Grab your Bible. We're starting in John 4:46. "So He"—that's Jesus—"came again to Cana in Galilee, where he had made the water wine. And at Capernaum there was an official whose son was ill." This official had probably been sent from King Herod's palace. Meaning, he's a really big deal. Important. And he's got political power and lots of money. Everybody would bow down to this official.

When this man heard that Jesus had come from Judea to Galilee, he went to Him and asked Him to come down and heal his son, for he was at the point of death. This journey would've been about twenty miles and taken a day to get there on foot, but look at Jesus' response. "Unless you see signs and wonders you will not believe" (John 4:48).

If it seems like a rebuke, that's because it is. But look at what Jesus doesn't say. Jesus doesn't say, "Why in the world would I hear your prayer request? I mean, you used to work for the guy who tried to kill me when I was two years old. You want to talk about that for a little while?" He doesn't talk about any of King Herod's past or the things he was associated with—like the systematic killing of Jews. He just stares at the man and focuses on the eternal while this man is focused on right now and what's most urgent. The official has no real response, so he says, "Sir, come down before my child dies" (John 4:49).

I've talked about this a lot, but there is no pain like kid pain. There's just not. If you're a parent, you understand. If you're not but will be, you'll understand then. There's just no pain like kid pain. This official has money, power, and prestige, but when his son is on the verge of death, none of those things matter because none of those things can heal him. His money can't heal him. His position can't heal him. His power can't heal him. His prestige can't heal him. And so, hearing of Jesus, he humbles himself and travels a day just in case this man Jesus can do something about it. We know the dad is desperate because he doesn't even really reply to Jesus' rebuke. He folds. He's basically saying, *"Okay, Rabbi. This isn't about me, this is about my son. Please come with me and see him? He's at the point of death."*

One of the things that happens when something's wrong with your son or daughter is you begin to ask yourself, *Is this all me? Did I do this? Are they suffering because of my sin or mistake or mess-up? Did I not pray over them enough? Not bring them to church enough? Is this my fault?* Let a kid struggle with an addiction, or doubt, or any kind of mental health issue, and I don't care how good your theology is, you begin to be gripped with, *Is this my fault? Did I do something wrong?* Let a child deal with a physical ailment and there's some-place in your brain that just goes, *God, are you punishing me via my kid? What's going on here?*

Can I remind you of Luke 15 and the story of the prodigal son? The youngest son goes to his dad and essentially says, "*You are dead to me. Give me what's coming to me!*" (v. 12). And then Jesus says that the younger son goes and squanders it all away on reckless liv-ing. Let me ask you a question: What did the dad do wrong? Was it his fault? The short answer is NO. He represents our heavenly Father. So, sometimes you have done nothing wrong and your kid is still in pain.

I don't care how much money you make, I don't care how nice your house is, I don't care what your position at work is, there's not a parent among us who wouldn't trade it all in an instant just to heal a child that's sick. This dad is right here. He'd trade it all.

Let me turn the mirror. Have you ever cried out to God like this? You ever had a son, or a daughter, or a mom, or a dad, a spouse, a loved one at the point of death, and you're saying, "Jesus, please come down before my child dies?" I've been there. Crying out to God, "God, just please fix him. I know you can. I know you can. God, please, please, please." This is what this dad's doing. This is vastly different from going to your disciple group during prayer time when the leader asks, "Do we have any prayer requests?" and you respond with, "I have an unspoken." That is not what we're talking about here. This thing is painful and it is spoken.

This dad is on his face before Jesus just in case Jesus is who He says He is. "Please, please, please, heal my boy." Now look at what Jesus does. John 4:50: "Jesus said to him, 'Go; your son will live.'" That's not a lot of information, is it? I mean, He just gets right to it. One of the things that I think is incredible here is that geography doesn't bother Jesus. He's not bothered at all that the son is not right there. Why? Because He is God in the flesh, and so a little geography does not hinder him at all. Now look at what happens. The man believed the word that Jesus spoke to him and went on his way. I look at that and I think what a minuscule amount of information. He doesn't ask how, doesn't ask for verification, doesn't get a receipt. Nothing. He believed and went.

Let's turn the mirror again: Do you believe Him? Because by the end of this chapter, I'm going to invite anybody who needs to be healed physically, emotionally, relationally, spiritually, anybody who's broken who needs God to do something in your life, to put something back together, I'm going to invite you to pray with me and be prayed over and—where possible—anointed with oil. And we're not praying like Presbyterians who say, "If it be your will." That's not what we're going to pray. We're going to pray like Pentecostals.

We're going to ask God to send down fire from heaven on some people. But before we get there, I'm pressing you—do you believe? More specifically, do you believe He—Jesus—is able to heal you? For everyone who said yes, stick with me. We're coming back to you. For everyone who said no, let me press you further. Do you want to believe? Are you willing to be willing? Because God wants you to just want to believe. God can do a lot with people who simply want to believe. If that's you, I've got some really good news—Jesus never measured someone's faith with His faith-meter and found them deficient (Um…sorry. You're not quite cracking into the miracle-making zone with that little bit of faith…). He never does this. Why? Because it's not the amount of faith you have that matters, but the object of your faith. Amount versus object. Big difference.

We know this because in Mark 9 there's another dad who brings his demon-possessed son to Jesus, but before he can get to Him, the disciples give it a go and they get into a denominational dispute. Staring at his tormented son, the desperate man says, "*Jesus, I brought my son to be healed by you and these can't cast out the demon"* (vv. 17–18).

Jesus looks at the man and says, *"Anything is possible for one who believes."* The Bible then says the dad cries out. Not thinks about it and replies, but his immediate response is this, *"I believe. Help me overcome my unbelief"* (vv. 23–24). Maybe the most honest prayer in all of Scripture. Especially when you're dealing with something that doesn't make sense to you. Like, "Why is my son sick? Why is my daughter sick? Why won't God answer my prayer? Why won't God heal my marriage?" When you're praying for that thing over and over and over, and God's not answering it the way you hope He will. That's this man and in that place, his response to Jesus is brutally honest—*"I believe. Help me overcome my unbelief."*

Now let's return to John 4, where Jesus is met with the same little, itty-bitty-bit faith, and a man whose unbelief seems bigger than his belief. The man asks, *"Will you heal my son?"* And Jesus says, *"Go; your son will live."* And the man believed the word that Jesus spoke to him and he went on his way. Pretty cut and dried, isn't it?

But look at what happens next. The man leaves. Returning the twenty miles home. And as he was going down—that means like down to his house—his servants met him and told him that his son was recovering. And so, he asked them the hour when he began to get better. And they said to him, check this out, "Yesterday at the seventh hour." That'd be 1:00. That was when the fever left him. And the father knew that was the hour when Jesus had said to him, "Your son will live." Now, think about this. He meets Jesus in desperation, *"Will you please heal my son?"* Jesus says, *"Your son will be healed."*

Let me tell you what faith is—faith is acting as if you actually believe that God is who He says He is and He always keeps his promises. Paul says, *Be anxious for nothing, but in prayer and supplication, make your requests known to God, and the peace of God that transcends understanding will guard your heart and mind in Christ Jesus* (Phil. 4:6–7). Then when God says to you, "You will be healed," from that moment to the moment you experience that healing, you begin to walk in the kind of faith that transcends understanding. And here's what that means. That means when the doctor's report comes back again and it's still not exactly what you were hoping for and what you were praying for, and then people look at you and ask, "Hold on, hold on. It's still there? How come you're not freaking out?"

Here's what you're actually saying: "I don't know. What I do know is that I have this peace that transcends understanding because my heart and mind are being guarded in Christ Jesus." That's what this man does. But the story isn't over. Look at what happens. "And he himself believed, and all his household" (John 4:53). Romans 8:28 says, *For God is at work in all things for the good of those that love him and are called according to his purpose.* Meaning, God often uses our pain as a platform for His glory. I could stand here all day and share with you stories of how, time after time after time, God took what looked like an unanswered prayer and then worked in that situation for His glory to be shown. I can't tell you the number of times I've prayed, "Dear God, would you please do it this way?" And he doesn't and it makes no sense to me whatsoever—and then when I look back, I can see how God was using the pain that we were walking in for a much bigger thing that He had in store. Why? Because God can use the worst mess for his own message. John goes on to record, "This was now the second sign that Jesus did when he had come from Judea to Galilee" (John 4:54). Remember, in the Gospel of John, he doesn't call these things "miracles"; he calls them "signs" because a sign is not the point. A sign does not point to itself. A sign points to something greater. And the sign here is this: There will come a day when—for all those who are in Christ Jesus—there will be no more sickness. And there will be a day when we step from this experience here on earth into His very presence.

And in that day, you and I will see the Son of God face-to-face. And we will hear these words, "Well done, good and faithful servant" (Matt. 25:21). And He will wipe away every tear from our eyes. Think about this. When Jesus reaches out to wipe that tear, what do you think you will see in the palm of His hand? A scar. And I'm sure if we were all there, at the cross, witnessing the Crucifixion of the Son of God, we may have been thinking, *God, have you completely lost your mind? What are you doing here?* But God sees the end from the beginning. He can see past the cross, through the empty tomb, to the ascension, and all the way to His return. He sees it all. And God would say, "No, I don't think you understand. I am at work in all things for the good of those who love me and are called according to my purpose."

John 5:1 says, "After this, there was a feast of the Jews, and Jesus went up to Jerusalem." Remember, every time, no matter where Jesus is, He's got to go up because this is Mount Moriah. Zion. Mount Calvary. The highest place in Israel. "Now there is, in Jerusalem by the sheep gate, a pool." If you ever go to Israel with me, I'll take you to the sheep gate and the pool of Bethesda. What you need to know is that this is not the VIP entrance. It's kind of close to the temple, and it's where the shepherds would bring the sheep on their way to be slaughtered. The pool at Bethesda actually had two pools, one on each side of the road. In one, people ritually cleansed, and in the other, shepherds cleaned their sheep. This was that pool.

The sheep gate has five roofed colonnades and scattered about on the ground like pick-up sticks are a multitude of invalids, blind, lame, and paralyzed. Notice how in the Gospel of John, Jesus has zero problem at all bouncing back and forth between the VIPs of the club level and the least of these in society. One minute He's walking with Nicodemus, a religious leader. The next minute He's sitting at a well in Samaria talking to a girl that custom would demand He not talk to. One minute He's hanging out with an official from King Herod's palace, and the next He's walking among the invalids.

Jesus doesn't just hang out with the clean and the healthy. He came for the dirty and the sick. Our church is way more like the pool of Bethesda with a multitude of invalids. Come visit on a Sunday and you'll see what I mean. Look around. We're kind of like the island of misfit toys for churches in our city. If you're busted up and bruised, if you walk with a limp or can't walk at all, if you've got some issues, then let me welcome you to our church. Come in person or watch us online. We're more like an emergency room than country club. You don't have to get your act together before you go to church. None of the rest of us do. You'll fit right in.

Our church, The Church of Eleven22 (there are a host of other great churches out there but let me just speak about ours for a moment), is a whole bunch of people who need the Lord to do for us what we have been unable to do for ourselves. All of us are invalids scattered around the two pools. And when Jesus walks into Jerusalem that day, this is what He finds. A sea of sick people.

Back to John 5. Verse 3 says, "In these lay a multitude of invalids—blind, lame, and paralyzed." Now, if you pay close attention to your Bible, which I hope you do, you'll notice there's no verse 4 after verse 3. It jumps straight to verse 5. That strike you as odd?

This is why we use the English Standard Version as our translation of choice. The ESV translators have attempted to be as accurate as possible to the original manuscripts. The translators describe the ESV as an "essentially literal translation," meaning they are trying, as much as possible, to replicate the precise wording of the original text. That's why they place verse 4 in the margin. By doing so, they're admitting verse 4 appears in later versions of the text, but not in earlier versions. They do this by saying, "some manuscripts insert" and then include this: *waiting for the moving of the water; for an angel of the Lord went down at certain seasons into the pool, and stirred the water; whoever stepped in first after the stirring of the water was healed of whatever disease he had.* The translators aren't sure if this is legend or if it actually happened, but whatever the case, this word-for-word attempt at translation gives us a Bible that's as literal as possible and gets as close as we can, with the knowledge we have, to the original. Which, by the way, is incredibly accurate and trustworthy. At any rate, this is why everybody's hanging out on the edge of this pool. Verse 5 says, "One man was there who had been an invalid for thirty-eight years." Think about it. Thirty-eight years.

In the first century, that's a life span. A long time. And I want you to focus on that word, *invalid*. This is how people would've seen him, especially in the first century. And this is how we know him. Now look at the two words—*in valid*. As in *not valid*. That's how this culture would have seen him. He was not producing, so he was of no value. An "IN Valid" human being. But that's not how Jesus sees him. Jesus sees every single human being as valid, no matter what your physical state, no matter what your mental state, no matter what your condition, no matter what... You are not in-valid. How do I know this? Because when Christ died on the cross, He validated you. This is why 1 Corinthians 6:19–20 says, *Do you not know that you are not your own? You were bought at a price.* Do you know how valuable and valid you are to the Almighty God?

I was curious so I googled this—the most expensive animal on the planet right now is a horse whose last name is Pegasus. It's valued at $72 million. As expensive as that racehorse is, it's nothing compared to any human being on the planet, regardless of where they're from, what they look like, what condition they're born in, or whatever. Every human being is infinitely more valuable than this racehorse, but we live in a world that says the opposite. We live in a world that says, "No, no, no. Some people are just inconvenient. They're not worth being born."

The problem with this philosophy is that every single person on this planet—no matter what condition—is an image bearer of the most high God. Including this man who's been lying here thirty-eight years. Part of the reason people in the first century looked down on this man was the advent of a faulty theology, which we will see again in John 9. In John 9, we bump into a guy who's blind from birth, and some of the disciples ask Jesus, "Rabbi, who sinned, this man or his parents, that he was born blind?" (v. 2). You thought, in the first century—and honestly, people think this today too—that if something is wrong with you, it's because you did something wrong. Which leads to the question that people sometimes ask me: If God is almighty and God is all loving, then why sickness? Why pain? Why tragedy? Why bad things? Another way to phrase this is: Why do bad things happen to good people?

Not only is that a bad question, it's the wrong question. Here's why. There was only one good person and the worst thing happened to Him, but it was for the glory of God. That said, I understand why people in the midst of hardship ask, "Why suffering, why pain? Is the enemy attacking me?" Let me answer that this way.

There are five categories of pain. Understanding these can help you deal with it and better know how to pray.

Number one: We live in a fallen world. When sin entered the world, everything about everything was fractured. Upturned. Nothing was as it was meant to be. Sin was and is that big a deal. First Corinthians 15 says that *death is an enemy of God.* In God's initial creation, we didn't dig holes and put people in them. No funerals. No sickness. So the hardship you or I might suffer, whether it's a car crash or cancer, can simply be collateral damage from the enemy. Scripture says satan is the ruler of this world, and he does have a measure of power given to him by God, but before you get too worried, greater is He that is in us than He that's in the world. Which leads me to point two.

Number two: Demonic attack. Sometimes your suffering is a sniper attack from the enemy. This is why Paul in Ephesians 6 says *our battle is not against flesh and blood but against rulers, principalities, and powers, and spiritual forces of wickedness* (v. 12). You thought your problem was your ex, or your boss, or your teacher, but Paul says that the enemy is often behind all of those battles, working through those people. Sometimes people say to me, "You actually believe in demons?" I do, for sure. One of satan's primary tricks is to cause you to think he's not to blame.

You ever struggled with an addiction? Know a loved one who has or is? What do you call that? There's this thing that you know you don't want to do. You know it's going to harm you. You know it's going to kill you. And yet, in a way that you can't explain, you continually go down a path you promised you'd never go down again. And you don't want to go down. Something is enticing you and has a hold on you. That thing is not you. That thing wants to kill you. Wants your head on a platter. What do you call that? I'm not saying that everybody who struggles with depression is oppressed by a demon, but we know from Isaiah 61 and Luke 4 that *Jesus takes from us the spirit of heaviness and exchanges it for a garment of praise.* Paul also speaks of a "spirit of slavery" and a "spirit of fear," so we know they're real and can afflict us (Rom. 8:15; 2 Tim. 1:7). But let me clarify one thing: No believer in Christ can be "possessed" by a demon because "possessed" denotes ownership, and you are possessed by Jesus. His blood purchased you and His Spirit seals you. That said, you can be oppressed, and that oppression is exactly what Paul speaks of in Ephesians 6:12–17 and 2 Corinthians 10:3–5, *the weapons of our warfare are not of the flesh but have divine power to destroy strongholds.* Oftentimes the reason that Christians are getting their butts kicked spiritually is because they are not ready for the fight. If you prance through life as if there is not an enemy that wants to kill, steal, and destroy you, then you are a sitting duck. Aleksandr Solzhenitsyn, in his book *The Gulag Archipelago*, is talking about Russian police in the late 1930s arresting citizens and taking them to the gulags. The police faced very little resistance. Solzhenitsyn says, "A person who is not inwardly prepared for the violence committed against them is always weaker than the one committing the violence." Be prepared.

Number three: Coming on the heels of a fallen world and demonic attack is the effect of your own sin. Sometimes, it's just you. Listen, I love you, this is going to sting a little, but it's true. Sometimes people come to me and say, "Pastor, I think satan is attacking me." "Okay, tell me what's going on." Then they tell me and I have to tell them, "No, darling. All he's got to do is leave you alone, your wounds are self-inflicted." "But you don't understand, my finances…" And when they explain their mountain of debt, the problem is clear. "Listen. You're buying stuff you don't need with money you don't have. The enemy doesn't have to do anything." Or sometimes it's about their job. "The enemy is attacking me. I got fired from my job." And when they explain how, the reason is crystal clear. "I hate to tell you but you got fired from your job because you don't show up on time and when you do show up, you don't work. That is not the enemy, that's you being lazy."

Number four: Sometimes we suffer when others sin against us. There are situations when our suffering is not our fault but the result of someone else's sin. The problem we bump into here is that we like to claim this one a lot and feed the victim mentality. I'm not disagreeing with you, but before you go here, eliminate the other three. We like to play this card because it absolves us of responsibility.

Number five: This is tough for some people but that doesn't make it any less true—sometimes our suffering is straight from the hand of God. See Paul's prayer to remove the thorn in his flesh. God sent a demon to torment him. Put that in your theological pipe and smoke it. You mean God's handing out demons? He did to King Saul. He sent one to torment him. Look at the life of Joseph. Scripture says He—meaning God—put him—meaning Joseph—in iron fetters. In prison. God's promised languished in servitude and prison for more than a decade. And look at Job. Job's suffering was God's idea. He asked satan, *"Have you considered my servant Job?"* While the Bible says Job was blameless. It wasn't like he had it coming or deserved it. Job was a righteous man of God. Lastly, Scripture says God was pleased to crush His Son. The Father "crushed" Jesus. Scripture also says Jesus learned obedience through the things that He suffered.

We quote Genesis 50:20, saying, *What the enemy meant for evil, God used for good.* But that's actually a misquote. That's not what it says. It says, *What the enemy meant for evil, God meant for good.* God didn't use anything. The enemy did not go first and then God changed it for good. God meant it.

Back to our man lying beside the pool of Bethesda. Jesus sees this man, who's been here for thirty-eight years, and he asks him the million-dollar question: "Do you want to be healed?" When I first read that, I thought, *Jesus, why are you asking? Of course he wants to be healed. The man hadn't walked for 38 years. You think he wants a sandwich? You think he's waiting in line at Ticketmaster?* No, he's lying at this pool because this is where healing happens. Regardless, Jesus asks, "Do you want to be healed?" And when Jesus uses the word, *heal,* he means it in a wholeness kind of way. When you see the word *healed* in the New Testament, He's not simply saying, *"Do you want me to fix one little broken part of your life?"* He's ultimately saying, *"Do you want me to put your whole life back together so that you can love God with your all?"* That's what he's talking about here. The Hebrew word for that is *shalom.* And remember, the man is not allowed in the temple, so he has no access to God. Zero. Why? Because God said so in the law of Moses: "For no one who has a blemish shall draw near, a man blind or lame, or one who has a mutilated face or a limb too long" (Lev. 21:18). This is part of the crushing weight of the law, and without jumping to the punchline, this is one reason why the grace poured out on us from the cross is so unbelievable. This is Paul writing to the church in Ephesus, "But now in Christ Jesus you who once were far off have been brought near by the blood of Christ" (Eph. 2:13). For first-century believers, this is mind-blowing.

If the man does not want to be healed, we've got a problem, because the want-to comes before the how-to. I used to do a lot of marriage counseling, and before we did anything, I would ask them both, "Do you want to fix your marriage?" You would be amazed at the number of times they shook their heads and said no. Point being, it doesn't matter if you've got the how-to if you ain't got the want-to.

If you came to me today and said, "Pastor, we've signed you up for break dancing lessons. We got you a coach. You're gonna do great," guess who's not going to learn how to break-dance? Why? Because I don't want to. And as crazy as it is, there are a whole lot of people who don't want to be healed. I know this because every Sunday I watch people show up to church with the same stuff, and as I get to know them one truth bubbles to the surface. They don't really want to change. They want somebody to change their external circumstances without them having to look in the mirror.

The longer I've been in ministry, the more times I've seen there's a pretty good reason for this. People in pain begin to wrap their identity around it, and if you offer to take away that pain, they think they'll be left holding nothing. But that's not what Scripture says. Jesus exchanges ashes for beauty. Bad for good. He never leaves us empty. I relate it to a baby in a diaper: "I know it's gross and it's stinky, but it's warm and it's mine, so I'll just sit in it for a while." Sometimes you don't want to be healed because then it will take away your excuse for your bad behavior. Either consciously or subconsciously, you think, *Yeah, if God heals me, then I've actually got to work at this marriage again, and I can't just continue to sit up late at night looking at porn and blaming her for it.* Or for some of you, if God heals you, it'll take away your excuse for your rotten attitude all the time. In any case, you're using your infirmity to justify your sin. The question remains—do you want to be healed?

Look at what the man does. The sick man answered him, *"Sir, I have no one to put me in the pool when the water is stirred up. And while I'm going in, other ones step down before me* (John 5:7). Whether true or not, a legend had formed that when the angel stirred the water, the first one in received the healing. No one else. Some people are good at making excuses and some people are good at making it happen, never both. Nothing frustrates me more than excuses. This guy sounds like a twenty-first-century college student: "Well, it's not my fault—I need a safe space." Oh, Lord, pray about that for a second. Despite his answer, what we see here is the patience and mercy of God. By the way, that's what *Bethesda* means: "the mercy of God."

Even though this guy's giving excuses, Jesus is going to heal him anyway. Now just work with me here a minute. Scripture doesn't say this, but it would fit the character of Jesus. Maybe Jesus gets down on his level and says, "Look here, man. You're looking for healing in the wrong places. Whether an actual angel comes to stir this thing up, or it's a legend that this world has created around here, you are looking for this physical pool to do something that it can't do for you. The only way you're going to be healed is for you to look at Me and do what I tell you to do." And the same is true for many of you. Many of you are looking for healing in the wrong places. Now, let me be clear. God heals in all kinds of ways. Every good and perfect gift is from above. And so, He calls Himself the Great Physician. And then God gives us this common grace, like doctors, and nurses, and medicine, and technology, and counselors, and all of the above.

Sometimes healing comes through just the power of prayer, and sometimes through pills, and sometimes through people, but it all comes from the Great Physician. And so, in my mind, Jesus says to the man on the mat, "Look, man, this pool's got nothing for you. I am the One who can heal you." Then Jesus says to him, " 'Get up, take up your bed, and walk.' And at once the man was healed, and he took up his bed and walked" (John 5:8–9).

When I read this, one of the questions I ask myself is: Why tell the man to take up his mat? Think about it. Think about the condition of this man. How long has he been there? Thirty-eight years. Now imagine the mat. It's where he sleeps. Eats. Begs. It's the thing that keeps him from sitting directly on the ground. That's a nasty mat. He couldn't get up and go to the bathroom. That's what he used the mat for. For thirty-eight years it collected his sweat. His body odor. His everything. Trust me, you wouldn't want to get close to this mat.

You would think Jesus would say, "All right, hop up off the mat and burn it, then take a shower." But that's not what he says. He says, "Take up that gross and nasty mat and start toting it around. Everywhere you go." "But why, Jesus?" "So that when people look at you, they will realize that your pain no longer identifies you but is actually a platform for the glory of God." So the brother rose up and toted it around. Why? Because Jesus told him to. And he's not ashamed of it. Why? Because Jesus isn't ashamed of it. How is that possible? "There is therefore now no condemnation for those who are in Christ Jesus" (Rom. 8:1). Meaning, your mat doesn't tell you who you are.

Only Jesus gets to tell you who you are. Your past has no say in that. Jesus says, "Take up your mess and walk with it, and I'm going to declare my message and my victory through your mess." This means that any time the enemy tries to point at my mat and remind me of my past, I just point him at the cross and remind him of his complete, eternal, and irrevocable defeat. When he begins to whisper, "Who are you to preach to all these people? If they knew what you have done…" Problem is, he's right. What's more, he doesn't know all that I've done because all he can do is see the stuff that I did. He has no idea what crazy is going on in my mind. And yet, when Jesus tells us it is finished—"*Tetelestai*"—it counted for all of our nasty mats. Their claim on us was finished. That means yours too. You see, the enemy always tries to identify you by your scars. But in Christ you are identified by His.

God is not ashamed of you and He is not ashamed of your past. In fact, He's going to use it as a platform for His glory. Notice what he says. He says, "*Take up your mat and walk*" (John 5:8). Here's what he doesn't say. He doesn't say, "Take up your mat and when you get tired, just lie back down on it and wipe that nasty all over you." Why would we do that? That'd be dumb, wouldn't it? Can you imagine seeing this man crippled for thirty-eight years, lying back down in the filth? You'd look at him and say, "Whoa, dude. What are you doing?" Walking people don't lie on a crippled man's mat. But this is exactly what we as believers in Jesus Christ do when we continuously go back to those old sins. Those old habits. Those old things that were killing us. And it makes no sense in light of the gospel.

Because of Jesus, you don't have to do the stuff you used to do, because you're not the person that you used to be. You're not a cripple. You're a child of the King. Let's keep reading. "Now, that day was the Sabbath. So the Jews—" meaning specifically the religious leaders, like the Pharisees and the Sadducees "—said to the man who had been healed, 'It is the Sabbath, and it is not lawful for you to take up your bed'" (John 5:9–10). God gave us the sabbath as a gift. It was supposed to be a day of rest. A day to refuel with the Lord so that you would be ready for the upcoming work He had for you. The religious leaders put so many laws and rules and burdens around keeping that sabbath that it became a burden and not a blessing to the people.

I call these rule makers "church people." You ever met some really religious people who can't see the miracle because of the mat? I have met folks on a Sunday who watch videos of life-changing miracles, and they want to critique the manner of the miracle. Man, would you get serious? These religious folks couldn't see past the law in order to see the lavish love of God.

Let me say that again.

They couldn't see past the law in order to see the lavish love of God. They only see the mat. This is not new. Jesus faced the same limiting religiosity in Mark 7. The Pharisees are busting His chops as to why His disciples don't wash their hands the way Hebrew tradition would mandate. It was a manmade tradition that occurs nowhere in the Word of God. Jesus shakes His head. In my mind, He's thinking, *Guys, would you get a grip.* He then quotes Isaiah: "This people honors me with their lips, but their heart is far from me; in vain do they worship me, teaching as doctrines the commandments of men" (Mark 7:6–7; based on Isa. 29:13). He's telling them, "*You have left the commandments of God and are now adhering to your own manmade commandments, as if it's to my Word. And so, you've rejected God to establish your tradition.*" This by definition is self-righteous. He ends by saying they are "thus making void the word of God by your tradition that you have handed down" (Mark 7:13). This is a mic drop to the religious elite standing around Jesus. They know it and they hate Him for it. But if you look closely, we do the same thing. We lift up our traditions to the exclusion of the work and power of God. Isaiah says, "So shall my word be that goes out from my mouth; it shall not return to me empty, but it shall accomplish that which I purpose, and shall succeed in the thing for which I sent it" (Isa. 55:11). When Jesus quotes Isaiah 29, those standing around Him know full well what Isaiah 55 says. Jesus is saying it without having to say it. The point He's making is that the only thing on planet earth that can nullify or make void the Word of God is our traditions. It was a gut punch to them, and it should be a gut punch to every one of us church-going folk.

So the no-longer-crippled man answered them, "The man who healed me, that man said to me, 'Take up your bed, and walk'"

(John 5:11). Here's what he's saying: "Yeah, I appreciate the inquisition here, but He healed me. I'm walking. Something I haven't done in almost forty years, so with all due respect, I think I'll listen to Him."

Surprised by his answer, they ask, "Who is the man who said to you, 'Take up your bed and walk'?" (John 5:12). I love what happens next. The man shrugs and says, "I have no idea." Truth is, there's no problem with "I don't know." Scripture says, "Now the man who had been healed did not know who it was, for Jesus had withdrawn, as there was a crowd in the place" (John 5:13). Afterward, Jesus found the man in the temple, which is a big deal. He had never been in the temple. By law, he wasn't allowed. For the last thirty-eight years the world around him had labeled him an invalid. Kept out and not welcome.

Now he's in the temple, and he's freaking out. In my mind, he's jumping up and down on his new legs. He's also probably worshiping by himself because he had yet to take a shower. But Jesus finds him in the temple and He says to him, "See, you are well!" That word *well* is "shalom" or "whole." Jesus continues, "Sin no more, that nothing worse may happen to you" (John 5:14). We don't know for sure, but this could mean that sin led to his condition. If it did, Jesus could be saying, "If you continue to make the same dumb choices you used to make, it's going to lead to the same place. Sin no more that nothing worse may happen to you." The man could look at the mat tucked under his arm and ask, "What could possibly be worse than that?" Actually, hell. Hell is a lot worse than that mat. Jesus is offering him not just physical healing, but spiritual healing.

Which is the eternal miracle. Salvation.

Jesus answered them, "My Father is working until now, and I am working" (John 5:17). This was why the Jews were seeking all the more to kill him—not only was he breaking the sabbath, but He was even calling God His own Father, making Himself equal to God. And because He is God, He alone can change your life.

Last time—do you want to be healed?

Because of Jesus, your past no longer has the right to define your future. In Christ, your past pain can be a platform for God's glory. This may be a little unorthodox, but whatever. I want to close this chapter by praying for your healing.

Here's why. I'm not a faith healer, I'm a Bible obeyer. I did not grow up in this whole praying-for-healing thing. I got saved at a Southern Baptist camp, and I'd never been to a healing service. We anointed biscuits with gravy. But just because that was what we did doesn't make us right. James, the brother of Jesus, says this, "Is anyone among you suffering?" I know some of you reading this right now are going through the wringer. It could be kid pain. Could be physical. Marital. And through the inspiration of the Holy Spirit, James says this to you: "Is anyone among you suffering?" Then he says, "Let him pray. Is anyone cheerful? Let him sing praise." But he doesn't stop there. He gets even more specific. "Is anyone among you sick?" (James 5:13–14). And he doesn't just mean physically sick. Literally, that word means "broken." Anyone among you broken? Like, brokenhearted. It for sure includes physical sickness, but remember what Moses said to the people: *"And you shall love the Lord your God with all your heart, and all your soul, and all your mind, and all your strength"* (Deut. 6:5). (This is called the Shema.) That's what it means to be the whole self. Is there anything in your life physically, mentally, relationally, spiritually that is broken, sick, or out of line from the way God would desire and design you?

Every time in the Scriptures when the enemy really wants to stop a move of God, you know what he tries to do? He tries to move in and wipe out a generation. See Moses. See Joshua. See Jesus. You know who's been most affected by the coronavirus pandemic? It's our kids' generation. From depression and anxiety, suicides have skyrocketed. Maybe you too are depressed and you just can't explain it. Your circumstances should tell you everything should be all right, but you can't turn the all right on. If this is you, God loves you so much. And He's not done with you. Not by a long shot. He's got a purpose and a plan for you. The alarm clock and the empty tomb are empirical evidence to me that God loves you and wants you around here today and tomorrow. Maybe what's broken is relational. Maybe it's your marriage and you think it's beyond repair. Or maybe you're divorced and the lies of condemnation constantly get whispered in your ear. Or maybe it's this feeling of loneliness or hopelessness. Maybe it's an addiction.

James says this: "Is there anyone among you sick?" (James 5:14). The Bible says, "Hope deferred makes the heart sick" (Prov. 13:12). Some of you picked up this book today and you feel hopeless. Your heart is sick. That feeling of hopelessness does not come from your heavenly Father because hope is not found in a new set of circumstances. Hope is found in the resurrected Christ.

"Is anyone among you sick? Let him call for the elders of the church, and let them pray over him, anointing him with oil in the name of the Lord. And the prayer of faith will save the one who is sick, and the Lord will raise him up. And if he has committed sins, he will be forgiven. Therefore, confess your sins to one another and pray for one another, that you may be healed" (James 5:14–16).

This is a promise from God to you and me, and it's either true or it's not.

This means every single person who is in Christ Jesus will be healed. The difficult part for us is that He just doesn't specify when. Some of you are going to be healed this side of eternity. The rest of us will be healed when we step into eternity with Jesus. Why the wait? I wish I knew. Paul prays three times for the thorn in his flesh and God says, "*No, my grace is sufficient for you*" (2 Cor. 12:9). With that in mind, I want us to pray like Shadrach, Meshach, and Abednego. When Nebuchadnezzar built an idol and told everyone to bow down to it, these three said no. Nebuchadnezzar told them if they didn't, he'd throw them into the fiery furnace.

In the face of incineration, they said, "Look here, man, we know that God can save us, and we are believing that God will save us, but even if He doesn't, we're not bowing down to your stupid idol." There's a sovereign God kind of prayer right there. So, right now in this moment, we are coming before God Most High because He said, *We have not because we ask not* (James 4:2). "God, You told me to ask, seek, and knock, so I am. I have a sickness and I want to be obedient to Your Word, so I'm going to ask You to move supernaturally and mightily. Right now. I believe You can, and I'm believing in this moment that You will, but even if You decide not to, like You did with Paul and the thorn in his flesh, I am not going to bow down to fear and doubt of this world, because I know if the tomb is empty, anything is possible."

Are you sick? Do you need prayer? Do you need to be healed? One little caveat here. Remember the official, the dad, who asked for healing for his son. His son wasn't even there. So maybe you need to come on behalf of your prodigal. Maybe you need to come on behalf of your spouse who won't come with you. Maybe you need to come on behalf of that friend, or that family member who's in the hospital. Because to Jesus, geography doesn't matter.

You think you don't have what it takes to pray? James answers this unspoken, too. He gives the example of Elijah, the Old Testament prophet. "Elijah was a man with a nature like ours" (James 5:17). Here's my translation: *Elijah was just a dude who knew the Lord. Like you or me.* "And he prayed fervently that it might not rain, and for three years and six months it did not rain on the earth. Then he prayed again, and heaven gave rain, and the earth bore its fruit" (James 5:17–18). The invitation is simple. As is the response. Just come. Let me pray over you.

I believe community matters, so if you're in a faith community, like a church, call your church and ask them to anoint you and lay hands on you. If they won't, get another church because your church is not walking in obedience to Scripture, and you don't want to be there anyway. Some of you are already in a disciple group. Great. Even better. See all those people around you? They're the hands and feet of Jesus, so why don't you ask them to lay hands on you? Really. And then ask someone to anoint you with oil as a symbol of the Spirit of God on you. Of the shed blood of Jesus for you. As a symbol to remind you it's by his stripes you were and are healed. You may want to hold out your hands like you are receiving a gift from the Father. Now while you're being anointed and those around you are laying hands on you (mind you, this should be appropriate and never make you feel anxious or fearful), I'm going to pray. Oh, and if you're alone in prison or stuck on an island by yourself, Psalm 91 says, *He commands His angels concerning you, and they will lift you up* (vv. 11–12). In order to lift you, they've got to lay hands on you, so right now, if you'll just close your eyes, we're going to ask God to do what only He can do and command His angels. Oh, and yes, you can anoint yourself. No problem.

Pray with Me

Good and gracious heavenly Father, we love You more than anything. And Lord, we thank You that You are a healer. We thank You that healing is found in the name of Jesus. And God, we worship You, the healer. We do not worship the healing. Lord, I pray that for those who are cheerful, Lord, I pray that they would sing praise, and I pray for the man, the woman, the student who is struggling and sick, whether it's physical sickness or mental sickness or relational sickness. For the man and woman who have a broken relationship that you need to put back together, Lord, I pray that forgiveness and reconciliation would rule and reign in that house. God, I pray that we are able to forgive one another because You have forgiven us through the blood of Jesus that was shed on that cross. God, I pray for those who are struggling in their minds. God, whether it's depression, or anxiety, or addiction, Lord, I ask that they would be anxious for nothing. God, I ask that by prayer and supplication they would make their request known to You. God, I ask that they would come to You with the same intensity that those unwanted thoughts come after them. And Lord, would You please give them a peace that surpasses all understanding? Would You guard their hearts and minds in Christ Jesus? God, I pray for those whom the enemy has a grip on and who are struggling with self-harm. Lord, I pray that because You suffered and died on the cross, they would know that we don't have to. Lord, would You remind us that our value is found in You? We are not our own. We are bought at a price; therefore, may we honor You with our bodies?

Lord, I pray for an outpouring of the Spirit of God. Lord, I pray that we would be healed in Jesus' name for Your glory. Lord, I ask for those who need physical healing. We confess that You are the Great Physician. Every good and perfect gift is from You. So we don't care how the healing comes. It could be a supernatural touch from You. Or it could be through the miracle of doctors and nurses and technology.

Lord, I pray against the enemy. Lord, I pray against the spirit of fear right now. And fear is not a feeling; fear is the spirit and he does not come from you. Lord, I pray for a spirit of power and of love, and for a sound mind. And I pray that men, women, and students on this day would be healed. And that those healings are a sign. A sign pointing people to You. I pray this in Jesus' name. Amen.

CHAPTER 4

The Feeding of the Five Thousand— Do You Believe Even When Doubts Creep In?

I need to tell you a story. It's painful. It's also true. Hearing it is going to hurt a little bit. But hang with me. It's worth it. In May 2002, five guys were playing video games at the house of one of their girlfriends in Jacksonville, Florida. A few of the guys knew each other. A few didn't. One of the guys was Isaac Brown Jr. Like many teenagers, Isaac Jr. played football, but his love was basketball. He never met a stranger, and he was the class clown whose smile could light up a room. Everybody loved him.

Somewhere in that night, for reasons that were never clear, Takoya Criner stood and fired seven times at the others, killing Isaac Jr. and a friend. They weren't smoking dope, weren't drinking, weren't running with a gang, weren't stealing cars. They were punching buttons on a game controller.

A few hours later, as the sun came up, the police chief and chaplain knocked on the door of Isaac's home. His father, Isaac Sr., answered the door. Isaac Sr. is a police officer. Been on the force since '86. He was and is one of their own. If you've ever flown into Jacksonville International Airport, you've probably walked right past him. He's there a lot.

This is how Isaac Sr. remembers that day. I've written it this way because I want you to hear it in Ike's words:

Early that morning, the doorbell rang. Man, who can this be? And when I opened the door, my chief was standing there. And believe it or not, it didn't really surprise me, it didn't. My sergeant was there and I'm like, man, and my lieutenant, they were there together, and still nothing clicked. But behind my lieutenant, I saw the chaplain, I saw the police chaplain, Chaplain Crosby. And when I saw him, I knew something was wrong. And I think the first thing I said was, "Hey, Chaplain Crosby, why are you here?" He didn't say anything at the time, my sergeant spoke first. And he told me, he said, "Ike, I got to tell you that your son, Isaac Jr., was killed." And that pretty much did it there. That pretty much broke me down and it was kind of unbelievable. What do you do? What do you do? Pretty helpless, pretty helpless feeling.

Ike buried his son and sat in court every day until the jury found Takoya guilty of killing Isaac Jr. and a friend, and wounding another man. Takoya had no connection to Isaac. The shooting was as random as random can be. Isaac was just in the wrong place at the wrong time.

Now I need to leave you and Ike right there for a little while, but we're coming back. But before we go, I want to ask you to put yourself in Ike's place. Stare at that courtroom and his son's killer through Ike's eyes. What are the whispers screaming in your head? Maybe they sound something like, *Why did God do what God did? Why didn't He stop this? Why...?* You think Ike has a little rising anger? You think he'd like to kill his son's killer? You think Ike has a few doubts about who God is and the love of God? Would you? Let me ask it this way: What wouldn't you doubt? Just being honest; if it's me, it'd be tough not to doubt everything about everything.

As we dive in here, I'm asking you: What happens, what do you do, when it just doesn't make sense? When your doubts are raging? Because trust me, when Ike answered that door, doubt started screaming at the top of its lungs.

*   *   *

John 6 is going to walk us through an experience with the disciples where life gets really complicated. And their doubts creep in. What was once so clear, now is not.

Verses 1–2 start us off on a high note: "After this, Jesus went away to the other side of the Sea of Galilee, which is the Sea of Tiberius. And a large crowd was following him, because they saw the signs that he was doing on the sick." Which is great, but it takes a nosedive from there: "Jesus went up on the mountain, and there he sat down with his disciples. Now the Passover, the feast of the Jews, was at hand. Lifting up his eyes, then, and seeing that a large crowd was coming toward him, Jesus said to Philip, 'Where are we to buy bread, so that these people may eat?'" You should probably underline these words: "He said this to test him, for he himself knew what he would do" (vv. 3–6).

Stop right there. Do you know that the Lord will test us? The writer of Hebrews says that the son not disciplined is the illegitimate son. God disciplines us, or tests us, or sends us through trials, because He loves us. Because we are legitimate children of God. Now, if that is the definition of *legitimacy*, then I was raised super legit. My dad must have loved me a lot because he wore us out. And I know some of you weren't raised that way. You were put in time-out. Which is half your problem, but that's another book.

Most often the reason God tests us and allows us to go through trials is to remind us of our desperation for him. In fact, J. I. Packer says it this way, "Still he seeks the fellowship of his people, and sends them both sorrows and joys in order to detach their love from other things and attach it to himself."

Jesus doesn't always give the disciples the answers they're looking for. Or the ones they want. Sometimes He asks them questions that they can't answer so that they'll look to Him. And right here with Philip, that's what He's doing.

Before I go any further, for those of you who are having a rough time right now and getting your lunch handed to you, let me say this—the Father knows. He's not indifferent. Not checked out. Not surprised. Not pacing the halls of heaven popping antacids over your predicament. Let me say this directly—whatever you're facing has already been sifted through His sovereign hand. Remember this.

And so, Philip answered him, "Two hundred denari"—that's eight months' wages—"worth of bread would not be enough for each of them to get a little" (v. 7). Philip has studied the situation and immediately goes to pragmatism. Which makes me wonder: Was he not paying attention in Cana? Jesus has just sidled up to Philip and asked, "Philip, how are we gonna buy bread for all of these people?"

Given their experience at the wedding, you'd think Philip would say, "Don't know, Lord, but if you can turn water to wine, what can you do with bread?" But that's not what he does. He immediately looks to the impossibility of the temporary. One of his disciples, Andrew, Simon Peter's brother, said to Jesus, "*Well, there's a boy here who has five barley loaves and two fish*" (v. 9). And we're not talking about a large, delicious bass. Think sardine. Then Andrew, also looking at the impossibility of the temporal, points out, "But what are they for so many?" (v. 9).

The only one who seems to offer a solution to Jesus is the boy with the picnic: "Lord, we seem to be staring down at an impossible situation, and I know it's not much, but it's all that I have." All these doubters and adults scratching their heads and one boy speaks up.

It's amazing what God can do with just one person who's willing to take what's in their hands and put it into His hands, and then see what He can do.

This isn't a message on stewardship, so relax. I'm not really talking about money here. That too is another book. But I will point out that there are basically three attitudes when it comes to money and stuff. Attitude number one, the most prevalent in our country, is this: What's mine is mine. It's called selfishness. Attitude two is this: What's yours is mine. That's called stealing. It's also called socialism. Attitude three: What's mine is God's. That's called stewardship. And what this little boy understands is "What's mine is yours, God." And when we take what we have and we put it in the hands of Jesus, we have no idea what is possible. You should probably underline that too because what's about to happen, in case you're new to Bible study, is Jesus is going to feed all those people with that one boy's lunch. And remember, this doesn't happen if he doesn't take the little bit he has and put it in the hands of Jesus, trusting that what's in the hands of Jesus is infinitely greater than what he could do with all of it on his own.

Here's a question for you: Are you trusting Jesus with what He's put in your hand? Or do you believe you can do a better job with it than Him? Are you white-knuckling or open-handed?

Jesus responds, " 'Have the people sit down.' Now, there was much grass in the place. So the men sat down, about five thousand in number" (v. 10). Why does it say, "the men sat down"? Because in the first century, you counted heads of households. Meaning, there could be up to twenty thousand people on that hillside. *And Jesus took the loaves and when He had given thanks, He distributed them to those who were seated and also as much fish as they wanted* (v. 11).

This miracle is found in all four gospels. In the Gospel of Matthew, the Bible says that Jesus took the bread and the fish, gave thanks, and then handed the fish and the loaves to the disciples and said to them, "You feed them."

Think about this from the perspective of the disciples. Jesus takes five loaves and two little itty-bitty sardine-like fish, hands it out to each one of the disciples, and says, "All right, boys. Start giving it away." Now we're gonna find out in just a second here that every single person had as much food as they wanted to eat, with leftovers. But, notice. That did not happen in the hands of Jesus. Where does the miracle happen? The miracle happens in the hands of the disciples.

Think about this. You're the disciples. Twenty thousand hungry people. Jesus commands, puts something in your hand, and you think, *Um... Lord, this ain't gonna work. We're gonna look like a bunch of idiots.* Many times God will call us to do something, and in our own natural mind, we may look like an idiot. And you know what? You might. But if you don't take that step of obedience, you have no idea of the miracle that's waiting on the other side. Which begs the question—are you willing to look like an idiot for Jesus?

Honestly, I don't know how this happened. The disciples took the little they had and started handing it out. And as they walked in obedience they began to realize they weren't running out. In fact, they had plenty. More than enough. That's what's going on here.

But let's not miss the obvious—the miracle does not begin to happen as long as they hold it in their hands. The miracle happens when they take what Jesus put in their hands and give it away.

Make the connection for me. What has the Lord put in your hand? "And when they had eaten their fill, he told his disciples, 'Gather up the leftover fragments, that nothing may be lost' " (John 6:12). Again, "what's mine is mine" is selfishness. "What's yours is mine" is stealing. And "what's mine is God's" is stewardship.

Jesus wants us to be good stewards of it all. Doesn't want you to waste any of what He's given you. Not just the first and best but everything.

One older pastor told me, "Don't waste Jesus' bread." I can't say it any better. So they gathered up the leftovers and filled twelve baskets with fragments of the five barley loaves that had been left by those who had eaten. The Bible doesn't say this, but what happened to the boy, and what if he got to take one of the baskets home? The boy opened his hand and offered what little he had, thinking, *This is all that I have but I'm willing to give it to you, Jesus.* Then a few hours later he walks home with a basket full. How's he explain that to his mama?

Staring at the twelve leftover baskets, the people saw the sign that he had done, and said, "This is indeed the Prophet who is to come into the world!" (John 6:14). Their hearts are full, their minds are full, their bellies are full. But watch what happens: "Perceiving then that they were about to come and take [Jesus] by force and make him king, Jesus withdrew again to the mountain by himself" (John 6:15). We as people have a propensity to fit Jesus into our box. The moment we think that Jesus can meet our needs, we quickly try to get Jesus to be on our team. We begin to think, *Oh, look what He can do with fresh loaves, or fish and loaves. Imagine what He could do with the stock market. Imagine what He could do with Medicaid. Imagine what He could do with the Romans and getting them out of here.* He becomes a tool or an instrument in our hand rather than Lord of all. Truth is, Jesus did not come to take sides. He came to take over. And one day He will return and rule and reign.

You ever notice how no matter what someone's cause, they want Jesus on their side? But the gospel is greater than your cause. The gospel is greater than my cause. When the religious rulers try to put Jesus in political power, He won't agree and plays a little game of hide-and-seek until evening.

Helicopter up a minute. Jesus has turned water to wine, healed sick people, and fed the five thousand, which is really twenty thousand. From an earthly perspective, things are going great in the ministry. Matter of fact, they couldn't be any better. John 6:16–19: "When evening came, his disciples went down to the sea, got into a boat, and started across the sea to Capernaum. It was now dark, and Jesus had not yet come to them. The sea became rough because a strong wind was blowing. When they had rowed about three or four miles, they saw Jesus walking on the sea and coming near the boat, and they were frightened."

You think?

I don't know if you've ever been to the Sea of Galilee, but it's pretty awesome. Long, narrow, and surrounded by steep hills and mountains on both sides. Sometimes the wind from the east and the wind from the west hit the Sea of Galilee and change it from glassy to rough in just a second. No warning.

Rowing this boat are a bunch of professional fishermen who are now afraid, and the reason they're afraid is twofold: First, they're rowing and not getting any closer to land. Second, they see somebody walking on the sea. But watch what Jesus does and says, because He's about to speak the most repeated command in all of the Bible: *"Don't be afraid"* (v. 20).

At least 366 times in Scripture we are commanded to not be afraid. Why? I don't know about you, but every single day of my life, including on leap years, I need to hear these words: Don't be afraid.

Here's the thing—fear is not a feeling. Paul tells Timothy that God has not given us a spirit of fear (2 Tim. 1:7). Hence, fear is not a feeling. Fear is a spirit. A demonic spirit. And God has not given us a spirit of fear but of power, of love, and of a sound mind. Jesus commands "Don't be afraid," not because their circumstances are going to change, but because their savior is present with them. See the difference?

Unlike fear, scared is a feeling. And it can be a healthy emotion given us by God to guide us and give us wisdom. If a bear walks into your home, you feel scared, so you turn around and walk out. That's wisdom. Scared is no problem. When we're scared, we begin moving in a direction called courage. Praise God for courage. But fear is not scared. Fear paralyzes, and that's why fear is the opposite of faith. When Jesus shows up on the scene, His disciples are freaking out, so He says, " 'It is I; do not be afraid.' Then they were glad to take him into the boat, and immediately the boat was at the land to which they were going" (vv. 20–21).

Twenty-one verses into this chapter and we've already got two epic, faith-building miracles. He fed the multitude and walked on water. You would think at this point that these two events would be enough to sustain the faith of the disciples for at least a chapter, right? Not so. We as believers in Jesus Christ can get addicted to the mountaintop. Me too. I love those soul-filling experiences. But God does not bring us up on the mountaintop to just sit and soak, but fills us up with His Spirit so that we can be sent out into the valleys to do the ministry that He's called us to do.

One of the things we see throughout Scripture is that often the deepest valleys in the Bible come off the highest mountaintops. Think about it. Jesus gets baptized, which has got to be a high holy moment for Him. While He's standing in the water, the heavens open up and the Father says out loud, *"Behold my son in whom I am well pleased"* (Matt. 3:17). And then in the very next verse (4:1), He's led into the wilderness to be tempted by the devil.

Later, Jesus is transfigured on the mountaintop. Peter sticks his head into the middle of the Jesus-Elijah-Moses huddle and says, *"It is good that we are here"* (Matt. 17:4). Given what they're seeing, Peter, James, and John want to build tents for them and stay right there forever. And yet, in the next paragraph they step down into the valley where they find a dad with a sick son.

Then there's the Lord's supper. Jesus washes the disciples' feet and speaks of His body and blood. A few hours later He's arrested, beaten, whipped, mocked, spit on, struck, and crucified until dead, then buried.

High highs followed by low lows. Finding yourself on a mountaintop is no guarantee that a valley isn't soon to follow. But our location has zero bearing on Jesus' presence with us. He is with us. That's what one of His names means. Emanuel. God with us.

John 6:22–25: "On the next day the crowd that remained on the other side of the sea saw that there had been only one boat there, and that Jesus had not entered the boat with his disciples, but that his disciples had gone away alone. Other boats from Tiberias came near the place where they had eaten the bread after the Lord had given thanks. So when the crowd saw that Jesus was not there, nor his disciples, they themselves got into the boats and went to Capernaum, seeking Jesus. When they found him on the other side of the sea, they said to him, 'Rabbi, when did you come here?' "

At this point, the new disciples who recently started following Jesus are feeling super good about their life decisions. They left all to follow Jesus, and now as they look over the past couple of days, they're traveling with a crowd of twenty thousand people even though Jesus has not announced his next showing. People are rowing and walking from all over the region to follow after Jesus. Everyone in the crowd is thinking, *God is blessing us.*

But as always, Jesus knows their thoughts. So He answers them, "Truly, truly I say to you, you are seeking me, not because you saw signs, but because you ate your fill of the loaves. Do not work for the food that perishes, but for the food that endures to eternal life, which the Son of Man will give to you. For on him God the Father has set his seal" (vv. 26–27).

In other words, Jesus tells the crowd, *"You're not looking for Me, you're looking to see what I can do for you."* Ultimately, Jesus says,

"I will not be a means to your end, and if you keep chasing after Me to fill your belly, then you're chasing Me for the wrong reason." We are no different, and this would be a good time to flip the mirror: We don't follow Jesus because he makes our lives better. We follow Jesus because He is better than life.

Generally speaking, if you do life the way God has marked out for you—if you don't lie, don't commit adultery, don't steal, don't covet—things tend to go better for you. They just do.

But the abundant life found in following Christ is no guarantee that things go better for you. The abundant life in following Christ is that you get Christ. Rich or poor, well fed or starving, free or imprisoned, if you have Christ, then He and He alone sustains you. Jesus came that we might have life to the full, not full bellies. And full life is fully knowing him.

Someone from the crowd goes on to say, "What must we do, to be doing the works of God?" (v. 28).

This is the question all religious people want to ask. "Okay, we know you're God, we know you're good. We know we're not God. And we know we're not good. Given these, what must we do? What activity can we pursue? What box can we check?"

But this is the wrong question.

The right question is this: What must be done? Their question leans on their ability. Jesus' response points to the work of God in them. In fact, we are saved by works. Just not our own. We are saved by the finished work of Jesus on the cross. When He pushes up on His nail-pierced feet and declares "It is finished," He is saying that the debt has been paid and all that needs to be done has been accomplished. Now all you have to do is repent and believe. That's the difference. In response, Jesus breaks it down as simply as He can: "This is the work of God, that you believe in him, who he has sent."

Jesus puts it on the bottom shelf. Meaning, anyone can reach and attain this. His answer is as plain as it gets. What's the work that must be done? Trust Jesus. That's what he's saying. This is why I spent an entire chapter talking about *pisteuō*, the Greek word for "faith" or "belief," in *If the Tomb Is Empty*. Belief matters. A lot.

So they said to Him, "Then what sign do you do, that we may see and believe you? What work do you perform? Our fathers ate the manna in the wilderness; as it is written, 'He gave them bread from heaven to eat' " (vv. 30–31).

The reason that I covered these first two miracles before I got here is to show how quickly they forget. They're twenty-four hours from two super-legit miracles performed before their eyes by Jesus and then they have the audacity to say, "*Well, what must we do to do the works of God?*" Ever patient, Jesus says, "*It's simple. Put your faith in me. Believe in me. Trust in me*" (vv. 35–40).

Proof and practicality will never be enough. It just won't. The world around us is looking for scientific proof and a practical understanding before they believe. This response to Jesus is a posture that says, "Convince me and then I'll believe." Jesus is turning this on its head. He's saying, "Believe and convincing will follow." Reason will never be enough. Reason will never satisfy. The only thing that will get at this deep place in you is to be overcome by the presence of Jesus. In my church we call it the grace train of Jesus. When you are run over by the grace train, everything changes. I don't know how to explain it any better than that.

A great sermon and a great song will never sustain you. They may make you feel better, but they won't push you over the line and into true belief. Only the presence of a great savior will sustain you.

The people then say, "*Show us a sign because Moses called down manna from heaven*" (v. 31). Side note: What did the people who followed Moses do every single day? They complained and grumbled and said it was never enough.

Jesus is telling them and us that the only thing that matters is a relationship with Him. Period. Verse 32: "Jesus then said to them, 'Truly, truly, I say to you, it was not Moses who gave you the bread from heaven, but my Father gives you the true bread from heaven.'"

Once again, Jesus is going to speak on two planes. On one plane, He's talking about the physical experience that points to the supernatural realities happening in their presence. He says, "For the bread of God is he who comes down from heaven and gives life to the world." Their response is typical and shows how they have yet to lift their eyes above their own physical needs: "Sir, give us this bread always" (vv. 33–34).

Jesus' response is simple, but here He jumps up a plane. He's not talking about biscuits. "I am the bread of life; whoever comes to me shall not hunger, and whoever believes in me shall never thirst" (v. 35).

You and I have physical bodies and appetites, and the temporary things of this world do not quench the appetite. Nor do they sustain the appetite. Ultimately, it only increases the appetite. Jesus turns this discussion on its head, saying "*I am the only thing that will quench your eternal hunger and your eternal thirst.*"

Seven times in the Gospel of John, Jesus makes *I am* statements. Why seven? Because seven is the number of completion, and so every time Jesus makes one of these "I am" statements, He is saying, "I am completely God."

Why does this matter? Because "I am" is the covenant name of God. We find out in Exodus 3 that the Hebrew term for "I Am" is *Yahweh*. Say it: "Yah-way." It's supposed to sound like a breath. Breathe in. "Yah." Breathe out. "Way." Now say it all together: "Yahweh." This is God's covenant name translated: "I am that I am" or "I be that I be."

Anytime Jesus speaks an *I am*, He is linking Himself with the "I am" in the Old Testament. The same one that spoke to Moses is the same one speaking to them and the same one speaking to us. This would have blown their minds.

He goes on to say, "But I said to you that you have seen me and yet do not believe. All that the Father gives me will come to me, and whoever comes to me I will never cast out" (vv. 36–37).

For you theology nerds, this is where we get phrases like "unconditional election." And "perseverance of the saints." What we see here is really incredible. Jesus is going to talk about the reason we are able to have a relationship with God. Look at the last few words: "I will never cast out." This is a really big deal.

Some people often ask me this question: "Pastor, can a Christian lose his salvation?" And I say, "Well, that's the wrong question. The real question is: Can God lose one of his children? The answer? No way."

"But my cousin Jimmy has really walked away from the Lord and he's a long way from Jesus."

None of us knows the heart of another. I can't judge Jimmy. By looking at his life, you may be right. But this I know, and Luke 15 confirms, that we can walk a long way from God, or what we think is a long way from God, and yet He never leaves us. He's right there all along. Even when we're at our worst. This is why Scripture says, "While we were still sinners, Christ died for us" (Rom. 5:8). And then there's the flip side, which is a harsh reality: There are folks who walk away who, in truth, were never really walking "with" in the first place. Despite a lot of contemporary theology that preaches a contrary gospel that we're all saved, we're all children of God, and we'll all be in heaven together, there will be some people who will go to hell. It's tough for us to know the difference sometimes. If you are His, He won't lose His grip on you. Which begs the question—are you His?

John 6:38–40: "For I have come down from heaven, not to do my own will but the will of him who sent me. And this is the will of him who sent me, that I should lose nothing of all that he has given me, but raise it up on the last day. For this is the will of my Father, that everyone who looks on the Son and believes in him should have eternal life, and I will raise him up on the last day."

Jesus says, *"The only people who can come to Me are the people whom God draws to Me. The people who God wills to come to Me. And for everyone who would come to Me and believe in Me, these will receive eternal life."*

Some theologians love to say, "Okay, so which one is it? Does God draw or does everybody have to decide?"

Jesus responds, "Right, right." Some of my pastor buddies get hung up on this whole thing. Election versus free will. They go round and round. And look, I'm all for vigorous discussion about the Word, but here's my response—what can the dust do? Dust can't make itself alive. He breathed into us and we came alive. The initiation started with Him. He elected us. Not the other way around. In His lungs. Said another way, He chooses me and then gives me the ability to respond to Him, and yet if I don't receive Him, I'm going to hell. And I can take zero credit for following Jesus. I can't wrap my head around that. The good news is that He allows me the freedom and time to deliberate choosing Him until He gets tired of it and chooses Him for me through me.

Listen, if you're reading this and wondering if Jesus chose you, let's look at the obvious. You're reading this. How'd you get here? What more do you need? These words are like a two-by-four to the head. Wake up! Yes, right now God is drawing you to the savior. This is happening right now.

Verses 41–42: "So the Jews grumbled about him, because he said, 'I am the bread that came down from heaven.' They said, 'Is not this Jesus, the son of Joseph, whose father and mother we know? How does he now say, "I have come down from heaven"?'" The people who were the most religious can't see Jesus for who He is, because they cannot get over their own religion and tradition. Because of that, they're going to miss out on true life. This is why Mark 7:13 says, *It is the traditions of men that make void the Word of God.* Think about it. Nothing else on planet earth "voids" the Word of God save the traditions we hand down. Scary words.

Jesus continues: "Do not grumble among yourselves. No one can come to me unless the Father who sent me draws him. And I will raise him up on the last day. It is written in the Prophets, 'And they will all be taught by God.' Everyone who has heard and learned from the Father comes to me" (John 6:43–45).

Here's what Jesus has to say, which is very unpopular today: "*You cannot reject God's Son and claim to know God the Father. You cannot claim to know God and reject Jesus, because if you knew God, then you would recognize His Son.*"

"Not that anyone has seen the Father except he who is from God; he has seen the Father. Truly, truly, I say to you, whoever believes has eternal life. I am the bread of life" (John 6:46–48). Your Father gave manna in the wilderness and they got it.

Jesus is saying, "*I am the only thing that will satisfy the insatiable appetite of your soul. I am the living bread that came down from heaven. If anyone eats of this bread, he will live forever. And the bread that I will give him is my flesh.*"

Admittedly, this is where it gets weird. Can you imagine Peter and Thomas and the other disciples? "Did he just say 'fish'? He said 'fish,' right? Not 'flesh.' He said 'fish' because we've got twelve baskets' worth of leftover magical-saving sardines right here. Is that what he said? It sounded like 'flesh,' but that doesn't make sense. Okay, hold on, he's probably gonna clear it all up..."

"The Jews then disputed among themselves, saying, 'How can this man give us his flesh to eat?'" (John 6:52). These people don't even eat pork, much less a prophet, so they're a little confused.

Again, see this through the eyes of the disciples. They had to be scratching their heads: "Everybody chill out. It's fine, it's fine. He's gonna clear it all up right now. Last thing we need for our growing ministry is some kind of PR mishap. We don't wanna get canceled, we just got started. Jesus knows we've got momentum…"

Jesus, knowing their thoughts, then lays this on them: "Truly, truly, I say to you, unless you eat the flesh of the Son of Man and drink his blood, you have no life in you" (John 6:53).

The disciples had to be dumbfounded. "Did he just add blood to the equation?"

Jesus again. John 6:54: "Whoever feeds on my flesh and drinks my blood has eternal life, and I will raise him up on the last day."

I imagine one of the disciples stepping in right here. "All right, time out. We're gonna take five. A little brief intermission. Uh… Messiah is tired from walking on water last night, and feeding all twenty thousand of you. So if you'll just step out into the lobby, we've got some refreshments, leftover fish and loaves that were collected from the previous miracle. Remember the miracle?" Then they turn to Jesus. "Dude…what are you doing? You're screwing this up. We left everything for you and you're talking about cannibalism. What are you doing?! Look, we need to back up so why don't you go take a nap and we'll clean up this PR nightmare. When you're rested you can just tell them one of those stories again. Tell them the one about the dad and the two sons. Or, I know, why don't you call the Pharisees names? They love it. Better yet, how about a miracle? Just levitate. Then, when we've got their attention again, you can explain yourself. We got a good thing going here and don't want to mess it up." That's not what actually happened, but if I were one of the disciples in that moment, I think I'd want to have a private word with Jesus to straighten things out.

Here's the explanation: "For my flesh is true food, and my blood is true drink. Whoever feeds on my flesh and drinks my blood abides in me, and I in him. As the living Father sent me, and I live because of the Father" (vv. 56–57).

The phrase "feeds on my flesh" makes me think of *The Walking Dead*, and I'm pretty sure it did something similar with the disciples. Jesus says these things in the synagogue at Capernaum. Boom, mic drop. No explanation.

This bothers us as Americans. As westerners. Because nobody understands what He's talking about, and we feel like we deserve to have God explain all that He does to us, for us. I don't know who taught us that, but you can't find that in the Bible. He owes us no explanation, and we need to be reminded of this reality. We are not saved by our understanding of the teaching. We are saved by faith in Jesus Christ, by the finished work of Christ.

On one hand, I know a lot of very well-educated religious experts who have not surrendered their lives to the Lordship of Jesus Christ. In truth, they are still lords of their own lives. And on the other hand, I know a whole bunch of people who barely know the difference between the Old and the New Testaments, but they have surrendered. Totally. And they believe that when Christ died on the cross, His death counted for them. That He took their place. Here's the point—your and my salvation is not tied up in our incredible understanding of the whys behind everything that happens. Our salvation is tied to this: Do you believe that when Christ died on the cross, that counted for you?

Jesus speaks this to the disciples. He is speaking the same to us. And He explains nothing.

Verse 60: "When many of his disciples heard it, they said, 'This is a hard saying; who can listen to it?'"

You ever been there? You ever read that part in your Bible and you just wish it wasn't there? You ever read some doctrinal reality and you think, *That doesn't make sense to me*? What about when some of your own experiences don't line up with what you thought God would do?

This is exactly what is happening here. And Jesus is about to make it worse. Verse 61: "But Jesus, knowing in himself that his disciples were grumbling about this, said to them, 'Do you take offense at this?'" And they're probably saying, "Yes, we take offense to this. Growing up, our parents wouldn't even let us eat a medium-rare steak, and now you're telling us we got to eat your flesh and drink your blood. Yes, Jesus, this is offensive."

Verse 62. He does give a little hint. He says, "What if you were to see the Son of Man ascending to where he was before?" This is the key to understanding this text. Basically, He's saying that one day this will all make total sense.

"One day when my life, death, and resurrection are in the rearview, you will watch me ascend to the right hand of God the Father and all at once, you will see the full picture of the gospel. Then you will be able to understand what I am talking about. But right now, I'm not going to explain any of that to any of you. And even if I tried, you couldn't wrap your heads around it so between now and then, you're going to have to trust me. *Pisteuō*."

Jesus says this, "It is the Spirit who gives life; the flesh is no help at all. The words that I have spoken to you are spirit and life. But there are some of you who do not believe." Jesus knew from the beginning who did not believe, and who would betray him. "And he said, 'This is why I told you that no one can come to me unless it is granted him by the Father.' After this many of his disciples turned back and no longer walked with him" (vv. 63–66).

Don't miss that. "Many of his disciples turned back and no longer walked with him." The Savior of the World, the King of all Kings, is standing in front of them, and some walk away. Can you imagine?

Now let me flip the mirror again. He's standing here. Right next to you reading this book. He's just as present with you and me now as He was with them. Which again begs the question—will you walk away or follow?

And what does Jesus do about it?

If I was teaching in my church and I said something that was true and right and godly, but an entire section didn't understand and all decided to just leave, I'd be like, "Hold on, hold on for a second." And then I'd run over to that section, and explain, "That's not what I meant. Just let me explain. This is what I mean..." Because in as little as four sentences Jesus could clear up everything He was talking about. And in fact, He's talking about the gospel. He's simply saying, "If you don't have the gospel, then you can have no part with me. I'm not asking you to be a vampire or a cannibal, or do something weird like that." He could have explained that soon the church would celebrate communion, the body and blood of Jesus, as a sacrament to remember His broken body and shed blood. But Jesus doesn't explain Himself, and He watches the people walk away and does not go chasing after them.

This is a hunch, but I suspect one of the reasons they walk away is because they constantly wanted more signs. Constant reassurance they'd made the right choice. Instead, they cop-out: "He's changed so much. I was here in the beginning, and He would give out fish and loaves, walk on water, and change water to wine, which was really cool. But now He's got a posse and He's talking about eating flesh and drinking blood."

In short, their needs had not been met: "Jesus, I'm hungry. I used to come here and get fed, and now I'm not getting fed. Now He wants me to eat Him but I'm not into that. That's weird."

For some people, the teaching of Christ does not line up with their prior beliefs. Jesus won't behave. So many of the disciples turned back and no longer walked with him.

Watching them walk away, Jesus turns to the twelve. And He asks them, "Do you want to go away as well?" (v. 67). Real quick, you ever been here? I know I'm a pastor and we're not supposed to talk about this stuff. But Jesus is not into making larger crowds, He's into making disciples. And disciples believe when they don't understand.

Jesus is thinning the crowd. He's sifting out those who really believe and those who like the entertainment and the cooking.

Have you ever felt like walking away from Jesus because He said something hard and didn't do what you thought He ought to do? You ever had somebody pray over you and you believed, man, you believed with all your heart that God was going to heal you? Reconcile that marriage? Bring your prodigal son or daughter home? And yet you're sick, divorced, and an empty nester.

It's been weeks and you're like, "God, I don't understand."

I think that's what's going on right here. Jesus looks at the disciples, not the people who wanted their bellies filled, but the ones who followed Jesus. And He looks at them and proffers to the backs of those walking away, "*You want to leave as well?*"

For you, maybe it's a sickness. Maybe it's cancer. Whatever. And you begin to ask yourself, "God, I don't understand. Help me understand. Why do Christians get cancer?"

Or maybe you've done your part in the vows you made on that day with him or her. And despite your love, they turned their back on you. Betrayed you. Rejected you. What's worse, you've been faithfully going to church for weeks and months and years pleading with God for your unbelieving spouse and they're still gone. And what's more, they took everything in the divorce.

Or maybe it's that addiction. "God, would you please take this away from me? I don't want it. It's killing me. Wrecking my life." And yet you're still addicted and you can't understand why He won't just zap it out of you.

Or financial problems, and honestly, you didn't get there on your own. Your business partner stole the company out from under you while you were faithful and tithed. Now you're broke and filing bankruptcy.

What about that prodigal? You look at their life and you ask, "Is this my fault? Did I do something wrong? Did my sin cause this?

God, I prayed and believe the Word. How come you won't bring them home?"

Maybe you struggle with depression. Maybe for some of you, it's a bad church experience. The people who were supposed to be your shepherds were actually the ones who hurt you and abused you, and you think, *Well God, is that how that place works? If so, you can forget it.*

Maybe it's infertility. Let's just be honest. How do you get your head around that? I've been doing this for a long time. Been a pastor for twenty-five-plus years, and I am telling you it seems to me that some of the people who would be the greatest parents on the planet are the same people who have the hardest time becoming parents. And it also seems to me that some of the people who are the least qualified in our society seem to be the most fertile humans. Help me understand that one, God. I mean, can we just switch that up?

Or you lose a loved one too soon, and you try to explain why, but there is no explanation your brain will accept.

This is what's happening here. Jesus is speaking a hard teaching, and while He can step in and just explain it away in about two seconds, He doesn't. Instead, He looks at His disciples and says, "*You wanna leave too?*"

So what do you do? What are you going to do when you find yourself in that place?

Look, we all have our stories. We all have our pain. We all have our doubts. And the enemy wants you to believe your doubts and doubt your beliefs.

But faith in Christ requires us to believe our beliefs and doubt our doubts. This right here is where the rubber meets the road. When God doesn't do what you think He ought to do, or when God doesn't do what you think you would do if you were in His spot, what will you do?

Simon Peter's answer is what I come back to when I scratch my head and say, *Lord, what are you doing? Why don't you just heal them? Why don't you just reconcile them? Why don't you just let them have a baby? Why don't you just break the addiction? God, this is a hard teaching.*

When I begin to have that annoying feeling, those doubts, and I want to leave too, I remember Peter's words: "Lord, to whom shall we go? You have the words of eternal life, and we have believed, and have come to know, that you are the Holy One of God" (vv. 68–69).

That's it. That's what I want to scream out across the stratosphere. And notice the progression. We have believed…We have come to know. Belief came before knowing. Fact.

Simon Peter looks at Jesus, then he looks at the situation. He doesn't know what Jesus is talking about. He can't reconcile this whole eat-my-flesh-drink-my-blood stuff. And I imagine that Peter is looking at the rest of his ministry and the rest of his life, and thinking, *Well, I guess I made a poor career choice because the whole crowd is leaving, and now it's just gonna be me and you, Jesus.* And when Jesus asks, "*You wanna leave too?*" Peter is probably thinking, *Yeah, sorta.* But then he looks at all of his options and he asks Jesus this question. "*But where would we go?*" There's a lot Peter doesn't understand but one thing he does: To walk away from you, Jesus, is to walk toward something else. And every single one of us know a whole bunch of people who have turned away from the Lord and walked toward everything else this world has to offer, and here's the problem with every single person who has done that. They find no peace. They find no answers. They find no resolution. In fact, they find hell.

And if and when they do come back, they do so with scars and more pain and more hurt. Here's the point of all of John 6: We don't follow Jesus for full bellies. If and when the day comes in your life that you don't understand and you can't wrap your head around why God would do things this way, and not do things that way, and you want to walk away, here's what you do: You pick up your doubts, you put one foot in front of the other, and you keep following after Jesus because He's the only one who offers eternal life.

The way we know that God loves us is not because our current circumstances are great. The way that we know that He loves us, that He is for us and that He is with us and we don't need to fear, is because our sovereign Savior died on the cross to prove it once and for all. If you have never memorized Romans 5:8, now would be a good time: "God shows his love for us in that while we were still sinners, Christ died for us."

I'm not saying your current situation isn't tragic. It may be horrible—and you're right, your pain and hardship is a really big deal—but no matter how tragic your current situation is, Jesus lifts our eyes off of us and onto Him. Trust me, if we had time to sit down and to talk about the details of your life, I would weep with you, and I would mourn with you. Your pain is a big deal. But if you and I were standing at the foot of the cross at Golgotha two thousand years ago, and we didn't know the end of the story the way we do now, I think every single one of us would point our finger at heaven and say, "God, what are you doing? Have you completely lost your mind?"

And God would point to His Son. "No. I'm redeeming the world."

*   *   *

We started this chapter by talking about my friend Ike. Now let me tell you the rest of Ike's story...And again, I want you to hear this in his words. I don't want to tell you what he told me. I want him to tell you.

First, listen to Ike, talking about his family and his time sitting in the courtroom staring at his son's killer. "I always said, if you hurt one of my children, my family members, man, I'm going to get you. I'm going to get you, hate you. I'm supposed to hate you. I had convinced myself, God wanted me to get you, this is my child. And of course I get there, the courtroom, and he comes out, shuffling in chains, and I'm seeing him for the first time."

Now, read carefully what Ike is about to say.

"I loved him."

Did you read that? "I loved him." There is no logical explanation for this.

Ike again: "Didn't know him, never seen him before, didn't know his family, didn't know his background, but I loved him. And I still can't explain it. I didn't have the feelings I thought I was going to have. I know for sure now, it was God's love, God's grace, and later I would say to myself, *Wow, maybe He is doing something in me that I didn't even know was taking place.* Because I questioned myself. *What's wrong with me? What's wrong with me? Why don't I feel this way? Why don't I feel the way I thought I would feel?* But through all my whys and wondering, I still trusted that God was in control, and I just forgave him."

"I just forgave him..." These words shake some stuff loose in me at a really deep level.

Here's Ike talking about the aftermath. "After Takoya was sentenced and he went off to prison, I always kept him in my prayers, wondered: How's it going? What is he doing? How is he surviving? And so I wanted to talk to him, so I would write letters and I'd throw them away. He don't want to hear from me. What will he say? I don't want to hear from you, I'm doing three life sentences. And so all this is going through my mind, so I would never mail them. And one day I decided, hey, I'm going to write a letter, I'm going to send it to him. And I did just that. And in that letter, I said, hello, this is Mr. Brown. I said, I hope things are as well as they can be. I hope all is well. And I let him know that he was always in my prayers and

I'd always be mindful of him, thinking of him. And at the end of the letter, I said, I need to ask you for a favor. I said, I miss my son, Ike Jr. And I said, I'd like you to fill in for him until we all get to heaven. We can write, we can laugh, we can talk. And I said, and if not, I understand, and I mailed the letter off."

Let's just get to the nugget: Could you write that letter?

Now look at what happened. "It took about three weeks to a month to get a response back, and I get a letter and I'm scared to open it, because I don't know what it's going to say. I don't know if he cursing me out, leave me alone, I don't want to hear from you. And so I opened that letter and it said, 'Dear Mr. Brown, I now know that God is real. And I told God that if I heard from you, I would give my life to Him, the rest of my days.' And he was sharing this with me. And he said, 'Mr. Brown, you asked me for a favor. You asked me, can I fill in for him? Ike Jr.' And he said, 'I'm not qualified, but if you'll have me, from this point on, you're my dad, and I'm your son.'"

"I now know that God is real…"

How is this possible?

It's possible for one reason and one reason only—because the tomb is empty.

Now listen to Takoya's version of this story. He's talking from a prison cell, staring at three life sentences. "My name is Takoya Criner, and I'm currently serving a life imposed sentence. This man, Mr. Brown, that I had come to know and grew to love, and to now call my dad, my father, God has such a greater plan. We're just parts and characters in the road. This was an opportunity. God was using me and him as vessels, to not just show people that was around or close to familiar with our relationship or our situation, but the world, what love was, what love truly was. Some of the divine attributes of love. At first, it was strange. And over time, I was able to realize, this is beautiful. And I learned to embrace it more and more, and that love that I began to have grew more and more for my dad. And I was just waiting for this opportunity to be in his presence, to see and feel it. And when I was given the opportunity to see him for the first time, back in 2009, he ran up on me and wrapped me up in a bear hug. I didn't know what to expect, I was like, whoa, here you go. But I seen him, I didn't know what to expect. You know what I mean? I really didn't. I didn't because I was waiting for this opportunity. And when he ran up on me, I was in shackles and chains. I didn't know what to expect. He ran up on me, he wrapped me in a bear hug, told me he loved me, squeezed me tight. And it just felt, it felt good, man. It felt real good. I knew. That's when I knew it was genuine, for real. We is just flesh and blood, mortal beings. We are given a lot of things that we don't deserve, and that's what grace is. It was a beautiful thing. And this is why I embraced it, I embraced this opportunity."

Now, read what Ike has to say about his son Takoya. "Christ died for us. Through all of our mistakes, through all of our faults, He forgives us. It's just as simple as asking. He won't fine you, He won't hold it against you. He won't hold your mistakes against you. Just ask for forgiveness, believe God. I know it looks bad, I know you're struggling, you see no way out, but I'm telling you, if you would trust Him, I just tell you to trust God, no matter what. Trust God."

This is the gospel of Jesus Christ lived out. For Ike it's as simple as staring at his doubts and then looking at Jesus, *"Where would I go? You have the words of life and death."*

When Ike's world fell apart and his son was killed, he didn't know what to do. Nothing made sense. Why, God? Why would you do this? So he picked up his faith and his doubts and his pain and all his unanswered questions and he followed after Jesus. Not because his life all of a sudden became better. But because Jesus is better than life. Ike chose to love Takoya just as Jesus loved him. No matter what. This makes zero sense in the natural world. But it is the gospel.

That's what I call empty-tomb faith. And faith like that crushes the kingdom of darkness. Hell has no answer for love like that. Never has.

I want to end this chapter by doing two things. I want us to name our doubts. Speak them out loud. Go ahead. You can write them down in the margin if you like. I'm sure that as you've read along in this chapter, if you have doubts, they have risen to the surface and they've whispered in your ear. They have a tendency to do that. So, what are they? Do they sound like Ike's but with different names and situations? I'll bet they do. The enemy will always tempt you to doubt the love of God for you and those you love. He's done it since the garden. It's nothing new.

Now that we've named them, here's what we're going to do. And I've wrestled a lot with whether or not to do what I'm about to do, but here goes. I'm doing it. It may seem redundant, but I don't think so. I'm trying to listen to the prompting of the Holy Spirit, so just go with me here.

When Jesus said, "*Unless you eat my flesh and drink my blood*," he was pointing at what we call communion and at what communion means to us. We covered this pretty well in chapter 1 with water to wine, but I think we ought to do it again. Not because we didn't do it right the first time, but because I think Jesus is okay with us remembering Him. And I believe He wants to do a thing in this moment.

This would be a good time to get some bread and wine. You're going to need them. So, why don't you get both in front of you? For about 1,500 years, maybe longer than that, folks like you and me didn't have access to the words of the Bible. Definitely not in their pockets. Jesus knew this, so on that night of the Last Supper, He established what we know as the Lord's supper.

So, here we are in the middle of this book, because the tomb is empty. Communion is the proclamation that the tomb is empty.

Jesus is risen. If you're a dad, I want you to gather your family. I want you to act as the priest of your household. Single moms, you are equally as significant, so gather your children. College kids, grab your roomie. Bible study, gather round. If you're sitting in a cell block, invite your cellmate or go it alone. If you don't have bread and wine, go with what you've got. You can pretend. Jesus understands. I know this is hard for some of you, and the last thing you want to do is lay down your doubts. But I'm asking you to do just that.

Do you want to leave too? Bring that to the Lord's table and lay it down. But don't worry, you won't leave empty-handed. We are going to lay down our doubts and pick up the body and blood of Jesus in exchange. Beauty for ashes. Now that's what it looks like when you pick up your doubts and follow after Jesus.

Now I want to be really clear about this. This is the Lord's table, it's not my table. I do not determine who comes to this table. The Lord invites anyone who would believe, anyone who has put their faith in Jesus Christ. So if that's you, you are invited to the Lord's table.

No denomination keeps people in and out. Well, they do, but that's not the Lord's intention. You see, when Jesus says "unless you eat my flesh and drink my blood you have no part of me," here's what He could have done. He could have stepped into the crowd and said, "Here's what I'm talking about."

The night that He was betrayed, He gathered his disciples together as it was the Passover. And He took the bread just as they had done every year of their life. This dinner was not new to them. Jews had celebrated this since their deliverance from Egypt and the angel of death. Jesus broke the bread and He said, "*This is my body broken for you. As often as you eat of this, you do so in remembrance of me*" (Luke 22:19).

The disciples didn't know what He was talking about that night either because it hadn't happened yet. But the next day, they started putting the pieces together when His body was broken on the cross. As believers, every time we eat of His body, we are remembering that the sin we have committed was laid on His shoulders. Scripture says, *He became sin.* Think about that. All the sin committed by all the human race throughout all of history—including yours and mine—was placed on Jesus' shoulders. And he "became" it.

Why?

Because God is holy and just, all sin must be paid for. For God to dismiss sin would make Him unjust. Because of His mercy He delayed the payment. Because of His grace He made the payment. Making Him both the just and the justifier.

Don't let that slip past you—He made the payment in our place. With His Son. So go ahead and hold the bread in your hands. When we do this, we remember and we confess. But here's the thing—most of us think God keeps a tally sheet, and when we confess our sins, He checks them off His list. "One down, three billion to go." But that's not what we're doing. We don't confess our sins so that we might be forgiven of the sins we have committed. We confess that we have been forgiven by the broken body of Jesus on the cross. He forgave us on the cross. Past tense. A beautiful exchange. We're remembering this and receiving it. One of my friends likes to say when we celebrate communion, we're appropriating that forgiveness.

Our confession is that He is Savior and Lord, and that by the power of the Holy Spirit, we are receiving that forgiveness.

So let me speak this over you—this is the body of Christ broken for you. As often as you eat of it, remember that when He said it is finished, that counted for you.

Go ahead. Eat.

And then that night he took the cup. Again, the disciples had no idea what he was talking about here. He said, *"This is the cup of the covenant, my blood"* (Luke 22:20). Look with me back at the cross. In reality, there are two cups. There's the cup of the wrath of God poured out on Jesus, and then there's the cup of the new covenant. *Covenant* and *testimony* mean the same thing. The old covenant is the covenant of law. But at dinner, Jesus says, *"But this is the new covenant, the covenant of grace. Through this cup, you are not saved by law. I fulfilled every jot and tittle of that law in your place. I kept every promise and prophecy of the Scripture, every law of Moses in the old covenant. I am the fulfillment of that law."*

And now by God's immeasurable grace, you and I have been invited to the table. Jesus lifted the cup and said, *"As often as you drink of this cup, you do so in remembrance of me."* What are we remembering? That this body and this blood of Jesus Christ is His demonstration of His glory and His love for us. And because of this, we are made right with Him.

Now take the wine or grape juice or whatever you have, and drink. Do this in remembrance of Him.

Pray with Us

I'm going to do something a little different here. I've asked my friend Ike to write part of this prayer. And if you're listening to this on audio, I've asked Ike to read the prayer. So pray with me and my friend Ike:

Our Father, thank You for the opportunity to come before You. Thank You for grace and mercy and most importantly for forgiveness of sin and salvation. I thank You for Pastor Joby and his new book (Anything Is Possible). Because of Your resurrection, Jesus, I was immediately able to forgive and love the one who took the life of my son and accept him as my own. Because of Your resurrection, my son's killer was able to accept Christ as his personal savior, and me as his earthly dad. Together our salvation is assured. I pray this book reaches millions all over the world. My prayer is for everyone who reads this book to hold on to the promise Jesus made to those who believe in Him. "Most assuredly...he who believes in Me has everlasting life" (John 6:47 NKJV). Heavenly Father, our prayer is for the words of this book to jump off the pages as it's read by millions. We pray for the healing of our nation, as we wait on Your return. Even so, "come, Lord JESUS!" (Rev 22:20).

Thank you, Pastor Joby, for your leadership. Love and Prayers, Sgt. Ike Brown.

Now Pray with Me

Our good and gracious heavenly Father, God, we love You more than anything because You first loved us. God, I pray for the men, the women, the students who just don't understand right now. God, I pray for the folks who are having a difficult time in their lives, and they're attempting to walk away from You. Lord, I pray that their faith would not be grounded in their circumstances but instead be grounded in the good news of the gospel of Jesus Christ.

God, I pray that we, as believers, would snatch back our trust and faith from the things of this world...from the temporary things of this world, including the circumstances of our lives that don't make sense. And God, I pray that we would continuously, daily, take up our cross and re-decide once again, recommit ourselves, to put our faith in You, our sovereign Savior, who bled and died in our place, and who was resurrected on the third day, who ascended to the right hand of God the Father, and is the God that continues to work in all things. The painful things, the unexplainable things. The things we don't understand. The things that are our fault. *The things that have happened to us. That God would work in all things for the good of those who love You and are called according to Your purpose.*

And Lord, I pray that we would continuously answer the way Peter did, "To whom shall we go? For You are the only one who offers eternal life." *Please remind us that even when we are walking through tough times, through trials and tribulations, that these painful times will seem as light and momentary compared to the glory that You have in store for your children.*

So God, when we face troubles and trials and temptations and doubts, God, I pray that we would just pick up those things and continuously follow after You, because You are the one who offers eternal life. We pray in Jesus' name. Amen.

CHAPTER 5

The Raising of Lazarus—Do You Believe Jesus Can Raise the Dead to Life?

One of the really cool things about our church is that about a mile down the road sits one of the best medical facilities on the planet: the Mayo Clinic. Just having them here lifts the average IQ for the northeast corner of Florida. In my job, I get to meet some of these folks, both because they take care of me and they attend our services. One of those doctors is a man I've come to know and love—Dr. Asher Chanan-Khan. Born and raised in Pakistan, he grew up with Christian parents. He likes to say that "the Lord pursued me slowly and slowly. He just worked on my heart."

Dr. Asher is a professor of medicine at the Mayo Clinic, an oncologist and a hematologist. A specialist in blood cancer. He's into research and he's working to find a cure. That's his thing. He has spent his life doing just that. "I chose cancer because [when I was] growing up in Pakistan there were no cancer specialists. You had two options: surgery or die. Cancer was a death sentence. It devastates people. Then, in 2005 I went to get my cholesterol checked. A routine checkup. And they found this cancer sitting in my chest. They told me that there was a 90 percent chance I would die in two years. One hundred percent in five years. My only treatment option was surgery to take it out. So they did. After surgery, my walk with the Lord was more intentional. Something about the whole thing allowed me to know Jesus more closely, and I could sense God's presence."

So for two years they tested him closely and every test came back negative. No cancer. Five years, still nothing. He's beat it. "Life became normal. I started forgetting about cancer." Then his son Matthew was born and "I forgot about it altogether. I was cured. Life became vibrant, full. God gave me time with my son. And I was in remission fifteen years. Fifteen years. Before the cancer returned."

Every week, I stand on the stage and preach, and I can see Dr. Asher and Matthew because they sit on the second row. And they worship with their hands held high. It's beautiful. And he still spends his time seeking a cure for cancer for others. Let that sink in. Riddled with cancer, he's working on a cure for others.

Of course we are praying like crazy for him. For complete healing. Dr. Asher is also firmly rooted in the gospel and spends a whole bunch of time trying to lead all of his smarty-pants friends over at Mayo to Jesus. And if you're one of those smarty-pants at any of our hospitals in town or around the world, we love you so much. We're so appreciative of you. He's also rooted in the gospel and trying to share the good news of the love of Jesus with all his Muslim friends and family members.

With Dr. Asher and Matthew as the backdrop, I want to start by looking at John 11, but let me add some context first. John 10 is all about Jesus being a good shepherd. About how He loves His sheep. How He lays down His life for His sheep. In the Greek New Testament, the words *pastor* and *shepherd* are the same word: *poimēn*. The verb is *poimainō*, and it means to feed. The reason that my title is not "senior pastor of The Church of Eleven22" is because that role is already taken. *Senior pastor* and *chief shepherd* mean the same thing, and if you study our org chart you'll see we already have a senior pastor. Already have a chief shepherd. His name is Jesus. I am an undershepherd, and I get to work for Him.

So now let's dive into John 11. It says, "Now a certain man was ill, Lazarus of Bethany, the village of Mary and her sister Martha. It was Mary who anointed the Lord with ointment and wiped his feet with her hair" (vv. 1–2). By the way, John is writing this post-resurrection. Meaning, he can see back through the empty tomb, past the cross, into the events that have happened. And even though Mary and Martha and Lazarus don't know how this story ends, John does.

Part of the reason that John points this out is because Jesus is good buddies with this family. In Luke 10, we find out that Jesus had refrigerator rights at this family's house in Bethany. I hope you've got some friends who have refrigerator rights. Do you have people in your life who don't knock on the door? They just walk in, all Kramer style. (If you don't know Kramer, do yourself a favor and binge-watch *Seinfeld* this weekend.) They're like, "Oh, here we are." And they know where the K-cups are, and they know where the coffee mugs are, and they're in your fridge. Lars Peterson, we call him "Petey," is one of those people for me. You understand? This means you better not lounge round in my living room without appropriate clothing on, because Petey might just show up like the Holy Ghost in my house, okay?

But you need some people in your life who have refrigerator rights. These are the kinds of deep friendships that Jesus has with this family. So it says, "Mary, who anointed the Lord with ointment and wiped his feet with her hair, whose brother Lazarus was ill. So the sisters sent to [Jesus], saying, 'Lord, he whom you love is ill' " (vv. 2–3). Notice this. They couldn't send a text, so they've got to send a messenger. I think Martha is probably the one who puts the note together. "Hey, listen. Go find Jesus, because we need Him. Here's what I want you to tell Him. Tell him Lazarus is…No, no, no, no, no. Never mind. Don't put 'Lazarus.' Say this: 'The one whom you love is ill.' Maybe you can get His attention. Not 'the one who loves you,' but 'the one whom you love.'" Now, I don't know if John was a little offended by this. Maybe he thought to himself, *Well, that's my title.* Whatever. He doesn't bring it up.

Here's what I want you to see. Two truths. Jesus loves Lazarus. True. And Lazarus is sick. True. Both of these things can be true at the same time. And there are a lot of us who believe, and begin to think and feel, *God, if you really loved me, then maybe you wouldn't let me go through this pain.* The reality is that God's love for you does not prevent you from going through pain. But when we are in pain, notice what Mary and Martha do. They bring their need to Jesus. That's step one. It's what we all need to do.

Let me ask you this: Is prayer for you a first response or a last resort? Is prayer for you the thing that you do when you can't think of anything else to do, and you think, *Well, I guess I'll throw up a Hail Mary?* Or is it your first response? I hope and pray that you are the kind of believer, or you are becoming the kind of believer, who wakes up every single day and the first thing that you grab is not that stupid little smartphone, but I pray you grab ahold of Jesus and cry out, "Jesus, I'm gonna need You today. I don't know what's happening, but I know I am going to need You." Whether you're on the mountaintop or you are in the valley, whether you're in a sweet season in your life, then I pray you cry out to Him and say *Thank You.* And *I praise You.* The writer of Hebrews says, "Let us continually offer up a sacrifice of praise to God, that is, the fruit of lips that acknowledge his name" (Heb. 13:15). That word *continually* would mean every morning when your eyes crack open and you step once again into the day the Lord has made.

For Mary and Martha, prayer was the first response. They sent word to Jesus—which is what we do when we pray.

John 11:4 gets a little confusing: "But when Jesus heard it he said,

'This illness does not lead to death.'" Except it does. Some of the other translations will translate these words: "*This illness does not end in death.*" I think that's what Jesus means. This illness does not end in death. It leads through death. But it doesn't stop there.

Let's revisit a question I get asked all the time: Why do these things happen? If God loves me, why in the world would He allow me to walk through this pain? It's a legit question, and it's one thing to understand it theologically. It's another thing to experience it existentially. Sometimes, the mountaintop experience and the miracle that you're looking for is on the other side of the valley of the shadow of death. I pray this is the case for Dr. Asher. I'm just going to go on record—if I were God, Dr. Asher would not have cancer. Period. But I'm not, and furthermore, Scripture says, *Jesus learned obedience through the things that he suffered* (Heb. 5:8). Think about this for a second and it will mess with your theology. Why would Jesus need to learn obedience? Evidently the Father desired it. Since we're talking about cancer, I don't know why people get cancer. If it were up to me, Christians wouldn't get cancer. That's how it would work. But, if you're a terrorist? Boom, cancer. Christian, no cancer. That's just what I would do, all right? The moment you begin to plot evil against somebody, you'd be like, *I feel weird. Oh, is that a lump?* And you'd die. That's what would happen. But God didn't check with me. I'd also design chocolate to make you fit and lean. In my eating regimen, you'd eat chocolate and your friends would ask, "Whoa. What you been doing? Eating chocolate?" "Yeah." And broccoli would make you so fat you couldn't stand up. That's what I would do, but God didn't ask me.

No matter the reason for our suffering, Romans 8:28 is true for every single one of us—that *God is at work in all things for the good of those who love Him and are called according to His purpose.* And in the Greek, in Romans 8:28, God is the subject of the sentence. It's not the things. It does not say, "Everything works for a reason." No.

That's not what it says. It says, *God is at work in all things for the good of those who love Him and are called according to His purpose.* Big difference. This means God can use our sin, others' sins, demonic attack, and a fallen, broken world to accomplish His purposes and His will in our lives and His kingdom. The circumstances of our life are not the Lord of our life. The sovereign King of the universe is Lord of our life. And here's the thing—everything that happens to us is first sifted through His sovereign hand. This is tough for people, but tough doesn't make it any less true.

In John 9, when the disciples ask, "Rabbi, who sinned, this man or his parents, that he was born blind?" Jesus answered, "It was not that this man sinned, or his parents, but that the works of God might be displayed in him" (John 9:2–3). This means the deeper the pain, the greater the platform for God to show His love.

Don't believe me? Maybe one day, if you're a believer and you're walking the streets of heaven and you bump into Shadrach, Meshach, and Abednego, you can ask them about the furnace. God did not keep them from the fire. He just stood with them in it. Throughout Scripture, God did not always keep His people out of the valley of the shadow of death, but He walked with them through it. He prepared a table for them in the presence of their enemies. And He does the same with us.

That's what's about to happen here in John 11 and the death of Lazarus.

In the moment, when the pain hits, we can tend to focus on our circumstances and say, "God, what are you doing?" When you get there, I want you to remember that His love for us is not ultimately demonstrated in our current circumstances. His love for us is ultimately demonstrated at the cross. Walk with me back to the cross for a second and stand with me as we stare at Jesus. If we had seen it live, how many of us would have asked, "God, what are You doing? Have You completely lost control? They're killing Your Son!" And yet God would say, "I know it doesn't make sense, but three days from now, it will." So Jesus says, "It is for the glory of God, so that the Son of God may be glorified through it" (John 11:4).

Back to John 11 and another confusing verse. Verse 5: "Now Jesus loved Martha and her sister and Lazarus." By the way, Lazarus' name in Greek means "God is my altar." Surely Jesus is gonna help a guy with a name like that. So Jesus gets word that Lazarus is sick. Knowing Jesus like we do, and having read what we've read about Him, we tend to think the next verse in Scripture will read something like, "And so Jesus threw out some healing power all the way from wherever he is, and it went to Bethany, and boom. Lazarus hopped up and revival broke out in Bethany." We know that Jesus can pull off a long-distance healing. Remember the official's son?

That's what I would want it to say.

But that's not what it says.

Here's what it says. *Now Jesus loved Lazarus, so He stayed two days longer in the place where he was* (vv. 5–6).

Wait! What?!

No, no, no, Jesus. That's not how it's supposed to work. Except one thing—God's love and His apparent cooperation in our lives are not related. I talk to a whole bunch of people who will say, "Well, I can't believe in God, because I wanted him to do such-and-such and he didn't." I'm not saying your pain isn't real pain, and please hear me when I say I hurt with you, but belief and God's cooperation in your circumstances have nothing to do with each other. Why? I don't know. Maybe because He's God and we're not and we can ask Him when we meet Him.

If belief and God's cooperation in your pain and suffering are related, then why does Jesus stay two more days in the place where he was? Which, incidentally, allows Lazarus to die and his sisters to cry their eyes out? Let me just ask you: You ever feel like you've cried out to God and He ain't coming? I mean, seriously. You've been praying for your marriage, and praying for your marriage, and praying for your marriage, and you just don't understand why God won't change him. In fact, you're reading this chapter by yourself right now because he's out with the boys or playing golf. He's wasting his time sucking down beer and you're in here sitting under the gospel, and you're asking the Lord, "Come on, Lord. I've tried to do my best. I've tried to love him. I've tried to serve him. I see these videos of you putting these men and women back together. Put Jesus in the middle. And why can't I just have a marriage like that?" And you're crying out to God, and you believe that He loves you, but apparently He's not coming to answer that prayer right yet.

You ever been there?

Or maybe you're sick and you're praying for healing like we've prayed for Dr. Asher. And we pray and pray, and we know God can heal. And you've heard of Him healing other people. But for whatever reason, He's not healing you.

Or maybe it's your prodigal son or your prodigal daughter, and you don't know what to do. Your heart breaks. This is your child. When you brought them home from the hospital, you had all these hopes and all these dreams, and you did it right. You raised them in the church quoting, *Raise up a child in the way he should go, and when he is older he will not depart from it* (Prov. 22:6). And now they're gone and they've departed. To make matters worse, they've rejected you, and they're squandering away their life on reckless living, and all you want the Lord to do is just bring them home. You walk into church and hear someone talking about how the Lord answered their prayer request to get a good parking spot and you're thinking, *Forget the parking spot, can you just bring my kid home? Could you do that?*

You ever been there?

You pray and you pray and you pray and you pray, and you're feeling, "Lord, where are you?" And he doesn't show up. Here's the tough part, and I love you enough to tell you: God's not on our time. He's on His. And whether or not His timeline intersects with ours says nothing about His love for us. We don't measure God's love for us by our circumstances, but by the cross.

God demonstrated His love for us in this. While we were still sinners, Christ died for us (Rom. 5:8). Knowing his friend Lazarus has died, Jesus told the disciples, *"This is going to work out for my glory. And their good. You've just gotta hang in there."* John 11:7–9: "Then after this he said to the disciples, 'Let us go to Judea again.' The disciples said to him, 'Rabbi, the Jews were just now seeking to stone you, and are you going there again?' " His suggestion surprises them, and they're like, *"Are you sure, boss?"* Now listen to this answer. "Are there not twelve hours in the day? If anyone walks in the day, he does not stumble, because he sees the light of this world. But if anyone walks in the night, he stumbles, because the light is not in him" (vv. 9–10).

Does that help anybody? I know when Jesus said this, one of the disciples was like, "Mmm-hmm. That's good. That's so good, Rabbi. That's good. I'm tweeting it right now. Praise hands. Praise hands. Fire. Fire. Fire. Can't touch this." Oftentimes in church when the preacher says something that goes right over our heads we try to look spiritual by mooing instead of embarrassing ourselves by admitting that we didn't get it. Here's what He's saying: *"When the sun goes down, the workday is over. I'm the light of the world. As long as I am here, we got work to do."* But they still don't understand what He's saying, and we know this because He has to explain it to them in the next few verses. "After saying these things, he said to them, 'Our friend Lazarus has fallen asleep, but I go to awaken him.' " Now the disciples say to him, "Lord, if he has fallen asleep, he will recover" (vv. 11–12).

You ever try to explain to God how the world works? "God, I don't know if you're aware of this, but we got this thing called the stock market, and I'm pretty invested, and I need your help. All right? I needed it to go up, not down, and I'm getting crushed. And in Jesus' name, amen."

I would just encourage us, in our prayer time, to spend a little less time informing God of the situation and a lot more time listening or letting Him saturate you in His Word. The writer of Hebrews says, *He upholds all things by the word of His power* (Heb. 1:3). And *all things* still means "all things." God knows what's going on.

Let me ask this—do you have a little trouble understanding the Bible sometimes? I mean, does it always make total sense to you? Or maybe you're in church and the preacher says something that goes right over your head? If that's you, I've got really good news. You could make a great disciple. These guys understood almost nothing, and Jesus used them to turn the world upside down.

John 11:13–15: "Now Jesus had spoken of his death, but they thought that he meant taking rest in sleep. Then Jesus told them plainly, 'Lazarus has died, and for your sake I am glad that I was not there, so that you may believe. But let us go to him.' " Which goes right over their heads once again. And here's how we know. Because Thomas, who is later known as Doubting Thomas, and also called the Twin, said to his fellow disciples, "Let us also go, that we may die with him" (v. 16). At this point, Thomas is willing to lay down his life for Jesus.

I think it's kind of a bummer that he ends up with the name Doubting Thomas. I'm sure when he finally realized that his nickname had become Doubting Thomas, he was thinking, "No, no, no, I'm Ready to Die Thomas." I imagine the other disciples were like, "Whatever, Doubting Thomas."

But Thomas is an example of what actual discipleship is. Actual discipleship starts with that first step to come and see and check out Jesus for yourself. But over time and with maturity, you get to the place where you come and die to yourself as you follow after Jesus.

This is what Thomas is talking about. He's a step ahead, but they still don't understand all that's gonna happen.

Verse 17: "Now when Jesus came, he found that Lazarus had already been in the tomb four days." I think the reason He waits until he was in the tomb for four days is that there was a Jewish first-century legend that when you died, your spirit hovered around for a while. Sort of Casper the Ghost–ish. And it could come back to you under the right circumstances. But after three or four days, it had departed. Jesus waits because He wants everybody to know that Lazarus isn't sort of dead. Not kinda dead. Not mostly dead. Not Princess Bride dead. He's dead dead. All the way dead dead.

"Bethany was near Jerusalem, about two miles off" (v. 18). Stop. Do you know why this is in the Bible? Because Bethany was near Jerusalem, about two miles away. This is an actual historical event. This is not a fairy tale. This is not "A long time ago in a galaxy far, far away." I don't even like to use the word *story*. This is an actual event. It actually happened. In an actual place. Called Bethany. You can go to Bethany today. "And many of the Jews had come to Martha and Mary to console them concerning their brother" (v. 19). In the first century, large parties of mourners would come together, and they would help you lament and wail. In fact, if a large party didn't show, it suggested you weren't real popular. Knowing this, you could contract people to come be funeral criers for you so that people would think you were a bigger deal than you are. After you're gone. And I'm not even sure why that matters, but that was what they did.

Verse 20: "So when Martha heard that Jesus was coming, she went and met him, but Mary remained seated in the house." What I want you to see is how Jesus is going to handle the grief of two sisters. How many of you know that you can have the same mama and daddy and be nothing like your siblings in personality? Mary and Martha are completely different.

We find out in Luke 10, when Jesus goes to dinner at their house, that Martha is a type A driven. She's probably an eight or a three on the Enneagram. She likes to get stuff done. She loves to check things off her list. She's also a worker bee. She works her fingers to the bone. And now she's aggravated because she's putting everything in order, setting the table and so on, while her sister is doing nothing. So she goes to Jesus and she says, "*Jesus, can you help me out a little bit? My good-for-nothing sister is all crisscross-applesauce at your feet while I'm getting everything together. Okay? Prayer ain't gonna fix the peanut butter and jellies. You understand what I'm saying?*" (Luke 10:40). That's Martha. Anybody have a Martha in their life? She's the kind of woman who can't go to sleep when there's a dish in the sink. I'm married to one. It's crazy.

Mary, on the other hand, is probably a four on the Enneagram. She's an introvert. Feels all the feels. Just soaking in Jesus. So they're very different.

Martha hears that Jesus is in town and she's not waiting. Boom. She's outta there. Goes running to him, at which point she says to Jesus, "Lord, if you had been here, my brother would not have died. But even now I know that whatever you ask from God, God will give you" (John 11:21–22). Despite the fact that her brother is dead, she still believes. Now, she does use the moment to point out to the Savior of the World, "*You're late. I just wanna point it out. You're late. I gave you the info and plenty of time, and if you would have just been here when I told you, we wouldn't be in this mess . . . Okay? However, it ain't over, because you're here. And so I got a plan, Jesus, so if you'll just stick with my plan, everything will work out perfectly.*"

Anybody ever think about God that way? I do it all the time. I can't tell you the number of times. I'm like, "Lord, I've got this all figured out. If You would just do what I'm asking You to do, everything would be awesome. And I know You can do it. I know You can do miracles. I've read about it. I read about a time You healed a lady who just grabbed ahold of Your garment. You were just walking through Capernaum, and then You asked, 'All right. Who touched me? Somebody touched me.' And they did. Not only did they touch You, You healed them. So if You can accidentally heal some random woman in Capernaum, surely You can heal this person that I'm praying for. And when You do, I'll bring them up onstage during a service, and everybody'll become a Christian. Let's do that plan. Will You do that? Okay, ready, break."

Martha is driven, has no quit, and she's convinced this could still work, but the response she gets from Jesus isn't quite what she was hoping for: "Your brother will rise again" (John 11:23). Martha is thinking theologically. When the Messiah returns at the end of the age. So Martha says to him, "I know that he will rise again in the resurrection on the last day" (John 11:24). Again, Martha believes, and she has correct doctrine. Which matters. Doctrine does matter. You can't rightly love God without right thoughts about God. But Jesus isn't looking that far down the road. He's thinking short-term but, again, He doesn't explain it. "I am the resurrection and the life." (There's that *I am* statement again.) "Whoever believes in me, though he die, yet shall he live, and everyone who lives and believes in me shall never die." And then He asked this question. "Do you believe this?" (John 11:25–27).

There it is: Do you believe this?

She's got the right theology, correct doctrine, and all her ducks in a row, but she's still missing Jesus. "*I know if you ask God, He'll do whatever you ask.*" To which Jesus says, "*Your brother is going to rise again.*" Again, His words are going right over her head. She's like, "Yeah, yeah. I know. I know at the end, and everybody spends forever somewhere, and based on our relationship with you, we either go to Heaven with God or we're separated from Him forever." But it's here that Jesus redefines eternal life. "I am the resurrection and the life." What's the reason for the disconnect? Martha is looking at her dead brother. Jesus is looking at dead mankind.

I imagine Martha was just as confused as when He told the disciples to eat His flesh and drink His blood. She's standing there scratching her head and pointing at Lazarus' tomb. "Are we talking about the same thing? I feel like I'm talking about one thing and you're talking about another." In Colossians 3 we learn that Jesus is the firstborn from among the dead. In the Greek, that word "firstborn" is *prōtotokos*. From it we get our word *prototype.*

Let me explain. In case you haven't noticed, I like to hunt. A lot. And mostly I hunt with a bow. My favorite bow is made by Matt McPherson, who owns and runs Mathews Archery. I like Mathews for a lot of reasons, like they make the world's best bows, but I also admire and respect them because a lot of the money they make goes straight into missions and spreading the gospel around the world. If you ask Matt why he does what he does, he'll tell you it's to spread the gospel. So, I just tell Gretchen that every time I buy a new bow I'm supporting missionaries around the world. They're one of my favorite companies on the planet. Not to mention they help me fill my freezer every fall. Given the competition in the archery world, Mathews produces a new, or flagship, bow every year. Usually late November. It's awesome. I'm like a kid on Christmas morn. But a lot goes into that release. The engineers at Mathews don't just throw something together in late October. Before Matt and his guys can produce the flagship, they produce a prototype. The first of its kind. Then he tests it. And tests it. And tests it. Based on those results, he modifies and makes it better. Then he tests and modifies it some more. Only to do it all over again. The result is a perfect bow. So what you and I see on the shelf, or in Strike-Zone Fishing, our local pro shop and pretty much my favorite retail store in Jacksonville, is the result, or the mirror image, of the prototype. The first of its kind. The one upon which all the rest will be based.

Now back to Jesus and Martha. When Jesus is resurrected from the grave, He walks out of that tomb as the firstborn from the dead.

He's the *prōtotokos*. The one upon which and from which God the Father will resurrect all who would believe in Jesus and confess Him as Lord.

Here's the good news: Jesus the prototype worked. He defeated death, hell, and the grave. And because of Him and through Him, you and I, and Lazarus, will not stay eternally in a dusty, cold grave. We will be resurrected to life with Him. When Jesus looks at Martha and says, "I am the resurrection and the life," this is what He's saying. And for the record, I'm pretty sure there's bow hunting in heaven and Jesus no doubt shoots a Mathews. Just saying.

Having said this to Martha—which probably went right over her head—He then looks at her and asks, "Do you believe this?" (John 11:26). This is *the* rubber-meets-the-road question. "Do you believe this?" And it is an individual question. Jesus is asking Martha. And Jesus is asking you.

Now, she could have taken that question to mean two things. "Do you believe I'm going to raise your brother?" That's one way she could have heard it. Or, "Do you believe that I am the resurrection and the life? Do you believe that I am going to change your eternal circumstances? Are you putting your faith and hope and belief in Me? Do you believe that I am the Christ? That I am who I say I am?" And look what she says. She says, "Yes, Lord; I believe that you are the Christ, the Son of God, who is coming into the world" (John 11:27). I think Martha is starting to get it because she's making a really big distinction right here. A lot of people say, "I believe," but what they are really saying is, "Yes, I believe You can change my circumstances with a snap of Your fingers." Which He can. No doubt. Which we should be praying for. But in saying this, they—and oftentimes we—are just looking at the surface. What's immediately in front of them. But Martha is speaking to something deeper. More eternal. Martha is finally looking beyond her brother's grave, and it's probably here that she is finally looking into the eyes of Jesus.

Again, please hear me here. Theology matters. You can't rightly love God without right thoughts about Him. A part of the reason we study books of the Bible and I write books and preach sermons in which I just go verse by verse, and explain the Greek words and all that kind of stuff, is because if we put our faith in our feelings or our circumstances, or the things going on in our lives, we will flounder all over the place. A rudderless ship tossed at sea. What we need is to anchor our faith in the person and work of Jesus Christ, the character and nature of God. This is why the writer of Hebrews says, "We have this as a sure and steadfast anchor of the soul, a hope that enters into the inner place behind the curtain" (Heb. 6:19). When you look around and you can't understand why something is happening to you, you can lift your eyes and look to Him and understand. He's still got the whole world in His hands, and He loves you. How do I know this? Because He's the firstborn. He went first. For us. Before us.

And when she had said this, she went and called her sister. "Mary," *she said in private, "the teacher is here. He is calling you." And when* *she heard it, she rose quickly. She went out to him* (John 11:28–29). Now remember, Mary's a feeler. An introvert. She's just sitting in the house, and when she hears this, she runs to see Jesus. "Now Jesus had not yet come into the village, but was still in the place where Martha had met him. When the Jews who were with her in the house, consoling her, saw Mary rise quickly and go out, they followed her, supposing that she was going to the tomb to weep there" (John 11:30–31).

"Now when Mary came to where Jesus was and saw him..." Notice she does not speak first. She first falls down on her face. Emotionally exhausted. She's been holding it together until He arrived. Kneeling, she says, "Lord, if you had been here, my brother would not have died" (John 11:32). While I think they say it with different tones of voice, Mary and Martha say the same thing. My translation is simply this: "God, what are You doing? Can't You see what's happening here? We are in pain!"

You ever been there? I'll talk about this more in a later chapter, but I'm here now. Right this second. As I write this, I'm in one of the most difficult and painful periods of my life. And it has nothing to do with my house. I love my wife, she loves me. I love my kids. They love me. The Lord is in our house. But for reasons beyond our control we are in pain. But just because they are beyond our control does not mean they are beyond His. I can't tell you the number of times I've asked, "God, what are You doing?" At other times, I've asked, "Would You please reconcile this relationship? Why won't You reconcile the relationship? Why won't You heal so-and-so? Why won't You bring our son or our daughter back? God, what are You doing?"

Which leads me to ask you this question: Do you think it's okay to question God? You think it's okay to come to God and go, "God, I don't understand what You're doing here"? Well, Mary and Martha say as much to Jesus, and He rebukes neither. To neither woman does He point His finger in her chest and say, "You better watch it. Do you know who you're talking to? I'm the almighty sovereign King of the universe. I thought you into existence and I can unthink you out of it." That's not what He does. He just meets them right where they are. It's totally fine to ask God why. He can handle all your questions. He just wants you to bring them to Him and let Him answer them. Not the world. Listen to King David in Psalm 22:1. "My God, my God, why have you forsaken me?" Anybody ever felt that before? And think about this. Before Jesus ever quotes this on the cross, David prays it and the Spirit of God says to David, "*Yeah, Dave. That's good. Let's write that one down and put it in the book, because there are going to be some people who need to pray that until I return.*" "My God, my God, why have you forsaken me?"

Listen. God just wants the real you. He wants your arguments, your shouts, your cries, and your joys. The real you. Real questions. Real pain. Real hurt. With all the intensity you can muster. Because He's the only God who can do anything about any of them. And so when Mary finds Jesus, she falls at his feet and does exactly this. "Lord, if you had been here, my brother would not have died." The Joby translation is *"Lord, I don't understand what You're doing."*

"When Jesus saw her weeping, and the Jews who had come with her also weeping, He was deeply moved in his spirit and greatly troubled" (John 11:33). Deeply moved and greatly troubled. In my life and work, I've done a whole bunch of funerals. When I see people's loved ones get upset because the one they love has passed away, it never ceases to move me. Every time.

Just this year, I did my grandmother's funeral. She was in her nineties and loved Jesus, and she's in heaven, so it's not tragic. She lived a great life and she's one of the people the Lord used to bring me to Him, so she was really special to me. When I arrived at the funeral, I saw my brother. He's a cop down in Saint Johns County. He was sitting in the front row. And I knew if I looked at him during the service and saw him crying, I'd lose it. So before the service began he said, "Hey, bro. How can I help?" And I was like, "Russ, if you could just sit in the front row and be a rock, then I can just look at you and I'll be fine." And he was like, "I got you."

So I walked up there, spoke these words into the microphone: "Hey, I'm Joby." And I could feel myself starting to get choked up, 'cause she was lying right there in front of me. So, knowing I needed to pull it together, I immediately looked to my rock. Russ. My brother. The police officer who carries a gun, wears body armor, and busts down doors. And what was he doing? He was crying like a baby. He looked like De Niro with his face all turned inside out. I followed suit.

Jesus is moved. Most often in the New Testament, a certain Greek word is used to describe the emotion of Jesus. It means "compassion." It means "from or out of the gut." The womb, even. But the word used here to describe Jesus is not this word. And this is why I often spend time translating Greek to English. Words matter, and this word here is different. The Greek word here is *embrimaomai*, and it means "deeply moved in his spirit and greatly troubled." This word means sadness with emotional indignation. Another translation (NKJV) says He "groaned." You ever seen somebody get so moved and yet so mad that they cry? Or make those deep, guttural sounds? That's what's going on here simultaneously.

Jesus is both moved with great compassion and He's also really angry. But at what? He's ticked off at death. And I think He probably remembers back to that moment when He spoke everything into creation, and then He gathered together the dust of the earth and He breathed the *ruach* ("breath" or "spirit") of life into the very first man, Adam, and he opened his eyes, and he was face-to-face with God, the Father. Jesus remembers that because He was there. Fashioning each of us. Including His friend Lazarus. Jesus knows we were created for life with the Father. Not death. That's what's going on here.

And so Jesus says, "Where have you laid him?" And they said, "Lord, come and see" (John 11:34). Pay attention here because what we feel deeply Jesus feels more deeply. While they're crying, Jesus is going to weep. John 11:35, the shortest verse in the Bible: "Jesus wept."

I don't know who the first person was to face something difficult and then equate strength with lack of emotion. The whole boys-don't-cry thing. It's a lie. Strength is not withholding emotion. In fact, in Ecclesiastes 3, the Bible gives us a whole range of emotion. It says there is a time for every season under heaven. *There's a time to be born, to die, to mourn, to laugh. And there's a time for crying, and a time for dancing.* In twenty-five-plus years of ministry, I've found that if when it is time to cry, and you don't allow yourself to cry, then when it is time to dance, you won't be able to dance. It is okay to both feel and express the emotions that bubble up. Men, it's okay to cry.

Emotions are a gift from God to navigate life. They make a terrible decision-maker and a terrible lord, but they are quite a handy tool to navigate this thing called life. So when it is time to cry, we need to cry.

In this moment, Jesus sits down with Mary, puts his arm around her, and He just weeps. He is present in the moment and He brings His tears. You ever been around Christians at a tragedy? Maybe at a funeral. Christians can say the dumbest stuff. We mean well, but sometimes we just need to keep our mouths shut. We say things like, "Hey, it's the funeral, but why are we crying? We should be happy. They're in heaven." Whenever someone says that, I think to myself, *I'm about to send you to heaven. Get up out my face. What are you telling me about, man? I'm crying 'cause I miss him.* I get all the theological realities that we do not mourn as those without hope, but the Bible does not say that we do not mourn. We just mourn with hope. But that doesn't mean that it's not sad right now. And Jesus is sad right now. So, He weeps with this woman.

A few months ago, I got a text from a lady who used to attend another church but now attends ours. And the reason she joined ours is this: She had just lost her dad. He was healthy. Played golf a lot. Then he got sick and boom, he was gone. During her grieving, some other pastors came to visit. But I don't think they were all that pastoral because when they left, she was confused and so she reached out and asked me, "Pastor, they questioned my trust in God because of how much I was crying. Do I not trust God?"

And I responded "Wait, what?!"

Bottom line—that is spiritual abuse. Don't ever say that to someone grieving. If a lack of tears equals faith, then Jesus didn't have faith. And I don't either. Jesus cries when it's time to cry. Let me tell you how to *be* the church real quick. The Bible says that we're supposed to weep with those who weep. If any part of the body hurts, the whole body hurts. So, the next time a thing happens in our society and it significantly impacts a group of people who are a part of the body, and maybe they didn't grow up like you did, and maybe they have a different political persuasion than you do, then weep with those who weep. Because here's what Jesus does not do. He does not roll up on the scene and start asking a bunch of stupid questions. "Well, first, let's get all the facts. Okay? How did Lazarus die? Was it his fault? What was he wearing? Did he have insurance?" No. All He does is put His arm around her, and He weeps with her. He doesn't say dumb stuff. He just weeps with her.

The body of Christ is supposed to weep with those who weep. You cannot simultaneously empathize and defend. The two do not go together. So the next time you get the opportunity to minister to somebody, don't worry so much about what to say. Just keep your mouth shut, put your arm around them, and just shed some tears with them. That will mean more than you could ever know. I'm speaking from experience. If you feel like you have to say words, try these: "I love you."

Crying does not equal weakness. A few weeks ago, I was at a daddy-daughter retreat. One of the events was a daddy-daughter dance. Sure hope those YouTube videos don't go viral. Following the dance, every dad wrote a letter to our daughters. Ages nine to thirteen years old. And then every dad sat knee to knee, face-to-face, eye to eye with their daughters, and we read these letters and blessings over our daughters.

I've never seen so many muscled, tattooed, grown men crying like babies. Not one dad made it through. Not one. But that wasn't weakness. It was strength. In fact, if more daughters saw the strength of their dads' tears as they bless them, they'd stop listening to the lies of this world, and these stupid boys lying to them too. Amen. Dads? Be strong and cry.

Back to Jesus. He's crying. But let's ask the obvious. Why is He crying? He knows how this turns out. So why? I mean, how long is he gonna wait? Twenty minutes? Thirty? I don't know what the standard wait time is to resurrect your dead friend, but Jesus knew that day, this thing was going to end up awesome. And yet here He is crying.

One of my favorite things to do when it's not yet football season is watch past Georgia games. Especially 2021, the national championship year. Go Dawgs! Can I get a witness! But I don't watch reruns of when we lose. So, according to my DVR, Georgia is undefeated the last five years. But my kids don't know if the game I'm watching is a new game or a rerun. So they sit down and get into it. And let's say Georgia fumbles, and the other teams scoops and scores, and my kids are like, "Oh, no, Daddy!" And with great confidence I reply, "Oh, you of little faith. Believe, baby. Believe. The good guys win in the end." Why? Because I know how it's gonna end, so the middle stuff doesn't freak me out.

Jesus is the alpha and omega. He knows the beginning and the end. And yet for some reason He is weeping with Mary. Why? Seven times in the gospel of John, Jesus is going to say, "I am." He just said, "I am the resurrection and the life." This is the covenant name of God, "I am that I am," which means God is eternally present. That in the past, He is, and right now, He is, and in the future, He's already there. He is.

Maybe this is why the elders in heaven pray and sing around the throne, *Who was, and is, and is to come. Holy, holy, holy, is the Lord God Almighty*. Which means this: No matter what you're going through and no matter how it's going to end, Jesus is perfectly present with you in the right now. He is present with you in the midst of your pain and suffering. Regardless of the cause. That's what he's doing with Mary. He is perfectly present with her right now.

"So the Jews said, 'See how he loved him!' But some of them said,

'Could not he who opened the eyes of the blind man also have kept this man from dying?'" (John 11:36–37). I'll tell you one thing I've learned in pastoring a church through a pandemic: There's always a critic. I mean, Jesus is crying with this lady, and some people think, *Oh, that's sweet*, and other people think, *Nope. Not right.*

If you're a leader of anything, let me give you this advice for free. Whatever decision you make, you'll always encounter the three little bears. There's one group of people who are like, "Nope, not enough." There's another group of people who say, "That's way too much." And then there's the people who say, "That's just right." It was also true for Jesus.

Jesus, deeply moved again, came to the tomb, which was a cave, and a stone lay against it, and Jesus said, "Take away the stone." And Martha, the sister of the dead man, said to him, "Lord, by this time, there will be an odor, for he has been dead for four days." The King James translates it this way: "*But Lord, he stinketh.*" I love this next part, by the way. And Jesus said to her, "Did I not tell you that if you believed you would see the glory of God?" (John 11:38–40).

This is the rubber-meets-the-road moment where they're putting their faith into action, but Martha is worried about the real-world smell and she's tapping Jesus on the shoulder. "*Um, Lord, I don't know if we should do this or not.*" Martha is like a lot of people in my church. They believe on Sunday. During the sermon. But come Tuesday, and the Lord says roll the stone away, and their response is "Lord, that's stinky."

So let me ask you: What stone do you need to roll away? I mean that thing that the Spirit of God put down in your heart, and you know every time we talk about forgiveness and reconciliation, that person's name comes to your mind, and you believe that you need to go home and begin the process of reconciliation. The problem is, when you pick up the phone, you're like, "I don't know. I got a lot of reasons why this might not work." Or, maybe God has called you to give something radically generous. Like sell your house, or your car or your boat, and invest in the kingdom of God. When you're sitting in church, you think it's a great idea. Then you meet with your accountant and you're not so sure. "That stinks."

What about that ministry that He called you to start? What about that one-more that you quit inviting to church? What hurdle is standing in your way? What stone do you need to roll away? 'Cause I am telling you, Jesus is the only one who can bring Lazarus out of the grave, but He calls his followers to walk in faith and partner with Him in that miracle. We walk by faith and not by sight, and without faith it is impossible to please Him. So, where is He calling you to partner with Him? Think about that. If Jesus calls Lazarus out, and the disciples do not participate in doing what He says to do, I guess Lazarus just starves to death in the cave. God partners with us in the miraculous.

And so they took the stone away, and Jesus lifted up his eyes and said, "Father, I thank you that you have heard me. I knew that you always hear me, but I said this on account of the people standing around, that they may believe that you sent me." Apparently, God does not mind that we've suffered temporarily for an eternal good. "When he had said these things, he cried out with a loud voice, 'Lazarus, come out.'" Charles Spurgeon says that if he didn't call Lazarus' name, He would've emptied the whole graveyard because in the first century, graves were often communal and that one was full of bones. I love that. Then look at what Scripture says—*And the man who died came out* (John 11:41–44).

This is a picture of our salvation. We come alive when God calls us back from the dead. And, if you are in Christ, you have been called out of the grave. This is why Paul says, "But God, being rich in mercy, because of the great love with which he loved us, even when we were dead in our trespasses, made us alive together with Christ—by grace you have been saved—and raised us up with him and seated us with him in the heavenly places in Christ Jesus" (Eph. 2:4–6). If you unpack this, God does everything—makes us alive, raises us up, and seats us. Dust can't do anything on its own.

We see this to perfection in the life of Lazarus. Jesus didn't walk up to Lazarus' grave with a checklist of how to be better. How to improve. Doesn't give him a spreadsheet with a bunch of boxes to check. "Hey Laz, bro, if you can just score a 60, I can put in a good word for you with the man upstairs and you can get you out of here. Anything above a 59." But that's not what he does. He calls the dead man to come to life and come out of the grave. That's salvation. "For by grace you have been saved through faith. And this is not your own doing; it is the gift of God, not a result of works, so that no one may boast. For we are his workmanship" (Eph. 2:8–10).

If you have ever put your faith in Jesus Christ, it's because Jesus called you out of the grave. Maybe for some of you, the stone that needs to roll away is all your doubts. Maybe you've been putting your faith in your doubts and you just need to hear Jesus call you by name and say, "Come on out of the grave."

"The man who had died came out, his hands and feet bound with linen strips, and his face wrapped with a cloth. Jesus said to them, 'Unbind him, and let him go' " (John 11:44). The way the NIV translates it is this: "Take off the grave clothes and let him go" (John 11:44 NIV).

Why is it that the first command that Jesus gives for this man, who was called out of the grave, is to take off his grave clothes? Here's why: Because living people shouldn't wear grave clothes anymore. They stink, bro. They don't fit you anymore. Living people don't wear dead people's clothes. Jesus calls us to repent of our sins because when He calls you out of the grave, those past sins don't fit you anymore. You're dead to those things and alive in Christ. You don't have to do the things that you used to do because you're not the person that you used to be. The old you is dead, and the new you is alive in Jesus Christ. And honestly, only Jesus gets to tell you who you are.

If you're a believer in Jesus, one of the things the enemy is going to try to do in your life is define you by your scars and by your past wounds. He wants you to think that you are primarily that addiction. He wants you to think that you are primarily your divorce. He wants you to think that you are that affair. That you are that porn addiction. That you are your abortion. The mistakes, the sins, those things in your life. And yes, they are sins and you should absolutely repent, but once we do, He wraps us in a robe of righteousness. A spotless robe. And then He presents us to His and our Father, and no matter what we've done, when the Father looks at us He sees the sinless, spotless robe of His Son and not our sin. Some of us believe that on Sunday but come Monday, we're back in the rut. "But I don't think you understand. That divorce? That affair? That abortion? Whatever that thing is. That's the biggest thing that ever happened to me."

NO. IT'S NOT!

That's not the gospel of Jesus Christ. The moment that you surrendered your life to the Lordship of Jesus Christ, the blood of Jesus washed all of that away, and that death-to-life thing is now the biggest thing that has ever happened to you. Only Jesus gets to tell you who you are. And Jesus is telling every one of us to rise up, walk out, and take off our grave clothes. Put the porn away. Put the drunkenness away. Put the drugs away. Put the affair away. All of those things. Why? That stuff doesn't fit you anymore, brother or sister. Jesus has called you—and notice it's an individual call, by name—to walk in a manner worthy of the gospel of Jesus Christ. The enemy always wants to define you by your wounds, and yet Jesus walks up to our cold, dead bodies and shows us His hands, His feet, and His side. "Nope. I'm defining you by mine."

Notice, He doesn't tell Lazarus to do it on his own. He can't.

He's all bound up. The initiation starts with Jesus and Jesus alone saves us, but Jesus never saves us to be alone. He saves us into a faith family. He surrounds Lazarus with people who can help him take off those grave clothes. So let me ask you this: Do you believe? Do you believe that He can call you out of the grave? And do you believe that He can surround you with the right people? And do you believe that you could cast off those dead man's clothes? And do you believe that free of death, the tomb, and those scraps that represented who you once were, you could walk in the power of the good news of the gospel? That you could walk in a manner worthy of what God has called you to walk in? And that is to walk in a newness of life?

We started this chapter with my friend Dr. Asher. And in the same way we did with Ike, I want to let him close it. "Today it's in my spine. My chest. Sitting in front of my heart. This cancer is very painful. There have been days that I have not slept. Can't sleep. It's too painful. I literally crawl out of bed and onto my knees asking God, 'Help me sleep or help me bear.' The old me would like to control things. Seek the best help because I can. The new me is looking at the Lord. And I am perfectly fine with that. I'm fine with not knowing how this story ends. Yes, the cancer is back, but I'm here. And He is still asking me, 'You have time. What are you going to do with it?' The most important thing I learned is that God called me out. Personally. As He called Lazarus. He gave Lazarus time. And so He gave me time. How would Lazarus have lived? What would he have shared with people? What would he say happened? I am living the Lazarus moment. This time I'm not going to miss one second. I want to tell everybody that He is in control. Just trust Him. I want to live every minute to glorify Him, to thank Him for the time I've had on this earth. I'm here today, and today is the day that the Lord has made and I will rejoice and be glad in it. And I do. I do. Jesus said to her, 'I am the resurrection and the life. Whoever believes in me, though he die, yet shall he live and everyone who lives and believes in me shall never die. Do you believe this?' "

I love that man, and we're praying like crazy that Jesus will heal him and eradicate every cancerous cell out of his body. Jesus spoke those words two thousand years ago and He is still speaking them today. To you. To me. "Do you believe this?"

There it is in a nutshell. Do you believe Jesus can heal? Raise the dead to life. Today? Right now?

Some of you need to cry out to the Lord God, "He's sick. She's sick. My finances are sick. This relationship is sick. Physically, I'm sick. Mentally, I'm sick. God, I need your help." Some of you have been praying and waiting and crying out for a long time. I understand that—I prayed for the salvation of my dad for thirty years before God answered that prayer. Some of you are mad at God because of your current circumstances. And to you I say bring it. He can handle all you bring, including your anger. Bring those prayers with the same intensity to Him that you have in those imaginary conversations in your head. Some of you just need to cry because somebody told you that strong, mature Christians don't cry. Well, they lied. We need to cry. A lot. You need to let the tears flow, and watch what the Lord does through that release. And some of you need to come to pray for the Spirit to give you the strength to roll away the stone in your life. To walk in faith. Faith is acting as if you actually believe Jesus is who He says He is, and He always keeps His promises.

Some of you have been called to come alive for the very first time, to come out of the grave. To you I say, you've been dead long enough, come out. And pretty much all of us need to burn our grave clothes. We need to come before the Lord and say, "Lord, I need help taking off these grave clothes. I know it doesn't make sense, because I'm alive, but I have a daily tendency to put on these old grave clothes. God, would you please help me take 'em off? Forever."

My one request is this: Pray with somebody. If you're reading this book by yourself, then pick up the phone or go knock on somebody's door. I told you that you need four friends to let your mat down through the roof. Now's the time to call them. And if you don't have four friends, now's the time to find them and you'll know if they're your friends because they'll want to pray with you. If you've got a discipleship group, call them. And if you don't have anybody, call our church. Our people will pray with you. Whatever the case. This is not a Lone Ranger event. If you're in a prison cell alone, then cry out to the guy next to you or invite the Holy Spirit. He'll pray with you. God has called each of us into a family to help us take off our grave clothes and walk in newness of life. So grab somebody's hand. And let's lift the other one in worship.

Pray with Me

I've asked Dr. Asher to lead us in prayer and then I'll follow…

Dear Abba, I come to You beaten, broken, and humbled. Jesus, You are the Lord of my life, You are the King of this Universe. You are the alpha and the omega. My Lord, my God, You created me in my mother's womb and You alone have sustained me. You have numbered my days and filled them with goodness and purpose for the sake of Your glory. Jesus, I am not worthy, but You have loved me and engraved me on the palms of Your hands. In You alone do I rest my faith. In the confidence of Your mighty, everlasting presence do I open my eyes every day. All my infirmities and maladies are known to You. They shudder and melt away on Your command, and You restore me every day of my life. Jesus, in my meekness I kneel before You today, humbly asking for You to say the word and take the burden of this disease away from me (or ____). Restore my (his/her) body and make it a *testimony of Your unfathomable healing power, which continues to dwell among us because You love me (us).*

Our good and gracious heavenly Father God, You are good, and You are gracious. Jesus, I thank You that You did not come to make bad men better. You came to dead men and women to be called to life in You. So Lord, I pray for the resurrection in this place. God, I pray for healing. God, I pray for reconciliation. I pray for mental health, and I pray for all those kinds of things. But in the meantime, Lord, we just pray for Your presence, because Your presence changes everything. God, I pray against the lies of the enemy. I pray that we would know that our strength is not defined by a withholding of emotion, but that we would pour it out. We would pour it all out on the feet of Jesus.

Lord, I pray for men and women far from You that they would come running, and that they would know that You did not rebuke Mary or Martha. You met them exactly where they are, and God, I thank You and I praise You that You are the resurrection, and that You are the life, and we find those things in You. And Lord, I pray against the enemy as he tries to whisper those lies that we would be defined by our past wounds, and Lord, may we be defined by Your scars at the cross, because it is finished. Lord, would You please give us the strength to take off those grave clothes. If we are alive in Christ, then it makes no sense that we would still be wearing the clothes of the dead. Lord, I pray that as the enemy continuously tries to tempt us, we would see that life in You is so much better than going back to our old ways. We pray this in Jesus' name. Amen.

CHAPTER 6

Mary Anoints Jesus—Do You Believe Jesus Is Worthy of Worship—No Matter What?

Unexpressed gratitude is pretty much useless. Husbands, I know you may feel grateful inside for your wives, but if those words don't come out of your mouth it really doesn't mean anything. Wives, can I get a witness?

What you're about to see is a turning point in the Gospel of John. From John chapters 1 through 10, John covers the first three years of Jesus' ministry. Chapters 11 through 21 cover the last week of his life. If John's gospel were a video, this is about where he switches to slo-mo.

Starting in verse 45 of chapter 11, we read, "Many of the Jews, therefore, who had come with Mary and had seen what he did..." What'd He do? Flip back a few pages. He called Lazarus out of the grave. He raised a dead man to life. And everyone knew it because Lazarus had been in there four days.

The effect of this on the people around Jesus was that they "believed in" Jesus. As the promised Messiah. They *pisteuō*'d. Why? Because seeing is believing. Job says this very thing after his trial: "I know that you can do all things, and that no purpose of yours can be thwarted...I had heard of you by the hearing of the ear, but now my eye sees you" (Job 42:2, 5). Job had a right vision of God, just as these people now do who are following Jesus. I'm just telling you, if you roll up on a man who claims to be God, that's fine—anyone can do that. But bringing dead people to life? That proves it. Mic drop.

But some of them went to the Pharisees and told them what Jesus had done. So some believed and became followers of Jesus, and some tattled on Jesus. It's unbelievable to me. I've been doing this for a long time. Twenty-eight, twenty-nine years. Something like that. And this reaction to Jesus is unbelievable to me.

I see this every week in our church. People experience the same sermon, worship, and so on, and they see all the same evidence that Jesus is who He says He is, and they have polar opposite reactions to that evidence. Some people roll up in Bethany and they see Lazarus was dead and now he's alive and they want to argue with the way Jesus called him out. Others believe.

At the opposite end of the spectrum are the tattletales. "Jesus isn't doing it right." Ugh. Some people see and believe and some people see and criticize, it's just what happens. And the difference is found in the condition of the heart.

I can be preaching my face off, and some of the folks in front of me are into it. They sit down front, say "Amen," take notes, nod, cry. Yet sitting right next to them is someone scrolling Pinterest. I don't get it. That said, I don't preach because everyone always gets it. I preach out of obedience and because I was called, and then I leave the result to Jesus. But I still scratch my head sometimes. I am not saying that I am a very good preacher. In fact, I would say what I do is moderately delivered and exceptionally received. But it amazes me how different people react and respond to the same message or the same set of circumstances.

In John 11:47–49, the chief priests and the Pharisees gathered a council. By the way, this is what religious people do. God does a miracle and religious people vote on whether God did it right. They should be throwing a party, and yet they're throwing a fit because He does not fit into their religious box. And so they gathered together a council and they said, "What are we to do? For this man performs many signs. If we let him go on like this, everyone will believe in him, and the Romans will come and take away both our place and our nation."

There it is. There is the heart of every manmade religion. These men are not concerned about the law of God; they're not even concerned about taking care of the people of God whom they're supposed to serve. They are focused on one thing: their power. They want to make sure they don't lose their place, their temple, their authority, their title, their nation. Even if the people who they're supposed to serve continue under Roman occupation and oppression, that's fine as long as they get to stay in power. This is the heartbeat of manmade religion. The true foundation of manmade religion is focused on "me." I'm in control. The foundation of a relationship with Jesus is focused on Him, and He's in control. Big difference.

These religious men loved to walk into a room and say, "Whoa, everybody needs to listen to us and do what we say. We have the fancy hats, fancy titles, we decide what rules are, and you will obey." This is why they are so upset with Jesus. Because they can't control the outcome if people start following after Jesus.

"One of them, Caiaphas, who was high priest that year"—by the way, he's not a big Jesus fan—"said to them, 'You know nothing at all. Nor do you understand that it is better for you that one man should die for the people, not that the whole nation should perish'" (vv. 49–50). Now here's what's crazy—he's absolutely right.

He's speaking politically. He's saying, *"Hey, let's not screw this up for everybody because if there's an uprising here in Jerusalem, Caesar's gonna send the Roman army in and wipe us out. So why don't we just offer him up politically, allow the Romans to crucify him, and then the rest of us will be fine."*

What he does not know is that even though he is speaking self-ishly and politically, he is theologically accurate. Here's what's crazy: Caiaphas thinks he's in charge, but he's not. He's under the sovereign authority of the most high King. We know this because John is about to give us some commentary.

"He did not say this of his own accord, but being high priest that year he prophesied that Jesus would die for the nation, and not for the nation only, but also to gather into one the children of God who are scattered abroad" (vv. 51–52). You know where "scattered abroad" is? Well, for starters, it's my home. Jacksonville. And my hometown, Dillon. It's Dallas. Phoenix. LA (that's "Lower Alabama"). New York City. Stockholm. Paris. London. Melbourne. "Scattered" is us. Anywhere we are. If you're reading this book, then you're part of the scattered.

Now, here's the thing—God can use the ungodly to teach the truth. He can. And He does. God uses crooked sticks to draw straight lines, or the way my daddy used to say it, "Even a blind squirrel finds an acorn every once in a while. And even a broken clock is right twice a day." This is what's happening here.

Caiaphas thinks that he is self-serving and he's got it all figured out. Actually, he is simply a part of what God is doing. Verse 53: "So from that day on they made plans to put him to death." You'd think they'd worship Him for raising the dead. Nope. They try to kill Him.

Why? Again, it goes to power, prestige, position. The religious leaders look at Jesus, and at what's happening, and they think, *If He really is Messiah, I'm not needed anymore. He might take my job. Might take my control. Take what's mine.* Now I know you're sitting reading this and you're like, "How could they think such a thing about Jesus?"

Easy. You know who else thinks the same thing about Jesus? You do. We all do. This is the constant battle for us. Who is Lord? Him or me?

Don't believe me? Let me switch gears real quick. Let's talk about money. Let's talk about your giving. Your tithe. Are you robbing God?

Okay, feel that little twinge that surfaces when I just mention money. That twinge is evidence of the struggle. Because you're worried either I or Jesus will take your money. If you're a follower of Jesus, none of your money is yours. Right? All of it's His. Everything you have is a blood-bought grace gift from Jesus Christ. He's just letting you hold on to it.

This chapter is not primarily about money, but look at your reaction. Some of you just went, "Oh, okay. Thank God I'm back in." But let me ask you: What holds you? Does He hold you, or does your money have a hold on you? Some of you think, *I'm not going to follow Jesus because He might take my money. Or He might take my freedom. And I like doing what I want when I want.*

This means, ultimately, you want to be in control of you because when it comes down to it, you trust only yourself. Here's the thing about following Jesus—you cannot be in control of your life. Jesus said to *deny yourself, pick up your cross, and follow Him* (Matt. 16:24). Ultimately, to follow Jesus means there's a death in your future. Your death. "Follow me" means "come and die." When we follow Jesus, we lay down all our "rights." We have a right to nothing except what He gives us. We are no longer lord of our life. For Jesus to be your Lord means that we are turning over control of all our life to Him. And you're like, "Whoa, He might take my worldview? I've heard what the church believes about sex and marriage and money, and I agree with some of it but not all of it."

We can be hypercritical of the Pharisees as we read the New Testament, but here's the truth—we are them. And then we walk into church, or pick up this book and start flipping pages thinking we are in control. And at our root, that's what we and they are afraid of most. Losing control.

Part of the Good News of the Gospel of Jesus Christ is that when you claim Him as Lord, you lay it all down, you say, "God, I'm taking all of my hopes and all of my dreams and all of my desires and all of my sin and all of my condemnation and I am just laying it at Your feet." And when you do, a funny thing happens. You realize all your hopes and dreams and all of those things were too small. Because Jesus is better than life. But to do that, look what is required. "Deny yourself." Don't skip over that. Stay right here a minute. Let me poke you a little: What would it look like, right now, today, for you to deny yourself? What is He calling you to deny? Either Jesus is Lord or we are. There's no neutral ground. No Switzerland.

I also want you to notice there were two reactions when Lazarus walked out of the tomb. When confronted with the irrefutable miraculous power of the Son of God, the religious elite wanted to kill Jesus. The rest worshiped. This has been the case since God cast satan out of heaven and it is true today. Kill Him or bow. Those are your two options. Choose carefully.

As a result of this, *Jesus therefore no longer walked openly among the Jews because they were trying to kill him, but He went from there to a region near the wilderness, to a town called Ephraim, and there He stayed with his disciples* (John 11:54).

Basically, Jesus is laying low. He found a safe house. "Now the Passover of the Jews was at hand" (John 11:55). This is the third time in the Gospel of John that we see the Passover come up. This is partly how we know that Jesus did ministry for about three years.

The reason that Jesus is laying low is not because the religious leaders or even the Roman authorities were in control. Jesus was controlling the calendar because He knew He would be crucified at Passover.

The Passover is a holiday in the old covenant to celebrate the exodus. Briefly, let me back up (to the book of Exodus). God's chosen people were enslaved in Egypt. To free them, God picked an unlikely leader, Moses, who had a pretty nasty track record. God comes to him one day while Moses was minding his own business at work and he says, "*I want you to go to Pharaoh and I want you to say to Pharaoh, 'Let my people go.'* "

And Moses scratches his head. "*I don't think it's gonna work. Who should I say sent me?*" And God gives Moses his covenantal name, Yahweh, "*I am that I am. You tell him, 'I am' sent me.*" Not convinced, Moses asks, "*Well, he's the most powerful person on the planet. How's he gonna believe me?*" And God says, "*I'm gonna send ten plagues.*"

Each one of the plagues was a direct affront to one of Egypt's gods. Meaning, this is a head-to-head matchup between a man who said he was god—that is, Pharoah—and God. Every one of the plagues was to prove to Pharaoh that the one true God, Yahweh, is greater than all the little-*g* gods that the Egyptians worshiped. Like the blood god, the gnat god, the locust god, the water god, and the moon god, and all of them. Yahweh was tearing them down one by one.

But He saved the best for last. The last plague was the plague of all plagues. It was the plague of the firstborn. That even means Pharoah's firstborn. The tenth god to be toppled: Pharoah. Moses goes to Pharaoh and says, "*Listen, there's an angel of death that's coming through Egypt.*" And then God tells Moses to go to his people and say, "*Get a perfect spotless lamb, shed the blood of the lamb, and you put the blood of the lamb on the doorpost of your house. And when the angel of death comes through, the angel of death will pass over whoever has the blood of the lamb on the doorpost of the house.*"

The Hebrews did, the Egyptians did not. As a result, the Hebrews lived, the Egyptians died. Because after that day Pharaoh said, "*All right, get out of here. You're free.*"

Jesus is controlling the date of His own death because He is the Passover lamb. Remember what His cousin, John the Baptist, said way back in the beginning of the Gospel of John: "Behold, the

Lamb of God, who takes away the sin of the world!" (John 1:29). John is saying that Jesus is the perfect spotless Lamb. He dies a sinner's death in our place, and for whoever believes, the blood of the Lamb is put on the doorpost of their own heart. So that when the angel of death and judgment comes your way and sees the blood of Jesus on the doorpost of your heart, he passes over you and you go from slavery to freedom, into the promised land.

That's Passover.

"Now the Passover of the Jews was at hand, and many went up from the country to Jerusalem before the Passover to purify themselves. They were looking for Jesus and saying to one another as they stood in the temple, 'What do you think? That he will not come to the feast at all?' Now the chief priests and the Pharisees had given orders that if anyone knew where he was, he should let them know, so that they might arrest him" (John 11:55–57). And so everybody's got an eye for Jesus, seeing if he's going to show up. "Six days before the Passover, Jesus therefore came to Bethany, where Lazarus was, whom Jesus had raised from the dead" (John 12:1).

In John 11, Jesus asks Martha, "Do you believe?" And she says, "*I believe. You are the resurrection and the life. I believe that You are the Christ.*" Then they show up to the tomb and He says, "*All right, roll away the stone.*" And I previously asked you, "What stone is Jesus telling you to roll away by faith?" Martha came up with a whole bunch of excuses. Have you? I rarely check up on homework, but did you roll away that stone of doubt and unbelief?

Why not? The answer is simple, and we see the reason in Caiaphas. Control. You want Jesus but you don't want to take your hand off the reins of your own life. You want Jesus to raise your life, your finances, your marriage, your name, your problem, to life and yet you want to maintain lordship over you. You thought that just because we'd finished that chapter that we were finished with that lesson. Jesus knows better.

Did you do what He told you to do? Or have you already forgotten about it? Martha says, *"I believe You're the Christ."* And she did. And I believe you do too. When you're reading this. But when you close this cover, and you're back to your life, what do you do with the stone of your doubts? Did you offer excuses or, by faith, do what He told you to do? I hope you did. Because what good is a live Lazarus if he's stuck inside a tomb? He'll die of starvation. And so will your faith. Let me encourage you—feed your faith. Roll away the stone.

"So they gave a dinner for him there" (John 12:2).

We find out in the Gospel of Mark that the dinner is happening at Simon the Leper's house. I love this part. Read that again. Simon the Leper's house. Here's the obvious problem—you can't eat with somebody who has leprosy or you'll get leprosy. So, I think it's pretty safe to infer here that Simon has been healed of leprosy.

Let's say Simon is throwing a gratitude party. That's what he's doing. He used to have leprosy, but he doesn't anymore. He hears Jesus is in town and so he throws a party. Then he thinks to himself, *Gee, who should I invite? I know, how 'bout Lazarus. He's got some stuff to be grateful for. He was dead. Now he's not.* "Hey Laz, what're you doing today?"

"Not much. Truth be told, I wasn't even planning on being here."

"Cool, why don't you come to the party?"

One of the things that bums me out about us as humans is how quick we are to name people by their former condition. Simon the Leper is not a leper anymore. Why don't they call him Simon the Healed, Simon the Used-to-Be-Leper? Jesus doesn't call him Simon the Leper. He just calls him son, His friend. And so Simon is throwing a gratitude party. By the way, I think that's the way we ought to look at church. Every time we gather together as believers in the name of Jesus Christ, guess what's happening? A church, an ecclesia, is just Simon the Leper's house. Just a whole bunch of people who used to be blind and used to be lame and used to be dead and then we met Jesus and now we're different. We're alive. Church is just a gratitude party. So, our gathering ought to be a big old gratitude party for who He is and what He's done. How different would our churches be if we saw church that way? How different would our worship be?

"So they gave a dinner for him there. Martha served." Of course she did. Serving is what she does. Bless her heart. She can't stop. "Lazarus was one of those reclining with him at table" (John 12:2). It's a big week for Laz, so he's just kicking it at the table.

But busy-bee Martha can't relax. "Hey, bro, can you give me a hand with the sweet tea?" And Laz brushes her off. "Sis, can you just give me a break. I was dead for four days and now I'm alive. You ever been dead before? It's a thing. Trust me. Can I just sit here with Jesus at the table?"

Then there's Mary. The last time we heard from Mary, she runs out to Jesus, falls on her face, and cries, "Lord, if you had been here my brother would not have died." What did Jesus do? He wept. Cried His face off. Guys, it's okay to cry. What did Mary do? She took a pound of expensive ointment made from pure nard, which comes from the Himalayas. Somewhere between Pakistan and China. A long way from Bethany and very expensive.

And she anointed the feet of Jesus. Wiped his feet with her hair, and the house was filled with the perfume. Don't miss this—this is worship. It's beautiful worship. Look at all three of these siblings. All three respond differently to the presence of Jesus. And all three responses—service, rest with, and worship of—are highly appropriate.

All of us are wired in one of these three ways. Some of us get all worked up and want to know: What can I do, how can I sign up, how can I serve? Praise God, that's legit. No prob. Then some of you are like Lazarus. You respond by just wanting to abide. When the Lord stirs in you, you just wanna get your Bible and a big cup of coffee and spend an hour right there. Just reclining with him at the table. Praise God. He loves that, too. And then there's some of you, when the Lord stirs you up, you wanna get out the tambourine and the banner and just wanna go all Pentecostal. Praise God. Wave it. Make a joyful noise. No problem.

Here's what I want you to see. All three of these are right and good, and all three should be evident in the life of the believer. If the abiding and the serving and the worshiping aren't all there, something is wrong. Something is way bad wrong.

I know you may be wired more one way than the other, but that does not give you an excuse when the Bible commands you to lift your hands and sing loudly in the sanctuary. It's part of what we are called to do. It's part of how Mary responds. I mean, because think about it, I don't know exactly how it went down.

I don't know if Mary had planned this out, but when Jesus is reclining at the table, at some point, she gets up, goes to her house, and comes back with the most valuable thing she has—a pound of nard. Its value is equal to what you would pay a day laborer for three hundred days. Somewhere between, I don't know, eighty and one hundred thousand dollars in today's terms.

She takes her most valuable thing and offers it. At the feet of Jesus. And in doing so, she is saying, "Nope, not anymore. He is most valuable to me." And so she doesn't care about the dinner party, she just breaks this thing open. The Gospel of Mark says she starts with his head and gets all the way to his feet and pours out her gratitude on him.

If you read *If the Tomb Is Empty*, you know I've never been very good at trying to get people to love what I love. For instance, I keep trying to convince Gretchen to love sweet tea. Been trying for twenty-two years, but she don't like it. I don't know what's wrong with her.

I've also been trying to get my kids to have the same love for C. S.

Lewis literature that I do. Nope, they're not into it, okay. I'm trying to get my church to love the National Champion Georgia Bulldawgs. Half are, half aren't. I can't figure it out.

Now, all that's silly, for sure, but here's the thing that keeps me up at night as a pastor. I love Jesus, I mean, love Him. And I want others to love Him too. Sometimes I wonder what are the dangers with a church like ours. Multiple campuses, large attendance, all the people watching online, and a multisite megachurch, and I worry that people are just getting caught up in the crowd. 'Cause we're the new fad. The new thing. And I worry that people are missing Jesus. Here's me in a nutshell. I want you to love Him. It's why I do what I do. Period. I don't want you to just come sit in one of our seats and be entertained for a little while and then walk out and try to adjust your lifestyle a little. The same could be true of your reading this book. You could leaf through the pages. Laugh. Cry. Be entertained. And miss Jesus.

Sin management is not the point. The point is Jesus. That you would discover and deepen a relationship with Jesus Christ. Because when you love Him, turning over the reins and making Him Lord is the natural overflow of your heart. You want to. Psalm 42:1 says, *As the deer pants for the water, so my soul longs for You.* The evangelical church has jacked-up verses like this. Why? Because Christian bookstores made T-shirts with a deer standing at a stream, posing. You know what this is talking about? You know why the deer's panting for water? 'Cause somebody is trying to kill it. The deer is running for his life. He's afraid. He's running and running and running and he's parched and he's dehydrated and he's panting.

Deer don't pant from walking around streams of water. Deer don't pant from posing for pictures. The deer is panting because only one thing can quench his thirst. Does your soul long for God like this? How different would your life be if you did?

That's what I'm talking about. I've told you before, I can't get over the gospel. When we sing, " 'How Great Thou Art," the third verse says this: "And when I think that God, his son not sparing, sent him to die..." Then he pauses and adds, "I scarce can take it in."

That's me. My mind can't understand it. My heart can't contain it. I can't even fully understand how He would send His Son Jesus to die on the cross for a wretch like me. I don't understand why He would want to call me "son." I don't understand. All of my failures and faults, and broken promises, and yet He continuously lavishes His love upon me.

"I scarce can take it in. That on the cross, my burden gladly bearing, He bled and died to take away my sin." When you worship, is that how you worship? Is that how you sing? The reason we sing to Him at church, or wherever, is because it is an act of us just pouring out our lives to Him, pouring on our worship and our devotion to Him.

Does your love of Jesus Christ well up in you to the point that it overflows with tears and pours out onto His feet? Do you sing like a man or woman who was dead and is now alive?

That's what Mary's doing. By her actions she is saying, "My brother was dead and now he is alive. I'm gonna take everything I have and pour it on your feet." I want to sing like that. Like a man who has known death and is now raised to life. I wanna sing like a man who prayed for thirty years that God would save his dad, and then brought him to life. Because I did and He did.

Do you worship Him like somebody who was dead and is now alive? A few months ago, we commissioned about eightysomething deacons in our church. During the service, I was waiting on my part and I was sitting behind this older guy who we were commissioning. He grew up in church. His name is Mike. Super straitlaced. His wife told me when they first started coming, he said, "Hey, I'm into it, but I ain't raising my hands. And I ain't never raising my hands."

I like the guy a lot. He's a buddy of mine. Super funny. Super smart. Good golfer. And he's not the most expressive human I've ever met in my life. In fact, he's a urologist. Think about that. Think about his day every day. If you have to go see that kind of doctor, you don't want him walking in there like, "Woo-hoo," with this lab coat all jacked up and his hair like a crazy scientist. You want him super straitlaced. Yes, sir. High and tight. But during that service, we were worshiping and both his hands were high in the air. He was giving it everything he had. Why? Because of who Jesus is and what He's done for him. When we worship like that, when we pour out on the feet of Jesus, it changes the entire atmosphere. It just does.

Think about the dinner party. There's Simon up front. My guess is that Simon is serving food. You know why? He was a leper. He's never been able to touch anybody's food. You ever been in Israel? Everybody eats with their fingers, man, it's weird. Also, according to the law, anyone who touched him, or touched anything he touched, was ceremonially unclean for a week and was required to go see the priest and go through a cleaning ritual. But he no longer has leprosy.

Mary, at some point, breaks the vessel and then the smell of nard permeates throughout the entire place. It's invisible but everyone senses it. And people were like, "Uh-oh, what happened? Something's different in here." You see when believers in Jesus Christ pour out their worship on the feet of Jesus, it changes the atmosphere.

But while some worship, some hate. Haters are gonna hate. It's what they do. Judas, who is about to betray Him, says, "Why was this ointment not sold for three hundred denarii and given to the poor?" (John 12:5). He's critical of how Mary is worshiping. She's not doing this right. Not spiritual enough.

Pay attention to this. He's like a staff member. He's the treasurer. He's the CFO of Jesus, Incorporated. And he's critical of how somebody else is worshiping. Let me just say as bluntly as I can: The moment you find yourself criticizing how other people and how other churches choose to worship, you may be siding with Team Judas and not Team Jesus. Watch yourself.

John addresses this. "[Judas] said this, not because he cared about the poor, but because he was a thief, and having charge of the money-bag he used to help himself to what was put into it" (John 12:6).

Let me poke you a little. Are you a thief? That's right—are you a thief? I keep coming back to money because it's a really good measure and indicator of the lord of your life. If everything we have is given to us by God, do you help yourself to the money bag of what belongs to Him and say, "You know what? That's for me"? Religious people are really good at having a theologically sound argument for why it's okay to be a thief.

Judas is an example of what can happen to all of us if we're not careful. We too can get caught up in the machine. And we, like Judas, can become a consumer and not a worshiper because Judas was there to consume the goods and services of Jesus. While Mary was there to worship at the feet of Jesus. This is a warning for every single one of us. It's not all about us.

For a worshiper, it's all about Jesus. A consumer rolls up and he's like, "I hope this church meets my needs." A worshiper says, "I hope this church points me to the one who has already met all of my needs." A consumer comes in and says, "Is this a good band?" A worshiper is saying, "I just want a worship leader who points me to a good Father." The consumer is the one who shows up saying, "I'm looking for entertaining preaching, and I want it to make me laugh." But a worshiper says, "I'm praying for some cross-centered preaching to saturate my soul, because when it does, I can't help but be different." The consumer says, "I hope this is fun for the kids." A worshiper says, "I wanna be part of the faith family that helps equip me to disciple my kids." A consumer walks in and says, "I just wanna sit down and be comfortable." A worshiper shows up in a place like this and asks, "How can I go to the very ends of the earth and take the gospel? Why? 'Cause it ain't about me."

Aside from the apostle Paul, Saint Augustine is probably the most influential Christian to ever live. Augustine says this: "How sweet all at once it was for me to be rid of those fruitless joys which I once had feared to lose. You drove them from me. You who are the true, the sovereign joy, you drove them from me and took their place, you who are sweeter than all pleasure." What he's saying is this: *I was so afraid that if I followed You, You'd take away the things that I liked. And what You did is You took them away and You replaced them with You and You are better.* Martin Luther says, "Oh, I wish to devote my mouth and my heart to you. Do not forsake me for if I ever should be on my own, I would easily wreck it all."

What does it look like for you to devote your heart and your mouth to him? Spurgeon says, "I thank thee that this which is a necessity of my new life is also its greatest delight. So I do at this hour feast on thee." Or, as the Bible says, "Taste and see that the Lord is good" (Ps. 34:8). Do you see how that's different from just going to church?

John Owen, a puritan pastor, says this, "Oh, and behold the glory of Christ herein would I live, herein would I die, herein would I dwell in my thoughts and my affections until all things below become unto me a dead and deformed thing no way suitable for affection that embraces." Is that how you live?

Brother Lawrence, a sixteenth-century monk, wrote a book called *The Practice of the Presence.* In it, he says, "I have at times had such delicious thoughts on the Lord I'm ashamed to mention." That might be too far. That's a weird thing to say, but he's talking about an intimacy that's different than just showing up, sitting in the seat, going home, with no heart change.

Mary has had a heart change. In John 12:7, Jesus says, "Leave her alone, so that she may keep it for the day of my burial." Here's part of what Jesus is saying. *"She's not just worshiping me for what I did, raising her brother. She's primarily worshiping me for who I am."* Mary understands what Judas does not and never will. Then Jesus says,

"For the poor you always have with you, but you do not always have me" (v. 8).

Now pay attention to this. Is Jesus pro poor people? A hundred percent. In Matthew 25:31–40, Jesus says, "When the Son of Man comes in his glory, and all the angels with him, then he will sit on his glorious throne. Before him will be gathered all the nations, and he will separate people one from another as a shepherd separates the sheep from the goats. And he will place the sheep on his right, but the goats on the left. Then the King will say to those on his right, 'Come, you who are blessed by my Father, inherit the kingdom prepared for you from the foundation of the world. For I was hungry and you gave me food, I was thirsty and you gave me drink, I was a stranger and you welcomed me, I was naked and you clothed me, I was sick and you visited me, I was in prison and you came to me.' Then the righteous will answer him, saying, 'Lord, when did we see you hungry and feed you, or thirsty and give you drink? And when did we see you a stranger and welcome you, or naked and clothe you? And when did we see you sick or in prison and visit you?' And the King will answer them, 'Truly, I say to you, as you did it to one of the least of these . . . you did it to me.'"

And they're like, "*Why? We went to church.*" And He responds, "*Yep. But when I was in prison you didn't visit. When I was hungry, you gave me nothing to eat. When I was naked, you gave me no clothes.*" And they say, "*Whoa, we never saw Jesus that way.*" And He says, "*Whatever you did not do for the least of these, you did not do for me.*"

And then here's the most important part. "*Depart from me, for I never knew you.*" People who know and love Jesus also love people. That's what that means. But here's the danger: Serving the poor is not the end. Worship is the end. Serving the poor grows out of that. Serving the poor without worship is what the writer of Hebrews calls "dead works" (Heb. 6:1). This is why A. W. Tozer said we were created and why we are here, "that we might worship God and enjoy Him forever."

Worship is the end and everything else is a means to that end. In many churches, people tend to elevate activities above the gospel itself. Jesus says don't ever do that. He is the only one worthy of our worship, and all that we do grows out of that adoration and that love.

One of my fellow pastors, Adam Flynt, gave me a new set of commentaries. I'll quote them here because I can't say it any better. "Judas loved money more than Jesus, but money is not God. Money is not alive. Money cannot raise the dead. Money cannot love you back. Money is meant to represent value. It is currency. We gain money for what we provide or how we serve, and then we exchange the reward we gained by our ingenuity or effort for things we need or want. Money will not shepherd us. Money will not teach us truth. Money will not give itself in our place. Money is not at the right hand of God interceding for us. Money will not give us its righteousness so that we are justified before God. Mary understood this. Judas did not. Money is a means to an end. Jesus is an end in Himself."*

Jesus is the only end worthy of our worship. That's what's happening at the dinner table. So take a seat at the table. Join the conversation. Do you worship like Mary and Simon, or critique like Judas and Caiaphas?

If there are not times when this stirs up in you, you seriously need to check your heart. Have you ever been overwhelmed by the grace train of the gospel of Jesus Christ? When that happened, what was your response?

When the large crowd of Jews learned that Jesus was there, they

---

* James M. Hamilton Jr., "John 11:45–12:11," in *ESV Expository Commentary*, vol. 9, *John–Acts*, edited by Iain M. Duguid, James M. Hamilton Jr., and Jay Sklar (Wheaton, IL: Crossway, 2019), 202–206.

came not only on account of him, but also to see Lazarus. Bethany's a little town. Who doesn't wanna see a dead guy raised back to life? That's what they came to see. "So the chief priests made plans to put Lazarus to death as well, because on account of him many of the Jews were going away and believing in Jesus" (John 12:10–11).

We have an enemy and there are three things he wants to destroy. First, he wants to destroy the Word of God. Remember the first thing he says to Adam and Eve: *"Did God really say ... ?"* (Gen. 3:1). It's the same thing he does to Jesus in his temptation. He wants us to doubt the Word.

Second, he wants to destroy the work of God. Lazarus' resurrection is the handiwork of Jesus. So the enemy wants to take him out. If you have put your faith in Jesus, you are the handiwork of Jesus. This is why the enemy wants to take you out.

Last, the enemy wants to destroy the worship of God. Worship is warfare against the enemy, and he hates it and he hates you. And he wants to destroy these things. Worship is a gratitude party for who He is—the resurrection and life—and what He has done in our life and the lives of those around us. Word. Work. Worship. The enemy hates all three.

To end this chapter, I think we should do all three of the things that the three siblings at the table did. I think we should serve like Martha served. If the Lord stirs you up, you should do something about it. You should serve. Do whatever He tells you to do. Next, we should recline with Jesus at the table. There is something about changing the posture of your body to humble yourself before the Lord and say, "Here I am, Jesus. I just wanna be with you." And then, we should respond like Mary. Take what is most valuable to you and pour it out on His feet.

Serve. Abide. Worship. He wants all three.

Remember Jesus' conversation with the Samaritan woman at the well? She said, *"Hey, your people say you gotta worship on* this *mountain. And my people say it's* that *mountain. Where are we sup-posed to worship?"*

And Jesus says, *"God is looking for worshipers who will worship Him in spirit and truth"* (John 4:20, 24). There's not a style of wor-ship He's looking for, there's a heart of a worshiper that He wants. He wants your heart poured out on Him. If there's something in your life and it's just too valuable for you, then lay it at the feet of Jesus. Bring all your hopes and dreams and desires and all your sin and all your condemnation, and pour it out on his feet.

If you've never raised your hands before, I dare you. I dare you to set this book down right this second, raise your hands, and wor-ship. You may say, "Well, it makes me uncomfortable." Okay, cool. I hope you're uncomfortable, because the cross was uncomfort-able for Jesus. Jesus went through some serious discomfort to tear the curtain between the presence of God and the people of God so that we could do what the Word says and lift our hands in the sanctuary.

We used to sing this song a lot called, "How He Loves." And there's a line in it that got everybody all messed up. It says, "So heaven meets earth like a sloppy wet kiss." I run in the young, rest-less, and reformed camp. They're not that young anymore, but that's my crew. They're real proud of how theologically accurate they are, which, don't get me wrong, matters like crazy. But when I'd go to speak at all their conferences, the other pastors of churches that we partner with were asking, "Y'all sing 'sloppy wet kiss'?" And I'm like, "Oh yeah, we sing 'sloppy wet kiss.'" And they respond, "Oh, what would Spurgeon think?"

I don't care.

The only way I know how to explain it is this—husbands, mar-ried guys, why'd you marry your wife? Why? Did you just assess the situation and you were like, "Yeah, I should probably lock this down 'cause I won't be able to get this later. And since it's a covenant, she's stuck with me"? Was that it? Did you look at her and think, *She could carry on my gene pool just fine?*

Of course not. That never entered our minds. When I met Gretchen, I don't know how to explain it. I had dated other girls, but this was just different. At the heart level, she got me all stirred up. I'd look at her and I wasn't thinking about the economics of our union. Truth was, I couldn't afford to get married. I had one thought—*I wanna be with that woman for as many years as the Lord will give me.* That's it. Now twenty-two years into it, I love her more now than I did then.

Sometimes even now, I sit down with her on the couch and I just try to tell her how much I love her and I get all choked up and start crying and then my kids walk in and they say, "Dad, what is wrong with you?" And I'm like, "You shut your face. Moments like this are the reason you exist. Get outta here. All right."

When I married G, I wasn't simply checking something off the to-do list. I loved and do still love that girl. With all of me. And so I pour out my love. When Mary worships Jesus, there's nothing romantic there, but it's very passionate. She is modeling what our response should be for Him. The church is the bride of Christ; our groom gave His life for us, and He's coming back to take us home. So we should worship like that. When heaven meets earth, it's a sloppy wet kiss. Sometimes people change it to "unforeseen kiss." That sounds creepy. Heaven. Oh stop. What are you doing? I didn't ask for that. That's inappropriate. I like "heaven meets earth like a sloppy wet kiss." Set aside your baggage. God loves you. In the story of the prodigal, when the prodigal returned home, Scripture records "the father saw him and had compassion and ran and fell on his neck and kissed him." That's a bad translation because he didn't just kiss him once. A better translation reads, *He covered his face in kisses* (Luke 15:20). Think about it. The creator of the universe, God the Father, wants to cover your face in kisses. Would you let Him if He offered? Because He is.

Every one of us lives on a continuum between gratitude and entitlement. And one of the things that I do, as a discipline in my life, is write a gratitude list every year. One thing for every year of my life. Right now I'm forty-eight, so there are forty-eight items. And when I feel my heart leaning toward entitlement, I bust it out and read them again.

Things like: my salvation, my wife, my family, being American, being Southern, fall mornings in South Georgia woods, stuff like that. Some of them are things that other people would think are inappropriate, like bourbon or a good cigar. So, what's your list? What are you grateful for?

Now let me address the elephant in the room—some of you reading this are sitting there with chemo dripping in your arm. You're bald, just had a double mastectomy, and you think I'm telling you to just jump up and be all happy. No, I'm not. Please don't hear that. I have seen preachers like me say and do things like that and I cringe every time they do. That is not the heart of Jesus.

Having said that, I need to add a personal note. I'm writing this chapter in a cabin in South Georgia, where I'm currently on sabbatical. Two weeks before, Gretchen, me, and several of our best friends flew to Scotland on vacation. Trip of a lifetime. One of my friends traveling with us was my buddy, Brad Bowen. One of my best friends on the planet. I led him to the Lord, baptized him, been on several mission trips with him, hunted pretty much everywhere with him, and we've been attached at the hip for more than a decade. Brad owns the construction company that has built all the campuses for our church. Chances are good, if you've sat in one of our services, Brad built your seat. After we arrived in Scotland, we played golf at Saint Andrews. Stayed in an ancient castle. Hunted stag on beautiful mountains. Ate in crazy good restaurants. The whole thing was dreamy and idyllic. When I look back on it, sharing it with G and my best friends was something I'll never forget.

And I don't really know how to write this next part, but at fifty-six, Brad didn't make the return trip home. He died on the mountain. We left to go hunting one morning like we had dozens of times together before. And Brad never returned. I can't even believe I'm writing that. My best friend went home, just not with us. I am not writing what you're about to read because I think it sounds good, will sell books, or will get me invited to speak at conferences. I couldn't care less. I'm writing this chapter because I believe it with every fiber in my being. I'm writing it because it's true. Here's my bottom line, and I'm saying it in agreement with the writer of Hebrews: "Let us continually offer to God a sacrifice of praise—the fruit of lips that openly profess his name" (Heb. 13:15 NIV). When you are on the top of the mountain, you worship God. And when you find yourself in the valley of the shadow of death, you just have to worship your way through it.

I praise God that I knew Brad. That he's safe. That he is in heaven. But hear me when I say this: It hurts like hell. I choose that word on purpose. Because God's original intent was not that we would die. Death is collateral damage from sin. That is why it hurts like hell. I am crushed. It's been a week as I write this, and I can't even talk about it and keep it together. And as if I needed reminding, as I sat in the tree stand this morning, reflecting on this chapter, I watched the sun come up, and it was this orange-and-pink-and-purple sunrise, which looked eerily similar to the orange-and-pink-and-purple sunset on Wednesday, October 13, in Scotland. The day Brad died. I am in pain and yet my God reminded me that He is in control, that I can trust Him and that my friend Brad is with Him.

And even when it hurts like hell, my response is that He's a good, good Father and He calls me His son. Ultimately, here's the truth of where I find myself: Brad has been resurrected with Jesus—he knows Lazarus, Mary, Simon, Peter, the whole crew—while I might have to wait a few days to experience it. The writer of Hebrews says this: "Therefore let us be grateful for receiving a kingdom that cannot be shaken, and thus let us offer to God acceptable worship, with reverence and awe, for our God is a consuming fire" (Heb. 12:28–29). Big picture, I don't understand everything, and my current circumstances aren't what I'd wished for, but this I know—Jesus' kingdom cannot be shaken. And I will worship Him even when I don't understand.

I may have to wait forty years, but I'll get to see him again. So if you're in prison, if you're on the chemo drip, if your wife just left, if…name your pain, let me encourage you as a fellow brother in Christ whose heart is broken more than I can say, just praise Him. Praise Him like there's no tomorrow. Praise Him like He's the creator of the universe and the lover of our souls.

In this world we'll face all kinds of troubles. And yes, this is troubling, but my heart is not troubled 'cause I know the good news. Jesus has overcome this world.

About ten years ago, Brad and I were hunting and I asked him, "Bro, how is a good-looking, smart, successful dude like you single?" Brad was never married. He just looked at me and smiled. "Well, to be honest, it was a lot of fun until I met you."

God radically changed Brad's life, and I got to see it happen. I'm grateful I got to know him. If you are troubled, if you are in pain, it's okay. I'm reminded of Jesus' words to Peter: *"Do you want to go too?"* And Peter responded, *"Where would we go? You have the words of life and death"* (John 6:67–68).

I realize this chapter may seem out of place. Mary's worship of Jesus is not a miracle, while Simon's healing is, and yet I don't focus on Simon. Why include Mary in a book on miracles? Because when presented with the miracles of Jesus, people respond in several ways. Some doubt, some believe, some are critical, some are skeptical, and some just want to kill Jesus. I'm trying to point out that gratitude expressed in worship is the right response. Mary responded with extravagant gratitude and fragrant worship. Poured out on the feet of Jesus. Think about how that smell permeated every room.

When King David learned that his son with Bathsheba had died, he rose, bathed, walked into the temple—and worshiped. When Job learned his crops were destroyed, fortunes erased, and children all killed, he tore his clothes—and worshiped. When Paul and Silas were in jail, held in stocks, probably hanging upside down—they worshiped. Let me implore you, regardless of your circumstances, to pour it all out on the feet of Jesus.

Some of you need to break your jar of nard and write a big, fat check. Some of you need to get over yourself, sign up, and serve at your local church. And some of you need to lift your hands out of your pockets and shout at the top of your lungs. Why? Because He is worthy of our worship whether we see the miracle on this side of the grave or not. Because regardless of our circumstances, He is worthy of our worship. Because there is the possibility that the miracle we are praying and hoping for is just on the other side of that small step of obedience.

Pray with Me

Our good and gracious heavenly Father, may I never get over the gospel. God, I am like the woman with the alabaster jar. You found me. You saved me. You rescued me. When I think that on the cross You were willing to lay Your life down for someone like me, who did not deserve it, I am overwhelmed with gratitude. May we be willing to pour out our hearts and souls and emotions onto Your feet as a thank-you. God, I pray that You would break strongholds of fear and pride in our lives that have caused us in times of worship to be timid or reserved. God, would You wake up Your sleeping church that can so easily take for granted all that

You have done for us. God, I pray for the men and the women and the students who are currently walking through the valley of the shadow of death. Lord, I ask that You would make it known to them that they need to worship their way through these tough times. You are always worthy of our worship regardless of our circumstances and our corresponding feelings. God, would You please by the power of Your Holy Spirit give us the ability to lift our eyes above the temporary things of this world and fix our eyes on You. God, when it's not going our way, would You help us lift our eyes up over the horizon and fix our eyes on Jesus, the author and perfector of our faith. God, may we then respond with a life that brings You glory. May we be a people that cheerfully takes what is most valuable to us and lays it at Your feet as an act of worship. We pray this in Jesus' name. Amen.

CHAPTER 7

The Bleeding Woman—Do You Believe Jesus Is Who He Says He Is?

In the prologue I told you about my Mimi, her internal bleeding, how they life-flighted her to Charleston, and how I hit my knees and remembered that Jesus said, *Ask whatever you will in My name, and it will be given to you* (John 15:7). So I asked Him to heal my Mimi. I also told you how the ask-whatever-you-wish command doesn't mean cash, cars, and prizes. Jesus is not a vending machine. But it still means what it says.

And so I hit my knees and I begged God to save my Mimi. All I could think was that she was bleeding out in this helicopter. But when the helicopter landed in Charleston, the bleeding had stopped. For no apparent reason. It was just gone. So the next day, I drove down to Marion, South Carolina, opened the door, and there was Mimi just vacuuming. "Oh, hey, sugar. Come on in."

You ever been there? You ever been so desperate that either God shows up or you're toast? Desperate in the sense that you've tried everything, called every doctor, and spent every penny, and yet you can't fix your own problem?

In this chapter, we're going to meet a lady who's there. She's been bleeding nonstop for twelve years, spent every penny she has, and the doctors can't help her. We meet her broke and desperate,

176 • *Anything Is Possible*

standing in the middle of the street, eyeing Jesus. Mustering her last ounce of energy to get within arm's length. But in order for you to understand both the culture and the mindset of this woman who lived two thousand years ago, and why she's standing in the street, I have to back up another four hundred years. The thing is, this woman believed God's Word. So bear with me.

To start, let me ask you a hypothetical: What would be the last thing you would say to your kids if you weren't going to see them for a long time? Along with that, have you ever watched a movie that left you hanging and you thought to yourself, *There's got to be a sequel. It can't end that way?* Malachi, the last book in the Old Testament, is God's last word to His children before four hundred years of silence. It closes the Old Testament, but it does so with a promise of more to come. The promise of a sequel. Keep in mind that we're coming back to a desperate woman, one of my favorite people in all of Scripture, but before we do, go with me with to Malachi chapter 3. In verse 3:16, God says, "Then those who feared the LORD spoke with one another." Notice the "those who feared." Despite the faithlessness of most of His children over the ages, there's a remnant in Israel that still believes in God. Still trusts God. Still obeys the covenant. *Those who feared the Lord spoke with one another and the Lord paid attention and heard them.*

Don't read by that too fast. *God paid attention to them*, and He is paying attention to you. *He hears you.* Never confuse your perceived lack of cooperation on God's part for God's absence. Let me say that again: Never confuse your perceived lack of cooperation on God's part with indifference and an unwillingness to listen to you. God is not a clockmaker God who winds you up and then checks out while you wind down. Your enemy would like for you to think that's exactly what He is, but nothing could be further from the truth.

Malachi continues, "And a book of Remembrance was written before him of those who feared the LORD and esteemed his name."

In this Persian culture, they would make these big, fancy, almost bedazzled-looking books and they would write your name in it, and then they would write your actions or your deeds, then the results of those deeds and, finally, the promises and rewards you would acquire as a result of those deeds. I don't know if you realize this, but the Lord keeps a book on us too. It's called the Book of Life, and in it He writes our name, but there's a twist. He does not reward us according to our righteous deeds, because we don't have any. Scripture says there is none righteous, no, not one, and further, *our righteousness is like filthy rags* (Isa. 64:6). The phrase "filthy rags" means "used feminine products." That means, left to ourselves, the best we can offer God is used menstrual cloths. But God knows this about us so, out of His mercy, rather than record all our sins and failures, He records His Son's righteousness. This is what theologians called "imputed righteousness." It means for all of us who have surrendered to the Lordship of Jesus Christ, we get credit for all the good Jesus did. This is the inconceivability, the I-just-can't-believe-it-ness of the cross. God gives us what we don't deserve and withholds from us what we do, choosing instead to pour out that wrath on His Son. When I tell you that I just can't get over the cross, this is the part I can't get over.

Malachi 3:17: "They shall be mine, says the LORD of hosts, in the day when I make up my treasured possession." God is setting up a day on which He will gather unto Himself a people and they will be, to Him, a treasured possession. Have you ever thought that from God's perspective, you are His "treasured possession"? God, who needs nothing, who cannot be paid off, who cannot be bought, treasures you.

Listen, if eBay taught us anything, it taught us the true value of a thing. Right? For example, you've got a thing at your house and you think it's worth a lot and you put it on eBay. Hopes high. "I'm about to get two-hundy." Seven days later, you end up with $2. Guess what it was worth? Two dollars. You ever considered what God is willing to pay to purchase you? First Corinthians 6:19–20 says it this way: "You are not your own, for you were bought with a price." So how much does God treasure you? What price does He put on your head? Again, walk with me back to the cross. Now look up. That's His Son hanging there, and the answer is that much. God paid for you with the blood of His very own Son, so you're not a nobody, not a nothing, not insignificant. You are God's treasured possession. The joy set before Him. He says, "They shall be mine... in the day when I make up my treasured possession." And then here's a little foreshadowing of how that happens through the gospel: "And I will spare them as a man spares his son who serves him" (Mal. 3:17). The crazy thing is that God spares us, who didn't serve Him, and crucifies His own Son, who did. Then He gives us credit for His Son's service and calls us His treasured possession. This is the love of God poured out on us.

Paul will say it this way in Romans 8:31–32: "What then shall we say to these things? If God is for us, who can be against us? He who did not spare his own Son but gave him up for us all, how will he not also with him graciously give us all things?"

Back to Malachi 3. God is going to claim unto Himself a people who will be His treasured possessions. And then in verse 18, He goes on to say, "Then once more you shall see the distinction between the righteous and the wicked, between one who serves God and one who does not serve him." This is the way the Old Testament ends. Which, by the way, is also the way the teaching ministry of Jesus ends.

We talked about this in the previous chapter, but let me rehash. In Matthew 24, the disciples asked Jesus what the end of the world is going to be like, and He tells three stories back-to-back-to-back. In Matthew 25, the last story is called the Parable of the Sheep and the Goats. In it, Jesus says, "*When I return, I will be like a shepherd that separates the sheep from the goats. And the sheep He'll put on His right and He'll say,* "Well done, good and faithful servant. For I was naked and you gave me clothes, I was thirsty and you gave me something to drink. I was hungry and you fed me." The people standing around Jesus are confused. They scratch their heads and say, *"We didn't see you like that."* To which Jesus responds, *"Whatever you did to the least of these brothers of Mine, you have done unto Me. Enter into the joy of My Father because you knew Me and I knew you"* (vv. 31–40). In other words, entrance into the Father's kingdom is not granted because you did those things out of some duty but because you knew Him. Period. Those things, that service, bubbled up out of love. Not obligation. That's why they're in. To the goats on His left, He said, *"Depart from me. When I was thirsty and hungry, and in jail, you didn't do anything for Me."* The goats are astounded. *"What? We never saw you that way."* To which Jesus responds, *"It's not that you didn't do those things, but the reason you did none of those things is because you did not know Me"* (vv. 41–45).

In the parable, Jesus is telling you and me that there will be a separation and a day of judgment. And when that day comes I want me and my family, and you, to be sheep. Not goats. We get more info in Malachi 4:1. "For behold"—that means pay attention—"the day is coming, burning like an oven, when all the arrogant and all evildoers will be stubble. The day that is coming shall set them ablaze, says the LORD of hosts, so that it will leave them neither root nor branch."

In 2022, some 2,400 years after Malachi prophesied this word, we don't take this very seriously. And I know fire and brimstone is not a very popular topic, but it's also not very popular to be a Jesus follower. So let me just lay it here before you, not because I'm mad at you, not because I'm trying to judge you, but because I love you. A day of judgment is coming when we will stand before the judge and He says that everyone who is arrogant will burn like in an oven.

So let me just ask you: Are you arrogant?

If you say, "Yes, I'm arrogant," then you're in good company. Me too. You've realized you've got a problem and need help, knowing you can't fix you. If you recoil at the suggestion and say, "Well, I'm not arrogant..." I hate to break it to you, but that in and of itself is an incredibly arrogant thing to say. And what's worse, not only are you arrogant, but you're lying about your arrogance by denying it. This is called sin against an almighty, everlasting judge, which requires an eternal and everlasting payment.

I know this hurts some of your feelings, but if you were in a car accident and your car was on fire and you were being burned alive, and I dragged you from the inferno, would you mind if you got scratched on broken glass? Of course not. Despite a culture that says we're all going to heaven, we're not. Some people, some of your friends, are going to hell. That separation will come on a day of judgment. What pains me is that some of you—that's right, someone right now reading these pages—are in danger of hell because you haven't surrendered to the Lordship of Jesus. Let me pause and tell you bluntly: If you are reading this or listening to it, then God is calling you. It's time to realize you're in a burning car and reach out for His hand. He wants to pull you from the blaze.

Jonathan Edwards, a dead Puritan preacher, said, "The bow of God's wrath is bent and the arrow made ready on the string, and justice bends the arrow at your heart and strings the bow. And it is nothing but the mere pleasure of God, and that of an angry God, without any promise or obligation at all, that keeps the arrow one moment from being made drunk with your blood. What are we that we should think to stand before him at whose rebuke the Earth trembles and before whom the rocks are thrown down. There is nothing that keeps wicked men at any moment out of Hell, but the mere pleasure of God. We are but sinners in the hands of an angry God."

I grew up with what some might call a rather eclectic musical taste. Anybody who survived the eighties is in the same boat. That said, some of those lyrics have stuck with me and they're still true today—albeit slightly different. One such truth about me, "I like big butts and I cannot lie." But I'm talking about the *but*s in the Bible. My favorite is "But God." My next favorite is in this next verse: "But for you who fear my name, the sun of righteousness shall rise with healing in its wings." Bookmark this. We're coming back to that verse because it matters. A lot. But let's keep going. "You shall go out leaping like calves from the stall" (Mal. 4:2).

I don't know if you've been around cattle much, but if you tie up a little calf for any period of time and then untie it, they prance and dance and jump all around you. On the day of judgment you want to be in the prancing crew because you fear the name of the Lord.

Malachi continues, "And you shall tread down the wicked, for they will be ashes under the soles of your feet, on the day when I act, says the LORD of hosts" (Mal. 4:3). God is going to do a thing through you, even after He saves you, to enact and bring about His kingdom in this world. This is why Jesus teaches us to pray, "Your kingdom come, your will be done, on earth as it is in heaven" (Matt. 6:10).

The way Paul says this in Romans 16:20 is this: "The God of peace will soon crush Satan under your feet. The grace of our Lord Jesus Christ be with you." In other words, once you know the fear of the Lord, the salvation of the Lord, then you walk in this gospel power.

Malachi 4:4 is a beautiful text on progressive sanctification. Theologians use this term to describe what happens to us when we surrender to the Lordship of Jesus Christ. That through the power of the Holy Spirit, we become more like Him. "Remember the law of my servant Moses, the statutes and rules that I commanded him at Horeb for all Israel." This is a biggie, and people get hung up on this, but He's answering the question of how a New Testament believer should relate to Old Testament law. We are *saved by grace, through faith.* That said, Jesus also said, *If you love Me, obey My commands*, and He said that before any of the New Testament had been written. So, how does that freedom work itself out in our lives? Let me offer you a way to answer the question for yourself. Jesus, in the new covenant, has set us free to obey Him. And His Word. He did not set us free from obedience. The way we live matters. Now, I'm not trying to put you under a law, what the disciples called a yoke, that not even our forefathers could carry. I'm trying to change how you view it. If you love someone with your whole heart, is there anything you won't do for them?

When He says, *Remember the law of the Lord*, he's talking about the Ten Commandments. Now, I don't know about you, but it's not the remembering part that I have a problem with, it's the actual obeying part. Nobody has trouble remembering the law of God. Not a single person has ever said, "What did he say about murder again? I can't remember." The apostle Paul in Romans 7 says, *I see this law at work in me. I want to do good and I can't pull it off. And I see this law at work, the bad things I don't want to do, super good at doing those. What a wretched man am I. Who would save a wretch like me?* Having admitted his own failure, look at what he says next—and it's the answer to the problem that is us. Romans 8:1: "There is therefore now no condemnation for those who are in Christ Jesus."

Malachi is basically a precursor to Romans 7. *I'm going to send you someone to do for you what you cannot do for yourself, which is to live out the law perfectly on your behalf.* Which is exactly what Malachi 4 says. These are the last words of the Old Testament: "Behold"—and when the Bible says *behold* that means look up, pay attention, get off your phone—"Behold, I will send you Elijah the prophet before the great and awesome day of the LORD comes" (v. 5). So first, Elijah is coming. Then the Lord. Which means, when you see Elijah, watch out.

"And he will turn the hearts of fathers to their children and the hearts of children to their fathers, lest I come and strike the land with a decree of utter destruction" (v. 6). Mic drop! Boom! It's over. If you've got like a real paper Bible, like King James used to carry in his pocket, when you turn from Malachi 4, there's a blank page. Or it might say "New Testament" on it. That page in your Bible represents four hundred years of waiting. When you turn that page, you're turning through four hundred years of silence from God. Of waiting for this one who is going to come in the spirit and the power of Elijah. Of waiting for the one who is going to prepare the way of the Lord.

So for four hundred years, the people of God wait.

*   *   *

Let me ask you—do you ever start praying for something on a Sunday, and by Tuesday you're thinking, *Where are you, God?* Remember, God's not on your timetable and sometimes it takes a minute. Can I get a witness? Sometimes His time is not our time. The remnant in Israel prayed and waited and anticipated for four hundred years. Four hundred years. And then you get to the gospels. Luke 1:5–17 says, "In the days of Herod, king of Judea, there was a priest named Zechariah, of the division of Abijah. And he had a wife from the daughters of Aaron, and her name was Elizabeth. And they were both righteous before God, walking blamelessly in all the commandments and statutes of the Lord. But they had no child, because Elizabeth was barren, and both were advanced in years.

"Now while he"—that's Zechariah—"was serving as priest before God when his division was on duty, according to the custom of the priesthood, he was chosen by lot to enter the temple of the Lord and burn incense. And the whole multitude of the people were praying outside at the hour of incense. And there appeared to him an angel of the Lord standing on the right side of the altar of incense. And

Zechariah was troubled when he saw him, and fear fell upon him. But the angel said to him, 'Do not be afraid, Zechariah, for your prayer has been heard, and your wife Elizabeth will bear you a son, and you shall call his name John. And you will have joy and gladness, and many will rejoice at his birth, for he will be great before the Lord. And he must not drink wine or strong drink, and he will be filled with the Holy Spirit, even from his mother's womb.' " And here it comes: "And he will turn many of the children of Israel to the Lord their God, and he will go before him in the spirit and the power of Elijah, to turn the hearts of the fathers to their children, and the disobedient to the wisdom of the just, to make ready for the Lord a people prepared."

For four hundred years they've been waiting and waiting, and then all of a sudden the angel Gabriel appears, and he's talking to a religious person. Zechariah. A person who works in the temple. Somebody who knows Scripture. Who should be the most ready for the coming Messiah, a person who has been going through all of the Levitical rituals every day of his life to get ready for the coming Messiah. But because it does not fit in his religious box, he misses the whole thing. The angel shows up and says, "*This thing that Malachi has been talking about, that you've been waiting on, it's about to happen, and your son, you're going to name him John, and he is going to play a pivotal role in this coming Messiah.*"

And then Zechariah argues with Gabriel: "*How's that going to happen?*" But Gabriel, who stands in the presence of God, basically puts Zechariah in time-out. He says, "*Look here, you're not gonna be able to talk until she gives birth. Shhh.*" And just like that, he's mute. You ever met a preacher who can't talk? Worthless. Zechariah comes out of the temple, and everyone asks him, "*What happened?*" But all he can do is "*Mmm*" (vv. 18–22). Can't even talk.

And then finally, on the day that his kid is born, tradition would say that you would name him after yourself. Zechariah Jr. But that's not what he does. He names the boy John. And because he still can't talk, he writes it on paper, *"Name him John."* And they say, *"Why would you name him John?"* (vv. 59–63). What they don't understand is that this is bigger than just his name. God is about to do a new thing. He's about to establish a new covenant. And this covenant is not just for people with Jewish last names. God is going outside the family. He's going to start saving Jew *and* Gentile.

And so the kid grows up and he wears weird clothes and he's got weird hair, and he yells at people all the time, and he eats weird food. The Bible calls them locusts, but everybody knows they're roaches. So, he's out there eating roaches—or maybe what we call a grasshopper—and screaming at people, *"Repent and be baptized. Prepare ye the way of the Lord"* (Luke 3:3–4).

Surprisingly, people start showing up to see this thing that's happening and when they hear him, they start getting dunked. That's why his name is John the Baptist. When I grew up, this confused me. I thought it was like Mark the Methodist and Pete the Presbyterian and John the Baptist. Truth was, *Baptist* is a transliteration of the Greek word *baptizo.* And it means "to dip or dunk or wash." And by doing this, he was preparing the way of the Lord. Then one day at the Jordan, his cousin named Jesus, or more technically, "Yeshua," who was a nobody with nobody parents from nowhere according to everybody there, walks up on the scene. When John sees him, he says, "Behold," which again means, hey, everybody, get off your phones. Pay attention. What I'm about to say is important. "Behold, the Lamb of God, who takes away the sin of the world!" (John 1:29). He goes on to say, *"Look, this is not about me. My job was to prepare the way, and now the Messiah is here. The serpent crusher that we have been waiting on since Genesis 3. I'm not even worthy to tie his shoes"* (John 1:30–34).

This mattered to that Jewish audience. What he did not say is, "Behold, another lamb of God that's here to cover the sin of the

Jewish people for another year." That was what they had been doing since Moses rolled out the law a couple thousand years before that. But the Lamb of God has come to take away the sin, not just of those people, but of anybody who would believe. Once and for all. Forever. This blows their minds.

So Jesus walks down into the water, and John the Baptist and Jesus have this conversation about who is supposed to baptize who. Jesus wins, so John baptizes Jesus, and in that moment the heavens open up and God the Father says, "*Behold my Son, in whom I am well pleased*" (Matt. 3:17). Which, by the way, is a beautiful picture of the gospel of Jesus Christ. At this point, Jesus has done no earthly ministry, and what God is telling him is the verdict comes before the performance: "*Before you ever do anything to earn anything, I am your Father, and I am well pleased in you.*" The Father does the same with us. He loves us because He loves us. We can't do anything to earn it, so we can't do anything to lose it. Remember that. And then the Spirit of God descends on Jesus like a dove and Jesus begins His earthly ministry, which lasts about three and a half years. Primarily, Jesus does three things, and the third one is most important.

First of all, He is a preacher and a teacher. Everywhere He goes, He tells stories and He teaches, but He doesn't teach like many preachers today, "Hey, here's four ways to get along with people better." He primarily teaches about who God the Father is, His kingdom, and how we are to relate to Him. One hundred eighty-nine times He calls God, the cosmic judge, "Father." And He invites us to do the same, which is mind-blowing to these people.

Second, He performs signs and wonders. But not just because He has the power to do miracles, but because they point to something else. Every single time Jesus performed an earthly miracle, He pointed to an eternal reality. When He restored the sight of the blind, when He brought the dead to life, when He walked on water, He was pointing to something greater. Like the Jacksonville city limit sign I wrote about in the prologue. It just points to something greater. Much greater.

When He performed signs and wonders, He was then and is now pointing to the Father heart of God. This is not to suggest He didn't care about those He healed or raised from the dead. Nothing could be further from the truth. But in every miracle, He always had something bigger in mind. And that something bigger was pointing to the glory of your and my Father.

And then the most important thing: *"I have come to live a perfect life, to die a sinner's death, and on the third day, I will be resurrected for the forgiveness of your sin"* (Matt. 16:21, 20:19; Luke 9:2, 18:33, 24:46; 1 Cor. 15:4).

This is why He came.

When people encountered Jesus, they had different reactions. Some people scoffed. Some were offended. Some didn't like Him. Most often this reaction came from religious people like the Pharisees and the Sadducees. People who had studied the Bible and believed they were most prepared to meet the Messiah when He showed up. But, when Jesus didn't fit in their religious box, they thought, *This can't be God*, and they rejected Him. Can you imagine walking down Main Street, bumping into Jesus, the Savior of the World, and being so focused on your right-now that you miss eternity? That's exactly what happened to many of the religious elite.

Some people encountered Jesus and they were just entertained. I mean, who doesn't love to see a good exorcism every once in a while? Or a nice healing? Or they were in the crowd when Jesus fed five thousand with a kid's Lunchable and they ate all they could eat, with twelve basketfuls left over. Some believed. Some didn't.

This propensity to look at Jesus and say, "What can you do for me now?" was not just true in the first century. This is true today when people encounter Jesus. Some people scoff. Some people get mad because "You don't fit into the way I thought you would do this, and so I'm gonna do this on my own." Some people are so busy with the right-now that they miss out on eternity. Some people show up to church because they want to be entertained. They're just thinking, *What can I get out of this? I need a date. Maybe I'll try a church girl. It worked in* Coming to America, *maybe it'll work for me.*

And some people believed.

So, we've come full circle. Back to the woman standing in the street eyeing Jesus. I want to spend the rest of this chapter talking about this one woman's belief. Go to Luke 8. Everything I've written until now was just a setup for what's next but it's vitally important because it explains *why* this bleeding woman was standing in the street. It also shows that she doesn't merely have faith in faith, but her trust is in the Word of God. Luke 8, beginning at verse 40: "Now when Jesus returned"—from calming a storm and casting out demons—"the crowd welcomed him, for they were all waiting for him. And there came a man named Jairus, who was a ruler of the synagogue." This guy is a really big deal. "And falling at Jesus' feet, he implored him to come to his house, for he had an only daughter, about twelve years of age, and she was dying" (vv. 40–42).

Now I want to stop before I go on, because some of you are so familiar with these Bible stories that you think of them as Bible stories. This is not a story. And if you grew up in Sunday school, you already know how this ends, and so you miss the desperation in the voice of this dad. This dad is going to lay himself out in front of Jesus and implore Him, beg Him, cry, and say, *"Jesus, I need your help."*

Can I remind you? I know I say this all the time, but there is no pain like kid pain. And if you're a kid, you have no idea how much your mom and dad love you. I know you're like sixteen or seventeen or however old you are, and you're brilliant and you know everything, but when you get to be about twentysomething and life gets a little tougher, you're going to have an awakening and realize how much your mama and daddy love you. I remember when I held JP, I did not know I could love something like this. And then I remember when I held Reagan Capri, and I thought, *I would die for you, or, if they treat you poorly, maybe make somebody die for you. We already have a prison ministry. I can run this thing from there. No problem.* If you have kids, I don't need to convince you. No pain like kid pain.

A couple years ago, I'd just boarded a plane in Atlanta and sat down in my seat, when I got a call from my friend, Hunter Brant. Since we were about to take off, I texted him back, "Hey, I just boarded a plane. I'll call ya in an hour."

A second later, he texted me back. "I need your prayers. We're driving to Wolfson's Children's Hospital right now. We think Christian"—this was his brand-new baby boy—"might have leukemia." And so taking off or not taking off, I called him immediately. "Hey, man, I don't know how long I have, what's going on?"

He tells me. And so I say, "Can I pray for you? I'm just gonna pray for you." So he's driving in the car. Christian's in the back, Mama's in the passenger seat, and I'm on a plane on the tarmac. And as I'm praying I just sort of forgot where I was. I forget I am in public, and I start praying and praying, 'cause ain't no pain like kid pain. This isn't even my kid, but my heart just begins to hurt for him and his mama and daddy. And I'm calling heaven down and praying for miracles. And then I feel something on my shoulder, and I look over, and my seatmate has put his hand on my shoulder, and he's got one hand in the air, and he's praying.

And he's going for it. And then the Delta attendant comes over to tell me to put my phone up, and she realizes what I was doing, and so she's praying. And when I finally get done, and I look up, man, I'm crying my face off. And I don't mean a little bit. It's ugly. And I'm not a good crier. I'm not. Some of you are good criers. Especially you older fellas, when you cry, I mean, you put that jaw out there, you're kind of like the Terminator. One tear. Bing. You look like Clint Eastwood. Not me, nope. I look like I'm trying to eat my bottom lip off. I got the whole head bob, chin wobble. I can't breathe. I start having those convulsions. It's not okay. I look like an eighth-grade girl who just watched *The Notebook*. I try to look at the guy next to me who prayed with me to say thanks, but every time I look at him, we both well up. We never talk. I never said a word to him the whole time. I tried to look at him, but "Nope, ain't talking to you." I'll meet him in heaven.

I don't know for sure, but I tend to think this is the desperation that drove both Jairus and the woman to Jesus. Jairus has got an only daughter. She's twelve years old. And he's thinking, *Maybe Jesus can do something about it*. He is in utter desperation. Jesus is making His way to minister to this girl. "As Jesus went"—He's going to Jairus' house—"the people pressed around Him" (v. 42). They're not into social distancing back then. They're touching, bumping into Him. Think mosh pit at a rock concert.

"And there was a woman who had had a discharge of blood for twelve years" (v. 43). In the midst of this, there is a miraculous interruption. Jesus is on his way to the home of someone who is very important, and yet He's interrupted by somebody that society would not consider important. In fact, she's an outcast. It's no accident that these two events are sandwiched together. 'Cause this woman has had an issue of blood for twelve years, and Jairus' daughter is twelve years old. Jairus is very esteemed, and he is surrounded by community in the synagogue, and this woman, based on Levitical law, would have been outcast from the synagogue. And while we know Jairus' name, the Bible does not give us her name. Which leads me to understand this.

There are no nobodies in the kingdom of God.

Jesus, the Son of God, died on the cross not just to save the somebodies, but to save everybody. That means you—yes, you—matter to Him. He is not too busy for you. And you are not a burden to Him. Something struck me this week as I'm studying this, and I'm gonna need a little bit of help from you. Throughout history, this woman has become known by a certain title in Bible study circles. We refer to her a certain way. Got any idea what it is we call her? "The woman with the issue of blood." Every commentary I looked up, every source I read, called her "the woman with the issue of blood." Can I just ask you . . . why do we constantly refer to people by their issues instead of by their miracles? I don't know if you notice, but we all got a few issues. Aren't you glad God didn't refer to you by your issue? "Hey, there's the guy with the issue of anger." "Oh, and his wife, the one with the issue of complaining. Ol' Mrs. Drip, drip, drip." We live in a world that wants to label us because then it can deal with the label, and it doesn't have to deal with us.

But not God. He's not God-somewhere-out-there. He's God the Father, your Father, and He's intimately concerned with every detail of your life. Between the pandemic, the political situation, and the racial tension, we live in a world that says, "This is your label, and we want to tear you apart." But here's the truth—this world doesn't get to tell you who you are. Only Jesus gets to tell you who you are. You are not your divorce. You are not your affair. You're not your orientation. You're not your political affiliation. You're not your bankruptcy. You're not your addiction. You're not your marital status. You're not your sickness. You are not your career. You are not what this world or the ruler of this world tells you you are. You are not your issue. You are who Jesus tells you you are.

Now look at how He deals with this bleeding woman. *This woman, who had a discharge of blood for twelve years.* Think about it. She's not supposed to be there. "And though she had spent all her living on physicians, she could not be healed by anyone." So not only is she an outcast, but she's broke, and she's desperate. For twelve years, she's tried everything this world has to offer, and now, somehow, she sees Jesus through the crowd. And she thinks, *Maybe, maybe, maybe Jesus can do something about this.* And the Bible says, "She came up behind him and touched the fringe of his garment." Pay attention to that. Underline that. I'm going to come back to it. "[She] touched the fringe of his garment, and immediately her discharge of blood ceased" (v. 44).

Now, let me share this with you. It isn't that deep, but you got to pay attention to it. Typically, when something that's dirty touches something clean, then the clean gets dirty, right? This is why you make the kids take the shoes off when they come in the house. 'Cause it's not like the clean house cleans their shoes. But the dirty shoes dirty up the whole house. So typically when dirty touches clean, the clean gets dirty. But with Jesus, when dirty touches clean, the clean makes the dirty clean.

And that's not just true with an issue of bleeding two thousand years ago. That's also true with our issue of sin. Second Corinthians 5:21 says, *That on the cross, God made Him who was without sin to be sin for us, that we would be made the righteousness of God.* God takes our dirt, takes our sin, crucifies it to the cross, and gives us, or imputes to us, His righteousness and makes us clean.

Now watch what happens. Even though her bleeding has stopped, He's not finished with her. Luke 8:45: "And Jesus said, 'Who was it that touched me?'" Now, I wish I had time to get all into this. But let me just tell you: Jesus is jacking with everybody right here. You think the almighty King of the universe doesn't know who touched Him? He knows. The Bible says, "He knows everything" (1 John 3:20). The Bible says, *He knows the words you're going speak before you know them* (Ps. 139:4). The Bible says that God numbers the very hairs on our head. And if you've seen my picture, you know that for some, that's an easier count than others.

Some people's hair turns gray, some people's turns loose. He even knows which hairs are yours and which one's you're renting. That's what He knows. So Jesus says, "*Who touched me?*" And when all denied it, Peter said, "*Master, everybody's touching you.*" "But Jesus said, 'Someone touched me.' " That word there is, like, to grab on to. To grasp. "Someone touched me, for I perceive that power has gone out from me" (vv. 45–46).

Jesus is saying, "*No, this one was different. Someone touched Me with intention. There was a transfer of power from Me to them.*" If I can implore you, please don't be the kind of person who cracks open this book and stands in the vicinity of Jesus, maybe even bumps into Him, but isn't touched by Him. Please don't miss Him.

"And when the woman saw that she was not hidden, she came trembling, and falling down before him and declared in the presence of all the people why she had touched him, and how she had been immediately healed" (v. 47). You know why she's afraid? Because she has an issue of blood, and in the book of Leviticus, the law says that not only is she unclean, but anybody she touches is also unclean. So, rightly so, she's afraid that if she tells everybody what her issue is, they're going do some contact tracing, and then start declaring the people around her unclean. And everyone around her, they're all unclean. And everybody she bumped into to get to Jesus is going to be unclean. Given my experience as a pastor and having counseled people, I can guarantee you that at some point in her life, she had religious leaders look down their noses at her and say, "What are you doing here?"

Now let me just say something on behalf of both pastors and the church. If any of you reading this have had somebody in my position, a pastor, look at you and say, "What are you doing here?" that brother is not playing for Team Jesus. He does not understand the ministry of Jesus. The church is a movement for all people to discover and deepen our relationship with Jesus Christ. If you ever come to our church, you'll see for yourself that we've all been banged up a little by some other churches. When I hear stories, my heart hurts. Folks have told me, "I used to go to so-and-so church but they told me I wasn't welcome." As I said, our church is like the island of misfit toys.

I need you to understand there is a reason you are reading these pages and I believe the reason that you are is because you believe with a touch from Jesus, you too can be healed. And who you are, or what you've done, or who you did it with, or what you're gonna do, or what your background is—it doesn't matter. Jesus will let you grab ahold of Him no matter what condition you find yourself in.

Some of you have been running from God because you've got issues, and you know what He would say if you would just kneel before Him and reach out and touch Him. You think He would say, "How dare you?" But that's not what He says. Jesus says to this lady, "Daughter, your faith has made you well; go in peace" (v. 48).

Daughter.

Hear that? Mic drop. He called her "Daughter."

"Daughter, your faith has made you well; go in peace." When do you think was the last time she was called "Daughter"? He does not define her by what's going on in her life. He defines her by who she is because of what He's gonna do with the cross. Basically what He's saying is this: "I'm not calling you the woman with the issue of blood. Because actually, I have an issue with blood too. And I'm gonna pour mine out, and it's gonna change you forever." And this is true for any one of us. For anyone who would believe that when Christ died on the cross, that counted for you. If you would believe, then we are given the right to be called children, sons, and daughters of God.

So, He calls her "Daughter."

And then He says, "Your faith has made you well." Faith in what?

I own a prayer shawl that somebody brought me from Israel. I like to put it on 'cause it makes me feel holy and spiritual. Orthodox

Jewish folks still wear them today. Then and now, it was a reminder to pray. It was a part of what Jesus would have had on in the first century. When the Bible says, *She touched the fringe of the garment*, or the edge of the garment, she had touched the little tassel thing on the corner. These tassels are called tzitzit and the Hebrew word is *knopf.* It can be translated as "edge of the garment," but it can also be translated as "extremity, or wing."

Remember Malachi? Malachi tells us in chapter 4, "For behold, the day is coming, burning like an oven, when all the arrogant and all evildoers will be stubble. The day that is coming shall set them ablaze, says the LORD of hosts, so that it will leave them neither root nor branch. But for you who fear my name, the sun of righteousness shall rise with healing in its wings. You shall go out leaping like calves from the stall" (vv. 1–2). Everyone in Israel knew "healing in its wings" was speaking of the coming Messiah.

I could go on and on and on about all of the meanings of the strings and the knots, but each was to remind the wearer of the law of God. There are five knots that represent the Torah, the first five books of the Bible. There are four wrappings. There are eight cords. One of them's a different cord to point to the Messiah. It represents the numbers of laws that come from God, the numbers of dos, the numbers of don'ts. God is both practical and tactile. So He gives us things to do that help us remember. In the first century, everybody did not have a downloaded copy of the Scriptures in their pockets. They had to remember it. Memorize it. And so as you were walking along the city and you would touch these knots, you would be reminded of the law of God.

Over twelve years, this woman has spent all her money. She's seen all the physicians. She did everything that this world expected of her, and the problem's not going away. Not gotten any better. In fact, it's worse. Let's be honest, she probably smells. And she has had zero contact with other people because, by law, if she does, they're unclean. She can't go to temple worship, or see the priest, so she also has zero contact with God. She's isolated and alone.

She's desperate.

But she's heard these rumors. About this man named Jesus. He walked on water. Cast demons out of people. The blind see. The lame walk. And dead people are brought back to life. Maybe He is the one the prophets spoke of. And then this same Jesus shows up in Capernaum—her very own town, and even though she's not supposed to go out in the crowd because she'll contaminate everybody else, she doesn't care. She believes. And He is her last hope.

I want you to watch this woman as she elbows her way through the crowd wondering, *What if He is who He says He is? What if the rumors are true? What if He can? What if He is the Son of righteousness with healing in His wings? What if I am found out?*

And yet she presses her way to Jesus.

But not only is she bleeding, she has to contend with the crowd. People have thronged to Jesus. Those big, strong fishermen who walk everywhere with Him. She has to fight. Elbow her way through. Does she let the fear lie to her? Does she let it paralyze her faith? No. One step at a time. Maybe she pulls a hood up over her face so she's not recognized. "Excuse me. Excuse me. Pardon me. Can I get through?" The crowd presses, she fights through, but twelve years of anemic blood loss have made her weak. She's losing sight of him. But then he slows slightly. Just enough. It's now or never. She lunges. Reaches out. Grabs the *knopf.* She feels the power enter. He feels it leave.

And in that second she knows that the Son of righteousness has come with healing in His wings.

Bam!

I don't know how much faith you have, but I've got great news for you. It's not the amount of your faith that changes things. It is the object of your faith that changes things. Jesus says, *Even the tiniest little itsy-bitsy mustard seed–sized faith in the almighty everlasting God can move mountains in your life* (Matt. 17:20). In the entirety of Scripture, Jesus never bumped into anyone, measured their faith with His spidey sense, and said, "You know, you're only at 37 percent. Go back until you break the halfway mark." He didn't do that then. He doesn't do that now. And He doesn't do that with this precious woman. In fact, He chose this town. This day. This road. Because He knew she'd be here. He's been waiting for this day, and while Jairus' daughter for sure matters, He slowed down for this bleeding woman.

Notice what happens. She's healed. Scripture says the source of her infirmity was dried up in that moment. In her mind, she probably wants to disappear in the crowd. Not make a fuss. But Jesus isn't finished with her. Not by a long shot. Because while her body needed healing, it's her heart that's broken. Look at what Jesus says: *"Daughter, go in peace."* Did you hear that? One singular word. Listen to it again. Hear it through her ears. He called her "Daughter." That means she's welcomed back in. She is that thing she's always wanted to be. She is and forever will be a child of God.

When we bring our mustard seed–sized faith, press through the crowd, lunge, and reach out, the world does not get to tell us who we are anymore. We are no longer going to be defined by our issue. Only Jesus gets to tell us who we are, and to the only begotten Son of God, the Son of righteousness who has come with healing in His wings, we are His children. Sons and daughters of the King. For all of us who come to Him, Jesus responds, "You are My daughter, My son, and I have a purpose for you. A plan for you. And that plan is not to live as an outcast for the rest of your life. Now, you are the sons and daughters of the most high King, and I want you to walk in that kind of peace, shalom, and wholeness that God has for you."

Here's the point. Malachi was telling the truth. The Son of

righteousness has risen with healing in His wings. His name is Jesus. And so I just have to ask you: Do you need healing? Do you have the kind of faith that this woman had? I mean, think about it. Jesus could have leaned down to her and said, "Listen, I know that everybody else has treated you like an outcast, but do you realize two thousand years from now, people are gonna be sharing your testimony, and your step of courage is going to embolden people to receive the kind of healing that you have received?" So let me ask you again: Do you need to be healed? If so, is your healing waiting on the other side of a small step of faith? Do you need to elbow your way to Jesus?

Some of you need to be spiritually healed. Some of you are spiritually dead, and you need a resurrection. Some of you for the very first time need to reach out to Christ as your Lord and your Savior.

I'm gonna do something very different here. If I was preaching, I would ask everybody to bow your heads and close your eyes and have this just be something between each of you and Jesus. But as I was studying this, I could not get over the fact that she fought through the crowd and did this in public. And so, if you're reading this and for the very first time you want to surrender your life to the Lordship of Jesus Christ, stand up. Make it known right now. Call someone. Tell someone. Email someone. Email me!

If you are that one, I don't know your story, but the Lord does, and you'll no longer be defined by your issues. God almighty says to you, "Son, your faith has healed you" or "Daughter, your faith has healed you." And he has a purpose and a plan and a peace for you.

Maybe you've known Christ for a while, but you're in a place of utter desperation too, and you need to be healed. Remember, this woman had the boldness to not go to a small group and state an "unspoken" prayer request; she fought through the crowd with everybody watching. If you need the healing that's found through

Jesus, I'm going to ask you to stand up also. I know it's weird. You're reading a book. But I'm encouraging you to make it known. Tell someone. Call someone. Text someone. Email someone. Email me!

Maybe for some of you, it's relational. You need relational healing. You see, this lady was an outcast, but she found peace in Jesus. Maybe some of you have broken relationships. Jesus can mend a broken relationship. And maybe for some of you, it's financial. This woman had spent all the money that she made, and she was broke, and you're in a financial pinch. Maybe for some of you, it's physical. You need physical healing. Listen, I've read the whole Bible multiple times. I have not found a term limit on physical healing in the Scriptures. The power of the Holy Spirit has no expiration date. Jesus says He doesn't change, and He healed people, and I believe He could physically heal you. Or maybe for some, it's your marriage. And you might think, *Pastor, my marriage is dead.* Well, I've got good news. If God can resurrect His dead Son, then He can resurrect a dead marriage. He can breathe the *ruach* of life into that marriage, and He can heal that marriage. And for some of you, it's spiritual. You feel like the nation of Israel. You've been crying out to God and you're in a time of silence. He won't talk back to you. I dare you to stand up, reach out, make it known, and touch Him.

For some of you, it's mental. You are beginning to believe the labels that this world has placed on you, and it's beating you down. For some of you, you need emotional healing, because the circumstances of your life are getting bigger and bigger and bigger, and oftentimes this is one of the hardest things for Christians to deal with. On the surface, your circumstances seem fine. Why would you have anything to be anxious about? Despite that, you continuously deal with depression and anxiety. And Jesus offers you healing. And some of you are ruled by fear, and you need to be healed of fear, because fear is not a feeling. Fear is a spirit. The Bible says, *God did not give us a spirit of fear* (2 Tim. 1:7). But he has given us a power, a spirit of power and of love and of self-control. And so the spirit of fear has no place in the life of the believer. Receive it, receive healing.

And so if you need healing—last call. I invite you to make it known because we're going to pray for healing. No kidding. Stand up. Wherever you are. This is like driving a spiritual stake in the ground. Make it known. I don't care if you're alone in your house, Jesus is the God Who Sees, and He sees you. If you are on an airplane, stand. Wherever you are, just stand.

Jesus said, "Whoever believes in me will also do the works that I do; and greater works than these will he do, because I am going to the Father." Which is where He is right now as you're reading this. Look what He says next: "Whatever you ask in my name, this I will do, that the Father may be glorified in the Son. If you ask me anything in my name, I will do it" (John 14:12–14). If Jesus was standing here, He could pray for everybody, but it'd be one person in one place, at one time, so everybody'd have to get in one line. That might take a while. Knowing that, God has unleashed the body of Christ to pray for one another. And the same Spirit that resurrected Christ from the grave lives in the soul of every believer. And so, if you know someone who is a believer, reach out to them. They are a part of the body of Christ. Would you let them know that you need prayer and healing? We are going to ask God to do what He said He was going to do, that the Son of righteousness has come, and there is healing in His wings. And if you're reading this and you're thinking, "Well, part of the thing I'm struggling with is I'm alone," and you don't have anybody, then know that Jesus promised that He would never leave us or forsake us. At the end of this chapter I'm going to give you my email address. You email me, and some folks from our church will pray for you.

And as you're praying, I want you to pray like everything depends on it, because it does.

Pray with Me

Let me pray for us. Our good and gracious heavenly Father, Jesus, I thank You that You are the Son of righteousness, and there is healing in Your wings. God, there is healing in Your Word, and the Word became flesh and dwelt among us. And God, I pray for physical healing right now. God, I pray that scans would be perfect this week, and I pray that tumors would shrink. God, I pray that cells would obey You, the King of the universe. God, I pray that diagnoses that were terminal would now be classified as miraculous. God, I pray for marriages. Lord, I pray that You would bind together, and that what You bound together, no one could tear apart. God, I pray for mental and emotional freedom. God, the enemy is a liar, and I pray that he has no room in the head of the believer. Lord, I pray that they would not be conformed to the pattern of this world, but they would be transformed by the renewing of their mind.

God, would you miraculously transform minds right now? Would men and women and students begin to receive a peace that transcends all understanding? God, I pray for financial miracles. Lord, I pray that people would put their trust in You and You alone, and not the uncertainty of riches. God, I pray that relationships would be reconciled, just as we have been reconciled unto You. And God, I pray because of Your miraculous touch, we would be different, that this week, as marriages are restored and addictions are broken and depression is relieved, and doctors proclaim miracles. Lord, I pray, as we bump into our friends and our neighbors and our coworkers, that they would see us and say, "What is different about you?" And that we would give testimony. That we touched the hem of the garment, that we believe, that we had faith that the Son of righteousness has come and there is healing in His wings, and that we are walking in a shalom that only can be explained by the Prince of Peace.

God, we pray this in the only name that matters, the matchless name of our Lord, our Savior, and our healer, Jesus Christ. And all God's people said.

Amen.

Email address: Joby.martin@coe22.com

CHAPTER 8

The Empty Tomb—Do You Believe God Raised His Son to Life?

Well, we're here. We made it. Literally, every previous page in this book has led to this one, so buckle up. We're talking about the most important event in the history of history and why anything matters at all. Let me start by asking you this—what happens when the unexplainable runs into the undeniable? We call that a miracle. And the greatest miracle of all time is the resurrection of Jesus Christ. The fact that He lives—right this minute—is the miracle of all miracles. And because He rolled away that stone, walked out shining like the sun, and is seated at the right hand of God Most High, then anything is possible.

That means He can walk on water, change water to wine, cast out demons, heal the sick, raise the dead. It also means that if the tomb is empty—and it is—then anything is possible in your life too. Why? I'm glad you asked.

Go with me to John 20:1–2: "Now on the first day of the week Mary Magdalene came to the tomb early, while it was still dark, and saw that the stone had been taken away from the tomb. So she ran and went to Simon Peter and the other disciple, the one whom Jesus loved." For the record, there were twelve disciples. One was named John. John had a nickname, and his nickname was "the one whom

Jesus loves." Now, the interesting thing is, the only place John is called this is in the Gospel of John, written by John. I'm not doubting it, I'm just saying that where I come from, you don't get to pick your own nickname. Just saying.

So, Mary said to Peter and John, "They have taken the Lord out of the tomb, and we do not know where they have laid him" (v. 2). Now, can we just stop right there? You wanna see an example of not getting it? Mary has been following Jesus for almost three years. She's heard Him preach, heard Him teach, seen Him do miracles, and throughout all the gospels, Jesus has said over and over and over, "*I'm gonna be handed over to the chief priest. I'm gonna be crucified, dead, buried, and on the third day be resurrected from the grave.*"

If you're a little slow on the uptake on this whole Jesus thing—and sometimes the Bible doesn't make perfect sense—I've got good news for you: You could make a really good disciple. You see, Mary, on Resurrection Sunday, still doesn't get it. Jesus is doing what He said He was going to do, and she doesn't know what's happening. She thinks somebody has stolen the body. Verses 3–4: "So Peter went out with the other disciple"—the other disciple is John, who is writing about himself in some weird third-person sort of way—"and they were going toward the tomb. Both of them were running together." This is very important—John wants you to know that when Peter and John left from wherever they were, they went together. Started at the same time. John did not get a head start. They were running together. John makes it clear in verse 4: "Both of them were running together, but the other disciple outran Peter and reached the tomb first." John wants you to know that not only does Jesus like him a little bit better than all the rest of us, but also in a footrace he can outrun Peter. Peter might have been able to walk on water one time, but on dry ground, John's faster.

Verse 5: "And stooping to look in, he—" John saw the linen cloth there, but he didn't go in. So, he may be faster, but he's not braver: "I am not walking into a tomb." I'm not exactly sure why John didn't enter the tomb, but two reasons come to mind. First, he's a good Jewish man, and being that close to what he believed would be Jesus' dead body would make him ceremonially unclean. The second reason might just be fear. The soldiers had warned them to stay away and sealed the tomb with an iron spike. They weren't kidding around—proven by the fact that they'd killed Jesus.

Peter evidently doesn't care about either, as shown by the fact that just a few nights before, he chopped off an ear in the Garden of Gethsemane. So Peter reaches the tomb and rushes in. No hesitation.

Remember in the prologue I talked about the tomb and how in Jesus' day, rich people would carve out the side of a mountain and basically create a little cave? The Bible says that the tomb in which Jesus was laid was Joseph of Arimathea's tomb, a rich man's tomb. And because he was a rich man, he carved out two rooms. One room was a weeping or a wailing room, where a family would go and they would sit and mourn and just look at the body. The tombs that I've visited were like catacombs. Meaning, there were multiple rectangular holes carved into the stone. When someone died, the family would wrap the body in about 100 to 150 pounds of linen and spices, set them to rest in the tomb, and then roll a stone across the opening, allowing the body to decompose over time. After the body decomposed, they would collect the bones of the body and put them in a bone box that remained inside the tomb. So, if you wanted to visit Nana, you could. Her bones would be labeled in the tomb. That was just how it worked. But Joseph's tomb was a little bit different because he was a rich man. He didn't have these little cave things to put the bodies in. He carved out three places where you could lay bodies, along with a preparation place in the middle. Because

Joseph's tomb was a new and unused tomb, it wasn't entirely complete when Jesus was laid there. Today, if you visit the tomb, you can see the place where they would lay a body, adjacent to the door, that was not finished. Still kind of rough cut. And the one perpendicular to the door is not finished. But catty-cornered across from the opening, that one's finished. And it's there we think they laid the body of Jesus.

Contrast this tomb with Lazarus' tomb. These two are totally different. Lazarus' tomb in Bethany was more communal. Used a lot. Generations of family had been placed in that tomb. Why does this distinction matter? Think back to how Jesus called Lazarus out of the tomb. He did so by name. Had he not, then every person ever laid to rest in that tomb would have walked out. He'd have emptied the graveyard. Instead, Jesus called out a singular man, which is again worth noting, because that's what He does with every one of us. Jesus calls us individually. By name.

Joseph of Arimathea's tomb was entirely different. It had never been used and was probably still in the process of being carved out, so when they arrive with the body, the only place that makes sense to lay a body would be the one area that had been finished—the one you can see from the entrance.

Verse 6: "Then Simon Peter came, following him." Why is Peter following John? Because John, for the second time now, just in case you missed the first one, wants you to know, "We left together, I got there first, and then a little later, Peter comes tagging along." Evidently, a footrace in the first century was a big deal. So, Peter came, following him, and went into the tomb and saw the linen cloths lying there, and the face cloth, which had been on Jesus' head, not lying with the linen cloth, but folded up in a place by itself.

Now, the details here are important. The Lord's not going to waste any words with us in the Scriptures. Remember, they had wrapped Jesus in 100 to 150 pounds of linen cloths. Here's why these details are important. This is evidence that the body was not stolen. I don't know if you've ever stolen anything, but typically when you steal something, you're in a hurry. You don't stop to fold up a crime scene so it's nice and tidy for the police. You understand? You scoop and score. But when Jesus is resurrected, He's not in a hurry. He gets up, unwraps His face, folds up the linen cloth, and lays it aside.

Now, here's why. In the first century, a dinner table didn't look like da Vinci's *Last Supper*. It wasn't like a scoring table with all the judges sitting on one side waiting on the photo. That was not how it worked. They would lounge around all over. Sitting and lying on the floor. If you were finished and wanted to excuse yourself, you would put your linen napkin over your plate, alerting the servant that they could clean up your area, because you were not coming back. Which is key—it was a signal. Crumpled napkin equaled "I'm not coming back."

But if you were going to excuse yourself, and you wanted to alert the servant that you were not done and that you were coming back, then you would fold up your napkin, leaving it where the servant could see it. Folded napkin equaled "I may not be here right now, but I'm not finished—I'm coming back." So, when John wrote this—and remember he's writing to a Jewish audience, and every Jewish person who read this would understand—He folded His napkin. He was not stolen. He left on His own accord. He's coming back.

Verse 8: "Then the other disciple, who had reached the tomb first—" Okay, can we just take a time-out here? You can't scoot by this stuff. John would want you to know, inspired by the Holy Spirit, in the holy Scriptures, preserved by almighty God for all generations to be proclaimed on the greatest day of the greatest miracle of all time, that God becomes flesh, and He dies on the cross for our sin, and He resurrects on the third day to conquer sin and death. And while all of that is happening, John would want you to know—not just once, not just twice, but three times—John wants us to know that he can outrun Peter.

Here's why I'm pointing this out. It's like John can't get out of his own way. On the greatest day in human history, he still wants us to know, "Yeah, yeah, yeah, Jesus came back from the grave, but I'm faster than Peter." Here's what I know: We all bring ourselves to the resurrection of Jesus. We bring all our insecurities, pride, arrogance, doubts, anxiety. We leave nothing behind. And here's the good news—Jesus will meet you right where you are. You got questions? Doubts? Join the club. None of that disqualifies you from stepping inside the tomb because Jesus meets us right where we are.

What if today you could have the same kind of experience that John and Peter have? And what if, despite your doubts, you come to the tomb today, step inside, and find there is no body? He's not there. And what if when you turn around you come face-to-face with Jesus and He says to you, "I am who I say I am." Would you believe? Like really? This is where the rubber meets the road. This moment. This is it. Do you believe that He, Jesus, is alive, or dead?

Because how you answer this singular question determines everything about everything.

So?

At the heart of the matter is this word *believe*. We talked about this at great length in *If the Tomb Is Empty*. In Greek it's *pisteuō*, but that can be misleading in our present-day culture. It means "to believe, trust, commit your whole life to." For a lot of people, especially in the South, if you ask them, "Do you believe in God? Do you believe in Jesus?" many would say, "Yeah, man, I believe." Of course we believe. In the same way we believe in college football, and NASCAR, and sweet tea. It's just what we do. And so we equate that level of belief with this word here. But it's not.

Let me sum up. And I admit I don't know how much of this story is true, but it makes the point, so just work with me here. In 1860, a tightrope walker by the name of Charles Blondin walked across Niagara Falls. Multiple times. Back and forth. Forward and backward. Then he pushed a wheelbarrow. Back and forth. Forward and backward. At one interval, he asked the crowd, "Do you believe I can push this wheelbarrow across that rope?" After having seen him do it, the crowd enthusiastically answered yes. Then he asked, "Do you believe I can push it loaded with one of you?" Again, the crowd answered yes. Then Blondin asked, "Okay, who wants to get in the wheelbarrow?" Interestingly, no one took him up on his offer.

To get in that wheelbarrow is to *pisteuō*. To put your whole trust and faith in Blondin. There is a difference between "believing that" and "believing in." Everybody at the falls believed Blondin could walk back and forth. They'd seen him do it. But not a single person believed in Blondin as evidenced by the fact that nobody hopped into the wheelbarrow. And so, when the Bible says, "He saw and believed," it doesn't just mean "believe that," it means "believe in." Big difference.

Right this second you are either sitting in a chair or reclining someplace to read this book. You are being supported by something. That means that at this moment you are *pisteuō*-ing in that thing. Trusting in it to support you. And I have no idea what you believe about the chair. I don't know if you know who created the chair, I don't know if you know who placed the chair. I don't know if you know who sat in the chair before you. I don't even know what you believe about it. I don't know if you know the engineering behind it and how it holds you up. I don't know what you believe about the materials that made the chair, and I doubt you called the previous owner and asked, "Can you talk to me about the faithfulness of this chair? Is it going to hold me up?"

But here's what I know. At some point before right now, you put your faith in the chair. You said, "All right, here we go." And you sat down. You put the full weight of who you are onto the chair and you trusted that it would hold you up. That's what this means. That's what these men did. They saw and believed.

So, my question is simple—do you believe with that kind of belief?

Now let's look at the disciples again. Verses 9–10: "For as yet they did not understand the Scripture, that he must rise from the dead. Then the disciples went back to their homes." Did you know that you can fully believe without fully understanding? That's right—you can fully believe in Jesus, trust Jesus, surrender your life to the Lordship of Jesus Christ, become a Christian, go to heaven when you die, experience eternal life, and do all that without fully understanding while you are here on this earth.

Look, there's a lot of stuff I don't understand. And yet, the anchor that I cannot get away from is this—on Easter Sunday, two thousand years ago, Jesus is alive. If you tell me that you're going to die, and I watch you die—especially the kind of death that Jesus died—and then three days later come back from the dead, I'm with you. Regardless of what I understand or don't understand. I'll drink your sports drink, I'll wear your tennis shoes, I'll cut my hair funny, whatever you want me to do. Why? Because if you can conquer sin and death, then I'm with you.

If you have a hard time understanding, if you're a little slow on the uptake on this whole Jesus thing, if you're like, "I don't know about this and that and, really, dinosaurs and Noah, and whatever," great. You know what? You could make a great disciple of Jesus. Because the one thing these boys did not understand is the centerpiece of all Christianity. That was the part they were missing. They didn't understand the resurrection. And without the resurrection, this is all just a fairy tale and none of it matters. But the resurrection changes everything, about everything, for everyone who would believe.

Verses 11–13: "But Mary stood weeping outside the tomb, and

as she wept she stooped to look into the tomb. And she saw two angels in white, sitting where the body of Jesus had lain, one at the head and one at the feet. They said to her, 'Woman, why are you weeping?' "

Now, listen, I don't think that angels are jacking around with her. I think the angels are legitimately confused, because they're angels, and they see the activities going on from a heavenly perspective. I think they're thinking, *"Woman, what is wrong with you? Why are you crying? You shouldn't be crying. This is the greatest day in human history. Don't you know that the Lamb was slain for the forgiveness of your sin? And, behold the Lamb, He's not here, He has risen. Don't you read your Bible? Did you not pay attention in Sunday school? This was the point of the whole thing. Why are you crying? This is dumb. It's like crying on your birthday, it just doesn't make any sense. Do you understand? I was in heaven a minute ago and they are partying like rock stars up there, okay? What is wrong with you, woman, why are you crying?"*

And she says to them, " 'They have taken away my Lord, and I do not know where they have laid him.' Having said this, she turned around and saw Jesus standing, but she did not know that it was Jesus" (vv. 13–14). She's so confused in her own sorrow that she doesn't even see Jesus.

Can I tell you my greatest fear for you? My greatest fear is that you'd be three feet from Jesus and you wouldn't see Him. Because you're so hung up on something going on in your life, or you've got this question that you need answered. I worry you could be like Mary, face-to-face with Jesus and you could still miss Him. It would be such a shame for you to be this deep into the pages of this book where we have dug deep into the miracles of God and yet have you miss the God of those miracles.

Mary thinks he's the gardener, so she pleads with him. *"They've taken away my Lord, and I don't know where they've laid Him"* (v. 14).

Verse 15: "Jesus said to her, 'Woman, why are you weeping? Whom are you seeking?' Supposing him to be the gardener, she said to him, 'Sir, if you have carried him away, tell me where you have laid him, and I will take him away.'"

Then Jesus says the most beautiful word. He calls her by name. *And Jesus said to her, "Mary," and she turned and she said to Him. "Rabboni."* And John says, *That means "teacher"* (v. 16). It also could be translated as "precious teacher." Listen, it's not until Jesus calls Mary's name that Mary sees Jesus for who He really is.

You've probably heard most of this before. Jesus, the only begotten Son of God, humbled Himself and left heaven to arrive here on a rescue mission. Actually, it was more of a prisoner exchange. Him for us. He lived a sinless life, was wrongfully accused, arrested, beaten, and scourged. Scripture says during this time He became unrecognizable as a man. That means they beat Him very badly. Then He was unjustly crucified, died, and was buried in Joseph's unused tomb. Three days later, when His friends came looking for His body, He wasn't there. Why? Because He's not dead. Dead people don't fold up their napkins. Dead people don't roll away stones. Dead people don't walk and talk.

The night that I became a Christian and surrendered myself to the Lordship of Jesus Christ, it was not because I received any new information. It was because I had a new revelation. I felt like Jesus called my name. None of the information was new. I knew the whole Jesus-dying-on-the-cross thing. But somehow, in my heart of hearts, in a way that was unexplainable and undeniable, I knew He called my name and I saw Him for who He is. It is my hope and prayer that somehow today or tonight or this morning, through the revelation of the Holy Spirit, you would believe as they believed. I pray that you would hear Him call you your name. That Jesus is who He says He is, that He did what Scripture said He did, and that He's alive right this second, seated at the right hand of God the Father, and that He is still healing the sick, casting out demons, raising the dead, and saving sinners like you and me. This is pretty much the point of this book, which is also the point of His book.

Go down to verse 19: "On the evening of that day, the first day of the week, the doors being locked where the disciples were for fear of the Jews..." Note that. The doors are locked. Why? Because they're afraid. The Jewish leaders just killed Jesus. They were seen with Him. They're pretty sure they're next. "Man, if they killed Him, they're coming for us next."

What happened to all the faith they once had? The faith they expressed at Caesarea Philippi, when Peter said, "Thou art the Christ"? The faith they knew when Jesus walked on water, fed the multitudes, and called Lazarus out of the grave? Where is that faith? Somehow, between then and now, it has vanished. Which, again, means this—if you have doubts, even a lot of doubts, then you could make a great disciple. It also means that the opposite of faith is not doubt; the opposite of faith is fear. Fear paralyzes, and faith always produces action. And in that room with the doors locked, they are paralyzed.

And so they're all huddled up, afraid, and they've got all the doors locked. And then it says, "Jesus came and stood among them and said to them, 'Peace be with you'" (v. 19). Now, sometimes I think the Bible is a little understated. Can we just agree on that? These guys were freaking out. "Hey, Peter, did you lock the door?" "Uh-huh. Bartholomew, did you lock the door?" "What are we gonna do?" "Man, we went but the soldiers were gone, stone rolled away, and somebody had stolen his body." And then Mary pipes up, "I saw him, I saw him," and they're like, "Shut up, crazy lady, go sit over there. Go pray or something." That's what's going on in this room when Jesus appears.

And in the midst of all that doubt and fear, Jesus appears. Evidently locked doors can't hold Him. Neither can a tomb. And just being honest, but when He says, "Peace be with you," I think He means, "John, change your pants, all right?"

They don't expect him to just show up. And here's the reality—some of you cracked open this book and all the doors of your heart are locked and you don't really expect Him to show up. "I ain't believing today." Here's the truth of you and Jesus—Jesus chose you, and yet He gives you the right to receive Him or not. And before all you predestination versus free will people get in a tussle, you can resist Him until He decides you're not going to resist Him. It's just what the Bible teaches. What can dust do? It can't make itself breathe. Can't make itself alive. Our first breath started in His lungs. *While we were dead in our trespasses and sins, He made us alive* (Eph. 2:1–5). We didn't do that. You can't. I can't. Jesus alone walks through the locked, fearful places in us and speaks, "Peace."

When I surrendered my life to Jesus, I wasn't looking for Him. He just walked up into my life and said, "Peace be with you." Proving he can walk through whatever barrier and barricade we put up. John 20:20–23 says, "When he had said this, he showed them his hands and his side. Then the disciples were glad when they saw the Lord. Jesus said to them again, 'Peace be with you. As the Father has sent me, even so I am sending you.' And when he had said this, he breathed on them"—you may want to underline that—he breathed on them—"and said to them, 'Receive the Holy Spirit. If you forgive the sins of any, they are forgiven them; if you withhold forgiveness from any, it is withheld.'" That means that the disciples have received the good news of forgiveness of sins. It's called the gospel. If they withhold the gospel they are, in essence, withholding the ability for men and women to have their sins forgiven. When we withhold opening our mouths and sharing the gospel we are, in essence, withholding the cure for this sin-sick world.

I've read this passage a lot. Many times. I am a professional Christian, this is what I do, okay. But I still pick up stuff that I miss. Here's another. See this little part: "He breathed on them," I read that and I'm thinking, *What is this all about? That seems kind of weird, doesn't it?* Put yourself in the context here. Smell it. See it. The guys are afraid, doors locked, and boom! There's Jesus. Last time they saw Him, He was doornail-dead, hanging on a cross outside the city where they burn the trash. This was a real event, so think through how it happened. Did He breathe on them birthday cake style? Get 'em all together and blow over them all at once? I don't think so. It doesn't say so, but I think He went down the line one at a time.

Here's what I think. By His resurrection, Jesus has just accomplished what we read in 2 Corinthians 5:21, *that God made Him without sin to be sin, that we would be made His righteousness.* That means Jesus is the substitutionary atoning sacrifice for our sin. *Substitute* means "to take the place of." *Atonement* means "to pay for." Every single one of us are wretched, blackhearted sinners. Period. This is the heart of the problem. We have sinned against an almighty, holy, and just God, which requires an infinite punishment. And there is nothing that we can do on our own to make the payment. So, in His mercy, Jesus says, "I'll make the payment." He goes to the cross, and on the cross he pushes up on his nail-pierced feet and He says, "It is finished." And what is finished is the full payment required to take away our sin.

To be reconciled means that the relationship could return to what it was intended to be. Go all the way back to Genesis 2, when God created the very first human being. The Bible says, in Genesis 2:7, "The LORD God formed the man of dust from the ground and breathed into his nostrils the breath of life, and the man became a living creature." That word in Hebrew here for "breath" is *ruach*. The word *ruach* can also mean "spirit." The Greek word for "breath" or "spirit" is *pneuma*, from which we get *pneumonia.*

And the Bible wants us to know God got nostril-to-nostril with the very first man, Adam, and breathed the *ruach* of life into Adam, and when he opened his eyes, he was face-to-face with his creator and he knew him as heavenly Father. And, things went exceedingly well for nearly half a page here in my Bible. And then the man and woman sinned, sin entered the world, and then that face-to-face relationship with God as heavenly Father was forever fractured, and they were banished from the garden. And that's why every single one of us has had this yearning, this desire to get back to that moment where you and I could be face-to-face with our creator. And not just to know Him as judge, but to know him as heavenly Father.

All throughout the Old Testament, people could not have a face-to-face with God. Not even holy people like Moses. In Exodus 33, Moses says to God, "*God, show me your glory,*" and God answers, "*Bro, you can't handle my glory. I will burn you up like a potato chip, okay. But just to give you a glimpse, I'll put you over here in the cleft of the rock, and when I pass by, you can check out the afterglow.*" This is a very loose translation, but you should read it for yourself in Exodus 33:18–23.

In the upper room, when Jesus appears and breathes on them, I believe it was this intimate, one-to-one, face-to-face, breath-on-the-nostrils thing He did with Adam. This is the start-over, the do-over, for our face-to-face relationship with our heavenly Father. The risen Christ steps out of the tomb and breathes life into each of us. Singularly.

So, what in your life needs resurrecting? Is it your faith? Your belief? Maybe you need to walk up to the tomb, take a look inside, and be reminded that He's not in there. He's risen. Our faith is based on an actual historical event—this man Jesus died, and rose again. He's alive. Right this moment. He's King of Kings and Lord of Lords. How big is He? Tonight, when it's dark, walk outside and look up. See all those stars? There's something like ten trillion. Jesus put each one there and He calls them all by name and somehow in the midst of all that, He decided to think you up, mold you from the dust, and press His nostrils to your face. Your first breath started in Jesus.

Not only does Jesus meet us in our sorrows and meet us in our fear and meet us in our humanity, He also meets us in our doubt. John 20 ends this way—Thomas wasn't there when Jesus showed up for the first time. And for eight days, Thomas is like, *"Man, I don't know. I mean, I hear what you all say. I hear that it happened for you and that it was real for you, but for me, I gotta see for myself. I don't think I could...I don't know, man"* (v. 25).

And do you know what Jesus does? Jesus does not chastise Thomas for his doubts, He proves Himself. He shows up in that room again and He proves Himself. He shows Thomas the scars on His hands and on His feet and in His side. And He goes, *"See, Thomas, I am who I say I am, and I always keep My promises"* (v. 27). And then in verse 28, after seeing it, "Thomas answered him, 'My Lord and my God!'" That's the moment Thomas surrenders his life to Jesus. That's the moment he believes. "My Lord and my God." I think Thomas has gotten a bad rap in Sunday school. I don't think we should call him Doubting Thomas anymore. I think we should call him "Believing Thomas." Look at what Jesus says to him. *"You believed or trusted because you've seen me. Blessed are those who have not seen me and have yet* pisteuō-ed*, who have believed, who have trusted"* (v. 29). Right there, Jesus is talking about us. You and me. Think about it, in that moment, Jesus was thinking about us in *this* moment.

John ends his gospel this way: *"Now Jesus did many other signs in the presence of his disciples, which are not written in this book. But these are written so that you may believe or trust or* pisteuō *that Jesus is the Christ, the Son of God. And that by believing you may have life in His name"* (vv. 30–31).

So that you may "believe in."

Let me ask you again: Do you need a miracle? I can't do that for you. So, here, let go of my hand and take Jesus'. Police officer Ike Brown said, "When you don't understand, you trust God." So he wrote a letter to the man who killed his own son and he said, "I know what your sin has done to my son, but I would like to adopt you as my own, if you would just say yes." The same miracle that occurred in Ike can occur in every one of us. Whether you need to surrender your life to Jesus for the first time, or you need healing, or you need reconciliation in a relationship, or you need a prodigal to come home, or you need a marriage healed, or…name your need, Jesus is here. Breathing new life. And please don't lose sight of the real miracle. It's not that Jesus owes us a change in circumstances. The real miracle is that we get *Him*, and He is greater than all of our circumstances.

Will you bring all your unbelief, fall on your face, and believe in?

If you've made it this far, then you're probably desperate and need a miracle. Despite the fact that your news feed, your biology class, and all our modern and postmodern ideologies tell us we're crazy to believe in miracles, you're here. All of us have a tendency to say, "I know He can heal everybody else's marriage, but maybe not mine. I've heard that maybe He's healed somebody else's cancer, but maybe not mine. I've heard stories that He may have broken the chains of addiction for somebody else, but maybe not mine." Maybe it's pornography, it's an eating disorder, it's, "Why do I care so much about what Instagram says about me?"

What is the miracle you need? Name it. Write it out. Don't be afraid. *You have not because you ask not* (James 4:2). So, let's name the need and ask Him. This is not "name it and claim it." It's name it and lay it at the feet of Jesus and trust Him. Is it addiction? Cancer? Marriage? Prodigal? What? Maybe you think your problem is too big for Him? He defeated death, hell, and the grave. He can handle whatever you bring Him. So, let's bring the need and cry out for a miracle. *Let us come boldly before His throne of grace asking to receive mercy and grace to help us in our time of need* (Heb. 4:16). This is our time and here is our need. Lay it out there. Or would you be bold enough to tell someone else? Maybe your discipleship group. Your spouse. Best friend. "Hey, pray with me about this, will you?'

Remember, Jesus never stuck His finger in the chest of those who came to Him and said, "Nope, not enough faith. Come back when you've mustered up more." That's like saying, "You have to get cleaned up to take a bath." You don't. He took them in whatever condition they came. The point is they came in faith. And the amount of faith they had mattered none to Jesus. Will you come to Him?

The key is faith. Here's the writer of Hebrews: "And without faith it is impossible to please him, for whoever would draw near to God must believe that he exists and that he rewards those who seek him" (Heb. 11:6). When I read that my eye focuses on "draw near" and "believe." And if, unlike Jesus, you are looking inside yourself measuring your own faith and thinking to yourself, *I don't have it*, I have good news. "Faith comes from hearing, and hearing through the word of Christ" (Rom. 10:17). This means if you don't have it, you can get it. It's simple. Listen. Believe. Do.

Listen. Believe. Do.

Pray with Me

Our good and gracious heavenly Father, it is because of the empty tomb that we can pray. Lord, we want to confess to You that we believe because the tomb is empty; You are assuredly the God of miracles. God, we lift up to You our one-mores. Those who we believe don't know you yet, but You have placed them in our lives so we may point them to You. God, we ask that You would save them soon. Like this week. God, we thank You that You are our heavenly Father and that You have instructed Your children to bring to You all of our hopes and dreams and faults and failures. God, we cast all our cares upon You because You care for us. Lord, we confess that if You did not withhold Your own Son but gave Him for us that we would believe, then surely You hear our prayers. God, we confess that Your timing is perfect and ours is not. Lord, please remind us that it is not our circumstances that determine Your love toward us, but the cross does. The cross is the exclamation point to Your love for us. That You demonstrated Your love for us in this, that while we were still sinners, Christ died for us. Jesus, we bring to You our doubts and unanswered questions like Thomas did. We thank You that You are gentle and lowly and do not chastise us when our faith is wavering. Lord, we thank You that You, the object of our faith, are way more powerful than we are. Lord, would You once again show Yourself faithful to us? We thank You for the promise that we would be blessed when we don't get to see the scars on Your hands and feet and yet we believe. God, we thank You and praise You for Your gift of faith. We pray all of this in the good and strong name of Jesus Christ, our Lord and Savior.

CHAPTER 9

The Gift of the Holy Spirit—Do You Want to Know Christ and the Power of His Resurrection?

Over two hundred pages ago, I walked you into an empty tomb on the outskirts of the Old City of Jerusalem and said, "See, He's not here. He lives." And because of that, anything is possible. And between there and here we've spent a lot of time talking about this Jesus. So who is He? I like Paul's description to the Romans: God "gives life to the dead and calls into existence the things that do not exist" (Rom. 4:17). Sometimes the King James Version just says things better, and this might be one such place: "God, who quickeneth the dead, and calleth those things which be not as though they were." I love those two phrases: "which be not" and "quickeneth." Think about it. Only God can give life to the dead. Are there dead places in your life that need life? Or in the lives of those you love? But He doesn't stop there. He calls into existence things that don't exist. That's just who He is. Calling stuff out of thin air. Some of you are at this place—you need Him to do exactly this.

But how do we get from what we read on the page to what we experience? Here and now? How can you and I approach a holy and righteous God and pray for, hope for, and expect the unexplainable, the undeniable, the miraculous in our lives? Some of you have been reading, and waiting for this chapter. The pragmatics of how. Like, just how does this happen? How do I get from there to here?

Buckle up and hold on tight.

John 15 is one of my favorite chapters in the whole Bible because Jesus invites us to abide in Him, and when we do, He promises to abide in us. *Abide* is a beautiful and all-encompassing word that means "to rest in." Completely. To stay close. To be in communion with. Depend on. Remain under. To place all your cares and worries in. It's an invitation to fully *pisteuō*—all the time. These are some really, really sweet words when we remember Jesus, the almighty King of Kings, calls us friends. The problem we bump into in John 15 is that Jesus is only hours from going to the cross for all mankind, so it's His last chance to offer a warning. To give us a heads-up as to what's coming. What follows goes from sweet to bitter real quick. So I just need to warn you: Parts of this are not going to feel warm and fuzzy but more like a theological beatdown. But there's a reason. Hang with me. Jesus is on the throne.

Here's how He starts. It's a gear shift, man. After Jesus says that we are friends with Him, He says in verse 18, "If the world hates you, know that it has hated me before it hated you." Let me just ask you from the beginning—does the world hate you? Does it? Because Jesus says, if you follow Him, it hated Him so the world's going to hate you. And it's not fun when the world hates you. Everybody thinks they're tough and all of that, but when the world turns on you and writes articles about you or podcasts about you or tweets about you or whatever it is, it is not a lot of fun. And because of these phones we always carry in our pockets, every opinion today is instant, global, permanent, and unfiltered. Just a few generations ago, if you had an opinion about somebody, you would write a letter to the editorial department of your local paper, and they then decided whether to print it or not. But today, we exist in a state of constant criticism of almost everybody. The Greek word for that is *Twitter.* You understand what I'm saying?

And in this environment, Jesus says the world's going to hate us. Now here's why the world hates us. Because the worldview of this culture is antithetical to the gospel. I need you to understand this. The way a believer sees this world and the way a nonbeliever sees this world are completely and totally different. As a believer in Jesus Christ, we believe our MO is to love one another, and the reason that we love one another is because every single person that you've ever come eyeball to eyeball with is an image bearer of the most high God, and when sin fractured that relationship, God sent his Son, Jesus Christ, on a rescue mission to reconcile us back to God. That's the model of what it looks like and how we're to love one another. To lay down our lives for one another. That's how we are to operate as believers.

Yet the world that we live in right now believes that there is no God and that you and I are semi-advanced yet totally accidental primates and that each of us is the center of our own morality. We have set ourselves up as our own God and no one can tell us what to do. These paradigms are polar opposites. What's crazy is we tell a whole generation that they are nothing but purposeless animals, and then we act surprised when they act like who we said they are.

So Jesus turns a corner with *"Don't be surprised, this world's going to hate you."* In verse 19, He goes on to say, "If you were of the world, the world would love you as its own; but because you are not of the world, but I chose you out of the world, therefore the world hates you." If you're looking around wondering if the world hates you, this will be a big fat warning. If you're looking around and thinking, *I don't know. I feel like I can get along in the world pretty good*, it could be because you belong to the world. We do not live in a culture that is in neutral. There is a drift to this culture and it does not drift toward godliness; it does not drift toward Christlikeness. This is why the writer of Hebrews says that we have this anchor of the soul. Because we drift, and there's never been a ship in the history of ships that has drifted in a straight line. This is why we need an anchor and a rudder. Jesus is both. If you do not fight against the current of this culture, then you will just go with the flow, and it does not flow toward life and godliness. And if you don't get a bloody nose every once in a while from forcing yourself against this culture, then it could be that you are indistinguishable from this world. Jesus says He chose us out of this world, yet some of us are still just going with the flow.

Then he says, "Remember the word that I said to you: 'A servant is not greater than his master.' If they persecuted me, they will also persecute you. If they kept my word, they will also keep yours" (v. 20). Here He is referring back to something that He's already said: "A servant is not greater than his master" (John 13:16). Now I need you to understand the context in which He said that, because sometimes we Christians will hate the world, and then when the world hates back, we're like, "Ha ha." But Jesus does not say that we're to be hateful or hate-filled. That's the world. Not us. There's a lot of jerks for Jesus, but that's not what He's calling us to be. In John 13, they're at the Last Supper about to share communion, but before they do, Jesus—knowing that all authority in heaven and earth has been given to Him, and in order to show His disciples the full extent of His love—gets up from the table, dresses Himself as a servant, and washes His disciples' feet. That includes Judas. Jesus washes the feet of the one who would betray Him. His enemy. And then when He sits back down at the table, He says to the disciples, "*No servant is greater than his master. I have set for you an example; you will be blessed if you do likewise.*"

Let me spell this out: Jesus is saying the reason that the world hates us is not because we're jerks, but because we love the people of this world unconditionally and reject the systems of this world wholeheartedly. The problem is most of us, particularly American Christians, love the systems of this world wholeheartedly and we reject the people of this world. And here's what's crazy: You—that's right, you—think I'm talking about somebody else. When in fact, I'm talking about you and me. That's what's crazy about this.

Jesus commands us—that's right, commands us—to love every person we ever come eyeball to eyeball with, or these days, screen to screen with, serve them the way Jesus serves us, and then reject the way this world says that we're supposed to do everything. And yet so many of us do this in reverse. We serve the world the way this world says to do things and categorize and reject people because they're not like us. It is the exact opposite of what Jesus has called us to do.

Still not computing? Let me give you three examples. You may want to take your shoes off so I can get all up on those toes. Ready for this? Let's just talk about the three biggies: money, sex, and power. So many people who claim to be followers of Jesus still do money just like this world says to do money. The average Christian in America gives less than 2 percent of their income to charity, and yet they feel like they're so generous. If that's you, you're not. You're greedy even if you don't think you are. The bottom-line, basement-level beginning of generosity, according to Jesus in the New Testament, is a tithe. And that's not just to any charity—it's directed to God through the advancement of His kingdom. That's the first 10 percent of everything that comes in. But most of us just tip God occasionally when we remember it, then pat ourselves on the back as if we're doing something awesome. The reality is we're just greedy, buying more crap for ourselves, for our own desires, and then bragging about it. We do money just like the world. If you were sitting in my church, and I was preaching this, it'd be really quiet right now. Not a lot of "Amens." Some of you would be whispering, "I knew it. All he wants is our money." No, all *you* want is your money. And people can argue the whole 10 percent thing until they're blue in the face and tell me that's old covenant and we're under the new covenant of grace. And to that I say, "Praise God." But here's the thing—the writer of Hebrews says we have inherited a better covenant based on better promises. If this is true, why on earth would we give less under the new than the old? Answer me that.

God doesn't want your money, but He understands how it tugs on our hearts, so He said, *Where your money is, there your heart will be also* (Matt. 6:21). And He gave His blood for your heart.

In case you're not offended yet, let me move on to the next one: How about sex and sexuality? We live in a world that says, "I do what I want with whomever I want whenever I want and I ask no one's permission." Well, you're right, you can do whatever you want. But if you do, you cannot claim that Jesus is your Lord. Because He isn't. You are. And you've set up your own set of rules, which are totally contrary to His.

When the crusaders would get baptized, they would do so holding their swords out of the water. In effect saying, "You're Lord of all of this, but you ain't lord of this." Then they'd go kill people in the name of Christianity. In our current culture, we get baptized with both hands out of the water. In one we hold our wallet and in the other we hold our sexuality. Bottom line: If He's not Lord of all, He's not Lord at all.

You want to keep going? Power. Scripture says Jesus did not come to be served but to serve and to offer Himself as a ransom for many. The model there is for us to do likewise—to humble ourselves and serve one another. Period. Yet the world says, "No, no, no. I am to build my status and my own platform. To lift myself above others. To get what's mine." Think about this. Jesus was in heaven with the Father, in perfect communion, and yet Scripture says, He—Jesus (Phil 2:6)—did not think equality with God something to be grasped, so He humbled Himself, taking on the form of a bondservant and coming in the form of a man—to do what we could not do for ourselves and die for us. And by the way, a bond-servant is a servant by choice. Not conquering. Have you ever thought about how ludicrous this is—the King of everything comes here on a rescue mission, a prisoner exchange. Him for us. Why? Why not just zap all of mankind with a lightning bolt and start over? When Jesus appears on earth, He is exercising a power never seen before. It's also the model for those of us who follow Him.

He says, "But all these things they will do to you on account of my name, because they do not know him who sent me. If I had not come and spoken to them, they would not have been guilty of sin, but now they have no excuse for their sin" (John 15:21–22). You and I have been put on notice; we have heard the truth, and we will be held accountable for it. Then John 15:23, He says this, "Whoever hates me hates my Father also."

People believe today that there's one God and many roads to Him or Her and you just pick your path and good luck, I'll see you there. Jesus does not agree with your theology. Whatever you feel, think, believe about Jesus, that's what you feel, think, believe about God, the Father. If you hate Jesus, you hate God, the Father. If you love Jesus, you love God, the Father. If you reject Jesus, you reject God, the Father. If you ignore Jesus, you ignore God, the Father. If you know Jesus, you know God, the Father. Jesus will not allow himself to be divorced from God, the Father.

He says, "*If I had not done among them the works that no one else did, they would not be guilty of sin. But now they have seen and hated both Me and my Father, but the word that is written in their law must be fulfilled, they hated Me without a cause.*" Kind of intense, right? And this is just His intro. He said, "*It's going to get rough. This world is going to hate you.*" Which leads to the question: All right, Jesus, so then what is the solution to the pain that we are going to experience because of our faith?

I feel like the disciples are looking at him, scratching their heads like, "Well, Jesus, if that's our future, we need some help." To which He's got really, really good news. In verse 26, He says, *"I'm going to send you a helper."* But when the helper comes...This word *helper* gets translated a bunch of different ways: *helper, counselor, advocate, comforter.* They're all legit. You know why? Because we need help and we need an advocate and then we need counseling and we need a comforter. The Greek word here is *paraclete.*

I'm gonna teach some Greek here, so hang with me. When I was in seminary, I had to memorize all these words. The way that I did it was kind of dumb, and you're going to think less of me as a scholar, but okay, whatever. I would remember by word association, so a hundred years ago, when I was in high school, I played football. You know what I needed when I played football? I needed a pair of cleats. "Paraclete." I needed a pair of cleats. Why? Because when you're playing, if you're wearing cowboy boots, they're too slick, you'll get pushed all over the place. A pair of cleats keeps you grounded, connected to a firm foundation, so that when your enemy comes against you, you can stand firm. That's what Paul means in Ephesians 6:11 when he says, *Stand firm against the enemy and his evil schemes.*

It means that you get your feet rooted into the Word of God, the solid rock foundation. The second thing a pair of cleats does is help you change directions. If you run out there on the wet grass of a Friday night in your sneakers and try to change directions, you'll slip and fall. But if you got a pair of cleats hooked into the ground, you can just change directions and go wherever you need to go.

As believers in Jesus Christ, we can stand firm against the enemy by being rooted in the Word of God because we got the *paraclete* helping us stand firm, stay rooted, and change directions. Jesus says, "But when the Helper comes, whom I will send to you from the Father, the Spirit of truth, who proceeds from the Father, he will bear witness about me. And you also will bear witness, because you have been with me from the beginning" (John 15:26–27). Jesus says, *I am going to send the Spirit of God to dwell in you. I'm going to send the* paraclete *to dwell in you.* And so in the next few pages, I want to talk about the role of the Holy Spirit on the earth and inside of the believer.

When I got saved in high school, the news of my salvation came as a shocker to my high school. They weren't totally sure. I left for camp one summer and I came home and I was a Christian. And I told people, "Hey, I'm a believer." And this one guy in my high school came up to me and said, "I understand you became a Christian." I said, "Yes, sir. I did." And he said this, "Did you believe in the full gospel?"

That was code, but I missed it. I thought, *I think so. I don't remember any blackout dates on the thing that I signed up for. I think I'm all-in.* But he was talking about the role of the Holy Spirit in my life. The question becomes: What is the primary evidence of the Holy Spirit in the life of the believer? And the way that you answer that has a lot to do with the kind of church you grew up in, if you grew up in church.

What often happens when preachers talk about the role of the Holy Spirit in the life of the believer is that we immediately reduce the role of the Spirit's life in your life just to the giver of the gifts of the Spirit. Which is crazy because we're going to find out in a little while all that the Holy Spirit wants to do is point people to Jesus, but when most people talk about the Holy Spirit, they often point to you and what you get out of the deal. Now, understanding your spiritual gifts is very important. As is faithfully walking in them.

And I've got really good news for you. If you are a follower of Jesus, then you have at least one spiritual gift, and no Christian has all the spiritual gifts. That's why we need one another. We come together like one body with many parts for the edification of the church and the advancement of God's kingdom. Here's what this means. If you're a believer in Jesus, congratulations, you're gifted. Some of you have never heard that before, right? Amen. Remember the gifted class back in middle school? We didn't have enough of those people where I lived to make up a whole class so we were kind of intermixed, kind of like the wheat and the tares. And on Thursdays, this smart lady from the high school would come into our middle school class and she would say, "All right, will all the gifted kids please come with me?" And all these kids would get up and leave.

And then I remember thinking, *Hey, what are* we *going to do?* And I'm sure the teachers are thinking, *Oh, we got some coloring sheets for you. Enjoy.* If you are in Christ, congratulations—you're gifted. The Holy Spirit has given you certain gifts, and I would encourage you to figure out what those are. We have an assessment tool online at https://coe22com/gifts. Now I would warn you, I'm always slightly hesitant on these assessments because this assessment is not the Bible. You should pay attention to what you're passionate about, what you're good at, and what other people say that you're good at. But it's a starting point.

Ultimately the only way to truly figure out your spiritual gift is to set sail and get to doing something, and then you'll begin to figure out what part you play in the body. What I mean by "set sail" is to just start serving. The wind does not fill up the sail that remains docked in the port. If it does, the boat just tugs on a rope and needs to be cast off. So, cast off. Sometimes these assessments can throw you off a little bit. When I was in college, I was at this college campus ministry thing; they were super into the gifts, and they gave us a test that was a little more charismatic than the Bible. When we got our results back, I was standing next to a buddy and he said, "Bro, what'd you get?"

I read him my assessment. "I got martyrdom." Which is awesome—but you can use it one time and then you're done, right? "What'd you get?"

He sort of turned his head sideways and lifted one eyebrow. "I got celibacy."

"I think I'd rather have martyrdom, man."

Back to the question: What is the primary evidence of the Holy Spirit in the life of the believer? The answer, according to Scripture, is not signs and wonders, although it may include that. But the answer according to Scripture—there's a hint in John 15:27—is that you will also "bear witness." The primary evidence of the Spirit of God in the life of the believer is evangelism. So, what, according to Scripture, does an evangelist do? To be fair, the only person called an "evangelist" in Scripture is Philip (Acts 21:8). Paul also tells Timothy to "do the work of an evangelist" (2 Tim. 4:5), but the only one given the actual title is Philip. So, what'd he do? In Acts 8, *Philip went down to Samaria and began proclaiming Christ to them* (v. 4). Notice the "proclaiming Christ" part, which means he was preaching to the kingdom of God and that Christ was and is the promised Son of God. Then it says the crowds paid attention to him as they heard and saw the signs which he was performing. *For in the case of many who had unclean spirits, they were coming out of them shouting with a loud voice and many who had been paralyzed and lame were healed* (v. 7). But don't stop there—move down to verse 12: "But when they"—the crowds—"believed Philip as he preached good news about the kingdom of God and the name of Jesus Christ, they were baptized, both men and women." Notice what's happening here. Philip, the evangelist, is evangelizing. And when he does that, preaching the kingdom and the name of Jesus, people believe, they're healed, demons are cast out, and folks get baptized. But notice—none of this happens without the proclamation that Jesus is who He says He is and does what He says He will do. This is "bearing witness." Which is the primary evidence of the Holy Spirit.

What the Spirit wants to do is point everybody to Jesus, and if the Spirit lives in you, then He will want you to point everybody to

Jesus. This is what He says in John 15:27 and John 14:12: "Whoever believes in me will also do the works that I do; and greater works than these will he do, because I am going to the Father." If you know Acts 1:8, Jesus says, *"But you will receive power when the Holy Spirit comes upon you and you will be my witness."* Or in Acts 2, when the Holy Spirit descends on every single believer, what happens when the apostles are full of the Holy Spirit and a crowd shows up? Peter preaches, and on that day three thousand people surrendered their life to the Lordship of Jesus Christ. That's the primary evidence of the Holy Spirit. Jesus Himself says in Luke, when He stands up in the temple and reads from Isaiah, that He came to preach good news to the poor, proclaim freedom for the prisoners, recover sight for the blind, and set the oppressed free. Notice the progression— preaching and proclamation, and then healing and deliverance. And then in Mark, when everyone was looking for Jesus to perform more signs, He said, "Let us go on to the next towns, that I may preach there also, for that is why I came out" (Mark 1:38). I'm not negating signs and wonders, and I pray we see a whole lot of them. This entire book focuses on our need for miracles. But I am saying that the priority of Jesus, and those who followed Him, like Philip and Paul and Peter and all the rest, was the proclamation of the kingdom of God, and that when they did that, greater works followed. I make the distinction because in the history of the church, there has been a tendency to reverse that. To seek the signs and miracles to the exclusion of the proclamation. I don't want to do that. I want to proclaim like Philip and make room for the Holy Spirit to do what He does without limitation.

In John 16, Jesus says, "I have said all these things to you to keep you from falling away. They will put you out of the synagogues" (vv. 1–2). This was a really big deal. This isn't as if I said to you, "Well, you can't come to church anymore." You may think, *Fine, I'll watch online.* That's not what this is. All of Jewish life centered around the relationships they had at the synagogue. This was costly. It meant their livelihood. Their relationships. They would become outcasts. Several years ago, Pastor Britt, Pastor Adam, and I were training pastors in East Africa. And one of us said something to them like, "It must be really difficult to pastor in Africa." And they looked right back at us and said, "It must be virtually impossible to be a Christian in America." And I responded, "What are you talking about?" And they said, " 'Cause it costs you virtually nothing. And the message of Jesus is that it would cost you everything."

This is what Jesus is saying. If you follow Me, it will be costly. He goes on to say, "The hour is coming when whoever kills you will think he is offering service to God" (John 16:2). For the rest of our history as people in the United States of America, we will approach September 11 a little differently. There were some men who thought killing image bearers of God would make their god happy. Jesus looks at that and says, *"Beware of that. That's what a Christless religion will lead people to."* Jesus goes on to say, "And they will do these things because they have not known the Father, nor me" (v. 3). There is only one true God. He sent His one and only Son to make a way, and Jesus is the only way. We do not worship the same God with different names. Jesus says, "But I have said these things to you, that when their hour comes you may remember that I told them to you. I did not say these things to you from the beginning, because I was with you. But now I am going to him who sent me, and none of you asks me, 'Where are you going?' But because I have said these things to you, sorrow has filled your heart. Nevertheless, I tell you the truth: it is to your advantage that I go away" (vv. 4–7).

You should underline that. Jesus is looking at His disciples and says, *"It is to your advantage that I go away. For if I do not go away, the helper, the* paraclete, *will not come to you. But if I go, I will send him to you."* A friend of mine named J. D. Greear wrote a book called *Jesus, Continued...*, and the subtitle is this: *Why the Spirit*

Inside You Is Better *Than Jesus Beside You.* It's rooted in this verse. I mean, think about this. Jesus says it's to your advantage that Jesus leaves and sends you the Holy Spirit. If Jesus gave us the option, "All right, you get choice A or B, either I can be with you, be your room-mate forever, or I can leave and send the Spirit of God to live in you. Which one would you choose?" I think we would have a tendency to choose Jesus. This is how J.D.'s book starts. Imagine if Jesus was your roommate and you ran out of food, you're like, "Jesus, we ran out of food." He could get two little chicken minis. He could do miracles on the sabbath and get Chick-fil-A on Sunday. Praise God. Imagine you're at a party and you run out of wine. (Hear that, Baptists? That'll shake you up a little bit.) You say, "Jesus, we're out of wine," and He says, "Don't worry about it. Boo-yaah, let the party keep going. All right?"

Or if your dog died before Jesus got home, say, "Hey Jesus, my dog died." He'd respond, "I got you, man. Lazarus, come forth, bring your dog back to life." If you're cat people, you'd say, "Jesus, my cat died." And then Jesus would help you dig a hole to bury it.

Based on John 14, 15, and 16, I'm going to give you nine roles of the Holy Spirit in the life of the believer. It's not exhaustive. And it isn't in order of importance. It's just the order in which I wrote them down.

Number one is that the Spirit of God empowers you to share your faith. We just talked about that. It's also one corner of the mat, so we've covered it.

Number two: According to John 14:16, the Spirit of God is God's presence with you. The Holy Spirit in the believer is the fulfillment of Jesus' promise at the Great Commission when He says, *"And I will never leave you or forsake you."* Let me tell you what happens when the presence of God is with you—fear flees from you. This is because the Bible says perfect love drives out fear. Paul tells Timo-thy, *"God did not give you a spirit of fear, but a spirit of power and of love and of self-control, and that spirit of power, love, and self-control comes from the Spirit of God"* (2 Tim. 1:7). This is why God says to Joshua, *"Be strong and courageous, strong and courageous, strong and courageous."* Three times in chapter 1 of the Book of Joshua (vv. 6, 7, 9). Why? Because he's weak and afraid, weak and afraid, weak and afraid.

But God does not tell Joshua he can be strong and courageous by simply looking at Josh and saying, "Hey bro, come on, you got this. All right? You're smart enough, you're good enough, and doggone it, people like you." Nope, he says, *"Be strong and courageous. Do not tremble or be afraid, for I am with you"* (v. 9). The Spirit of God drives away fear because God's presence is with us.

Number three: In John 14:26, Jesus told us that the Spirit of God would teach us and bring to remembrance the things that we had been taught. I sure do hope and pray there have been times in your life where you face certain circumstances and a Bible verse pops up in your head that you did not even know that you knew. Maybe you heard it from a sermon or you read it on your own, and that is the Spirit of God teaching you. If you've ever learned anything in my preaching or writing, that is evidence of the Spirit of God teaching you, not me. If you've ever read the Bible and understood what it was saying, that's the Spirit of God teaching you.

Number four: In John 16:8–11, Jesus says this: "And when he comes—" Now notice every time in the New Testament when the Bible talks about the Holy Spirit, it's not an *it*, He's a *He*. Because the Holy Spirit is the third person of the Trinity. The Holy Spirit is not like a potion that you top up every weekend when you come to church. It says, "And when he comes, he will convict the world concerning sin and righteousness and judgment"—so there's three of them right there, that *the Spirit of God will convict the world concerning sin, righteousness, and judgment*—"concerning sin, because they do not believe in me; concerning righteousness, because I go to the Father, and you will see me no longer; concerning judgment, because the ruler of this world is judged."

Let's break number four into A and B. Number four-A is this: The Spirit of God convicts the world concerning sin. If you've ever been convicted of sin, it's because the Spirit of God is doing a work in you. If you've ever shown up to church, and you realized, *Uh-oh, I think I've got a problem, and I think I am the problem. I don't just mismanage my money, I'm greedy. I don't just struggle telling the truth, I am a liar. I don't just have trouble with relationships, I have trouble with relationships because I want everybody to bow down at the idol of self*—and you begin to be convicted of sin, that is a work of the Spirit. Now, listen, I know the younger you are the more applicable this is—I know your kindergarten teacher told you that you were a snowflake and a puppy's breath and a Skittle. Well, she is a liar and a false prophet, that's just a fact, okay? You're not. Every single one of us by nature and nurture are wretched, crooked and depraved, blackhearted sinners, and it's worse than you think. And the defensiveness that you have right now reading this is your own pride, which is the granddaddy of all sins.

Number four-B is that we are convicted of righteousness. Here's what this means. When you begin to compare yourself—not to your own self-justification, because we can always win when we do that—but when we begin to see ourselves in light of the perfect, righteous Son of God, it is a work of the Spirit in our life.

This leads to number five: judgment. The role of the Spirit is judgment. And this world will be judged. Every single one of us one day will stand before a holy and just God and give an account of our lives. And when we do, we will not have time to explain how we're a pretty good guy and we're not as bad as some other people. But when we come into the very presence of God, we will do what anyone does and fall on our face. This is what Isaiah does when he encounters the glory of God; he says this: "Woe is me! For I am lost;

for I am a man of unclean lips, and I dwell in the midst of a people of unclean lips; for my eyes have seen the King, the LORD of hosts!" (Isa. 6:5).

Apart from Jesus Christ, you will be judged for eternity, and you will have to give an account for your sins. We call that hell. Listen, if you're a follower of Jesus, this life is as close to hell as you will ever be. If you are not a follower of Jesus, this experience right here is as close to heaven as you will ever be. And I know that some of you thinking, *Are you trying to scare me?* Look, you should be terrified. You should sleep with a bike helmet and a cup and one eye open. I'm telling you, judgment is coming. The crazy thing is that when I was trained in evangelism, here's what we were taught to do. We were taught to just go up to absolute strangers and ask them this question: "If you were to die tonight, would you go to heaven?" And I remember thinking, that's a little aggressive. I don't think you should bring up death to strangers 'cause it sounds like you're gonna murder them. That's what it sounds like, right? Kind of creepy.

But as I write this, our church performed seven funerals in two weeks. Seven. So, it's worth asking: Are you prepared to stand before your maker and give an account for your life? If you've never surrendered your life to the Lordship of Jesus Christ, I am begging you to repent, trust Jesus, and be saved. And here's what's crazy. And even though all these things are true, that we will stand before a holy and just God, it's still the kindness of God that leads us to repentance.

I can't lead you to repentance, no matter how much I yell at you. I can't do that. It's the kindness of God and the conviction of your sin and the conviction of righteousness and God's judgment. Repentance is God's warm invitation to you to think about sin as if it is a sickness, and Jesus is inviting you into Himself for you to be cured. He's inviting you into His family. That's what the conviction of the Holy Spirit does. He woos you into this eternal relationship with Jesus Christ. It's what He does. In John 16:12–13, He keeps going: "I still have many things to say to you, but you cannot bear them now. When the Spirit of truth comes, he will guide you into all the truth, for he will not speak on his own authority, but whatever he hears he will speak, and he will declare to you the things that are to come."

Number six: The spirit of God will guide you in all truth. We translate the Greek word for this as "meek." In the Sermon on the Mount, Jesus says, "Blessed are the meek" (Matt. 5:5). *Meek* rhymes with *weak*, so we think it's not that awesome, but that's not true. The Greek word for *meek* paints a picture of a horse with a bit in its mouth. A powerful animal, but the master of the animal has an easy time with the reins directing which way that horse should go. It means controlled strength. That's the role the Spirit of God plays. Straight up, that's the kind of man I want to be. When I tattooed Acts 11:24 on my arm—*and he was a good man full of the Holy Spirit and faith, and a great number of people were brought to the Lord*— that's the kind of man I want to be. I want to be easily led and guided by the truth of the Holy Spirit. In a world that's whispering lies to us all the time, I want to be a really well-trained horse, having given the reins to Jesus. All He has to do to get my attention is give just the slightest little tug of the reins one way or the other. And I pray, when He does, that I start moving that direction. Immediately.

Every single time some famous pastor falls, our staff and many other people ask, "Pastor, what happened?" I'm going to tell you what happened. The Spirit of God was speaking to that man and saying, "Whoa! Whoa! Whoa! Don't go that way, go this way." The problem occurred when that pastor said, "Get off me. I got this." Three of the most dangerous words you'll ever hear: "I got this."

I don't want to be an "I got this" guy; I need a helper. When the Spirit tugs on me, I want to respond with, "You got this. You tell me what to do and that's what I'll do." The Spirit guides us in all truth. We live in a world with a whole bunch of information and almost no wisdom, and wisdom is the applied truth of the Word of God in our current circumstances. John 16:14–15 says, "He will glorify me, for he will take what is mine and declare it to you. All that the Father has is mine; therefore I said that he will take what is mine and declare it to you."

Number seven: The Spirit of God leads us to worship Jesus. Every single time I preach on the Holy Spirit, somebody always says, "We don't talk about the Spirit enough." And I just wanted you to know the Holy Spirit doesn't want us to talk about the Holy Spirit that much; all the Holy Spirit wants to talk about is Jesus. If you cast the Holy Spirit in a play on a stage, He would work in the background. Be a tech guy. Run the spotlight. He would continuously shine the spotlight on Jesus. If you want a good picture of this, read Genesis 24. It's the story of Abraham's servant, sent to find a wife for Isaac. Phrased another way, it's the story of the father who sent his servant to find a wife for his son. Throughout the entire chapter, the servant is referred to more than forty times but is never named. This is purposeful on the part of the Holy Spirit. The servant remains in the shadows and never takes center stage. Who takes center stage? The bride. The servant is a type of the Holy Spirit drawing no attention to Himself but continually pointing to the Son and the bride.

It's important for us to understand how the Godhead works. My friend Ryan Britt likes to say, "You won't know who you are unless you know whose you are." So true. Ownership precedes identity. He's talking about our relationship with the Father. And I would add to that, if you don't know the who of whose you are, you'll never know who you are. And most of us have a real misunderstanding about how one God in three persons works. And I get that it's hard to understand. Okay?

If you think that you can fully understand the magnitude of the Godhead, it's going to be tough. All right? We have like a paper cup–sized brain standing in front of the Atlantic thinking to ourselves, *I can't get it all in.* Remember, He's God, you're not. And a lot of us have a misunderstanding about who God the Father, God the Son, and God the Holy Spirit is. All the time, we think the Father's the main one and the Son's the nice one and the Holy Spirit's the weird one. That is not how it is. One God in three persons. Do I entirely understand how that works? Not really. But neither did Philip—one of his disciples. That's why he asked Him, "Lord show us the Father and it is enough for us." Jesus said to him, "Have I been with you so long, and you still do not know me Philip? Whoever has seen me has seen the Father" (Jn 14:8–9). If this whole thing makes your brain hurt, you're in good company. But think about it. If we can fully understand Him, then He's not the almighty, infinite God.

And God is not in competition or in conflict with Himself. God is love, and the Godhead is cooperating for our salvation and His glory. And so the Holy Spirit always points us to Jesus for forgiveness and worship. And Jesus always wants to bring us to the Father for healing, that's His identity and perspective. And the Father sends us the Holy Spirit to help us and sends us the Son to save us. God Himself is in perfect concert with God Himself in three persons as an essence.

John 16:16: "A little while, and you will see me no longer; and again a little while, and you will see me." He's talking about His death and resurrection. The others are confused. "So some of his disciples said to one another, 'What is this that he says to us, "A little while, and you will not see me, and again a little while, and you will see me"; and, "because I am going to the Father?" ' " (v. 17). And so they were saying, "*What does He mean by a little while? We do not know what He is talking about.*" Anybody ever feel like that at church? You find yourself in church, and somebody like me is up there just sweating and preaching and you're thinking, *We do not know what he is talking about.* When you do not know what he is talking about, just bring that to the Lord. *Lord, we do not know what he is talking about.* Because it's what Jesus does. Jesus knew that they wanted to ask Him. So they're standing around, kind of clearing their throats, but they won't ask Him. Still, He knows.

When my son, JP, was younger, he would come up to me and he'd say, "Uh, Dad, I didn't finish my dinner, so Mom said I couldn't ask for candy. So I'm not asking for candy, but she didn't say you couldn't give me some." It was that kind of thing. They're standing there and He knows, so he says to them, "Is this what you are asking yourselves, what I meant by saying, 'A little while and you will not see me, and again a little while and you will see me'? Truly, truly, I say to you, you will weep and lament, but the world will rejoice. You will be sorrowful, but your sorrow will turn into joy" (vv.19–20).

What he's saying is this: *"It's going to be a rough few days, boys. But after three days, it's going to be worth it."* And then this is the example that he gives. I love this, sorta. He says, "When a woman is giving birth, she has sorrow because her hour has come" (v. 21). Can I get a mama amen right here? He uses words like *sorrow*, and later he's going to call it *anguish*. And Jesus is right. I've been in the room twice. Anybody that calls labor beautiful is lying to you. It ain't beautiful. It's awful, scary, intimidating, terrifying, gross, it's awful. But then you're holding that baby, and it's the most beautiful thing ever. Especially for the mama, because she forgets what she just endured. She no longer remembers the anguish for the joy that a human being has been born into the world.

Jesus is saying, *"I know it's traumatic, but it's worth it."* Look, all you mamas, I can't even understand what you've gone through. I've seen it twice, I don't wanna sign up for it ever again. You understand? And I was just witnessing. You know, I was a part of the very beginning of the situation, and I pretty much just ran taxi for the rest of it until, you know, they came home. And yet even when you go through all of that and then you hold your kid—parents, you know what I'm talking about. There's a love unleashed in here that you did not realize that you possessed. And what I love about it is this is the example that Jesus is giving when He talks about God the Father, God the Son, and God the Holy Spirit, because when you are married and make a baby, while it's not the same, it is a reflection of the Trinity. God is one God in three beings. When Gretchen and I got married, she was still herself and I was still myself, we're two people. And please don't twist my words and tell me that I'm telling you that we're all gods. We're not. It's just an illustration.

God says that the two become one flesh, and then because she loved me and I loved her, out of an overflow of our love for one another, we created literal image bearers of us. They have our names and they look like us and we love them and they aggravate the life out of ourselves. This is what's happening. So mamas, I can't even begin to imagine the kind of love that you have for that child that you carried and caused you great anguish, but Jesus is describing His death and resurrection in terms of a pregnancy and birth. "*So also you have sorrow now, but I will see you again, and your hearts will rejoice, and no one will take your joy from you because they can't take Jesus from you because Jesus put his spirit in you*" (v. 22). That's what he means.

Number eight: The Holy Spirit helps us pray. Romans 8:26 says that even when we run out of words, He gives us the words to pray. The Holy Spirit will always guide you to pray to the Father in the name of Jesus.

"In that day you will ask nothing of me. Truly, truly, I say to you, whatever you ask of the Father in my name, he will give it to you." What a promise. Whatever you ask of the Father in the name of Jesus, He can't wait to give you that. The problem is, we mostly ask stuff for ourself in our name and then get mad when He doesn't answer that prayer. And then He says, "Until now, you have asked nothing in my name" (John 16:23–24).

Think about this. Had the disciples asked for stuff? Sure. They asked for power. Two brothers sent their mom—talk about a wimpy move. "Hey Mom, will you go talk to Jesus, see if we can be senior

VPs of Jesus, Incorporated?" It's like the original helicopter parent right there in Matthew. And so did Jesus answer their prayer? Nope. Peter on the mountain of transfiguration: *"It is good that we are here. We should just camp out up here"* (Matt. 17:4). And Jesus is like, "Nah, man, what are you talking about?"

One time they asked for revenge. There was a city that rejected Jesus and so James and John asked Him, "Lord, do you want us to tell fire to come down from heaven and consume them?" *"Like Elijah did on Mt. Carmel?"* (Luke 9:54). You see, they have been asking for stuff—they just haven't been praying to the Father in the name of Jesus.

Jesus ends John 16 this way: "I have said these things to you in figures of speech. The hour is coming when I will no longer speak to you in figures of speech but will tell you plainly about the Father. In that day you will ask in my name, and I do not say to you that I will ask the Father on your behalf; for the Father himself loves you, because you have loved me and have believed that I came from God" (vv. 25–27). And this is as plain as day as Jesus can put it for the disciples. "I came from the Father, I have come into the world, I am now leaving the world and going to the Father."

He's saying, "I might have been born in Bethlehem, but I am not from Bethlehem. I'm from heaven. The right hand of God. I came here for a while and now I'm going back." And for whatever reason, this is when it clicked for them. His disciples say, "Ah, now you are speaking plainly and not using figurative speech!" (v. 29). The figures of speech they're referencing are the seven *I am* statements that Jesus uses to identify Himself in the Gospel of John: I am the bread of life, the light of the world, the door of the sheep, the resurrection and the life, the good shepherd, the way, the truth, and the life, and the true vine. In essence, they are saying to Jesus, "We appreciate the seven *I am* statements, but all that stuff went right over our heads before. Why didn't You just tell us? Why didn't You explain it instead of talking in all that code?"

"Now we know that you know all things and do not need anyone to question you; this is why we believe that you came from God." Jesus answered them, "Do you now believe? Behold, the hour is coming, indeed it has come, when you will be scattered, each to his own home, and will leave me alone. Yet I am not alone, for the Father is with me" (vv. 30–32).

And then here's the last thing, number nine. He says, "I have said these things to you, that in me you may have peace." The Holy Spirit brings us peace. And then He gives a little commentary: "In the world you will have tribulation. But take heart; I have overcome the world" (v. 33). That tribulation could be financial, that could be relational, that could be mental, that could be spiritual. You see, here's how this works: Jesus purchases for us peace on the cross, and He deposits His Holy Spirit in us so that we could experience that peace that He purchased. He says, "*I give you peace.*" Here's the point: The Spirit of God in you is greater than the circumstances around you. This world, your world, has trouble, and God offers peace that transcends understanding.

In these crazy times that we live in, are you experiencing trouble? Tribulations? And maybe I'll ask you this way—does anybody reading this want some peace? Maybe it's in your marriage. Maybe it's with a prodigal child. Maybe it's a broken relationship. If you were to say, "I'm facing some tribulation in the area of relationships," then Jesus would say He wants to give you peace, whether it's your fault or somebody did something against you. Maybe somebody sinned against you and you want to be able to forgive them so that you can walk in this kind of peace, but you've been holding on to the unforgiveness for so long that there's a bitterness, a hard-heartedness that's beginning to stir. Jesus wants to give you peace through the power of the Holy Spirit. Maybe some of you would say, "You know what? The tribulation, the trouble that I'm experiencing right now, it's in here—in my mind."

Today, we would call this a mental health issue. How many of you would say, "Hey, you know what? I need some peace in my mind. I struggle with depression and I struggle with anxiety. And when I look around at the circumstances, everything ought to be okay, but I can't turn the okay on." And then you had some Christians who told you a lie that somehow a Christian could not struggle with depression, except many people in the Scriptures did. Elijah, Jeremiah—even Jesus, in the Garden of Gethsemane, said that He felt like He was going to die. And maybe you would say, "God, I need help. I need the *paraclete* to give me some peace in my mind and take captive every thought." Maybe that's you, so that you could love the Lord your God with all your mind.

And maybe some of you need peace in your soul. I mean, you're a believer, man, but somehow you feel a million miles from God and you are thinking and feeling, "Lord, I don't know what happened. I feel like when I pray, the prayers don't make it through the ceiling and I'm alone." Even though you know theologically you can't be alone. You have this soul problem and it feels like you're alone.

Or maybe there's an addiction. Maybe there's this thing that you struggle with and you need some peace because it feels like chains of bondage. It's like a thing in the spiritual realm has got hold of you and keeps baiting you to walk down a road that you said you'd never walk down again, and then you look up and there you are again, and it's trying to kill, steal, and destroy you. You're crying out, "Jesus, I need some help." And the Spirit of God wants to help you and break those chains.

Or maybe it's physical. Maybe you would love to experience some physical peace. This word *peace* means "to put back together, to be whole." And maybe your physical body isn't whole, and maybe the scans were going okay for a little while, but this week you got some back and it's still there or it came back. If that's you, I want you to tell Him, "All right, God, I need help. I need some peace."

Is this you?

To you, Jesus says, *"Come to Me, all you who are weary and heavy burdened…"* (Matt. 11:28). Let me tell you what a heavy burden is. A heavy burden is when you lack peace in the heart and in the soul and in the mind and in the body. Jesus says, "You weren't meant to carry it on your own. You don't got this. You need a helper. *Come to me all you who are weary and heavy burdened and I will give you—"* here's the word "—*I will give you rest for your soul.*"

Another word for *rest* is *peace*.

If this is you, I want us to pray. I want us to pray that the Spirit of God does exactly what Jesus promised, because we believe Jesus is who He says He is, and He always keep His promise. He promised we would know trials and tribulations, and He promised to send us a helper and give us peace. Not like the world gives, because Jesus has overcome the world. And not only that, but He has sent His Spirit. The Spirit of Holiness. To help us. And I don't know if you've ever thought about it much, but while His Spirit is here, He—Jesus—is seated at the right hand of the Father interceding for us. It's like a two-for-one.

We are going to pray that marriages are restored. Prodigals come home. Addictions are broken. Physical bodies are healed. Souls are set free. Sins are forgiven. Why?

Because He's alive.

Because the tomb is empty.

Because He is seated at the right hand of God.

Genesis 1 says that the Spirit of God hovered over the waters in creation. And then everything God created, He did through His Spirit. When He made man, he breathed in the *ruach* of God, His very Spirit, and all of us became living, breathing human souls. Then Jesus showed up, and every miracle He performed, He did through the Spirit of God. Then He was killed. Dead. Was buried. And God raised the Son through the Spirit. Then Jesus ascended, and God doesn't leave us orphans, so fifty days later He sent His same Spirit to fill us, baptize us, live inside us. Empower us. Make us more like Jesus. Lead people to Jesus. The same Spirit that raised Christ Jesus from the dead lives inside of every one of us who is in Jesus and gives strength to our mortal bodies. I'm pretty sure we don't really understand the totality of this. In all honesty, it's tough. We're finite. He's infinite. But our inability to understand it doesn't make it any less true. So, I believe. And I say, "Come, Holy Spirit. Have Your way. Rule. Reign. Deliver. Save. Heal. And please, please, please, don't let us be a hindrance to any thing You desire to do. Come, Holy Spirit."

If you're in a discipleship group or Bible study or whatever you call it, this is the time for you all to gather around one another, lay hands on one another, and pray down heaven. This is when you anoint people with oil, and "the prayer of faith will restore [the ESV says "save"] the one who is sick" (James 5:15 NASB). If you're in a cell by yourself, then just know that the Holy Spirit will pray with you. If you're in a marriage, pray with your husband or wife, and if they're not a believer, then pray with someone who is. I have tried, as best I know how, to bear witness and lead you to the feet of Jesus where, now, in and through the power of the Holy Spirit—who's been sent on a singular mission to help you—I want you to let go of my hand and grab hold of His. You need Him, not me. So go ahead. Reach out. Now let's pray in belief and faith.

Pray with Me

Our good and gracious heavenly Father, God, we love You because You first loved us. And God, we pray, we pray in faith in You, though it may seem small in comparison to our overwhelming circumstances. God, I thank you and I praise you. It's not the amount of faith that matters; it's the object of our faith that changes things.

And so, God, we cry out to You. God, would You help us? Because we need Your help. God, would You restore marriages? God, would You bring forgiveness between husbands and wives? Where there is bitterness, God, would You bring reconciliation between people who have been broken? Surely, God, if sinful man can be reconciled to a holy God, surely brothers and sisters can be reconciled to one another. And God, we pray, we pray for clear, transformed minds. God, we pray against the lies of the enemy because when he whispers those lies of condemnation, he is speaking his native tongue, for the enemy is a liar and fear is a liar.

And You did not give us a spirit of fear, but of power and of love and of self-control. So, God, the enemy has no room in our heads. And God, we pray for souls to be reconnected to You. Spirit of God, would You just fill up the believer reading this right now? And God, for anybody who hasn't trusted You yet, we pray right now that You would rescue and redeem that soul, that they would surrender to you in this very moment. And God, we pray for physical health. God, we know that through the stripes of Jesus, we will be healed. And we know that You are the great physician, but God, we are just asking of the Father in the name of Jesus that we would experience that healing on this side of eternity.

God, would You put us back together, heart, soul, mind, and strength, that Your body, Your church full of the Holy Spirit under the blood of Jesus and the love of the heavenly Father would be able to love You with all. And so, God, we pray these things in the name, the only name that matters when you pray, we pray these because of the love of the Father, the blood of Jesus, the power of the Spirit, we pray it in Jesus' name. And all God's people said, Amen.

Epilogue

I want to end with a story. A true story. Something that has happened in my life in the last few months. I'm writing it because I don't want you to think I'm just spouting theory. One more pastor with a theology degree and a platform and little life experience. While I've been writing this book, Gretchen and I have had several opportunities to cry out to God and plead for the miraculous. For God to intervene. And maybe none more so than this last story.

Gretchen and I met Ben and Carrie Williams way back in 2008. I was youth pastor at Beach United Methodist Church, and the church was growing. They helped me and our team start what was at that time the 11:22 service. After about a year, that service had outgrown the entire church. I'm not touting numbers; I'm just saying we'd outgrown our space. Ben was key to that growth. And he was key to my growth as a leader. Ben is a PK, a "pastor's kid," and he grew up in the mission field. When I met him, he was leading worship at his dad's church here in Jacksonville. We met at Panera and from the beginning, I thought, *This guy's cool. He doesn't strike me as a typical worship pastor.* (Not that typical worship pastors aren't cool, but I think you get my drift.) We had this meeting—just the two of us—that Ben likes to laugh about now. Apparently I said something to the effect of "Hey, man. I just need you to know, in a family, if Mom and Dad ain't okay, then the family ain't okay." And Ben sort of raised one eyebrow. "Are you saying I'm the mom?" And I said, "Well yeah. That's what I'm saying." So, we hired him.

Our first service rolled around and I finally thought to myself, *Oh crap. I've never heard him sing. In fact, has anybody heard him sing?* And then he sang, and I thought, *All right. At least he doesn't sound like a sissy, so that's good.*

Fast-forward. We met Carrie and the kids, and our families started hanging out. And we didn't know each other at all. I mean, at all. And we went to dinner at Buca di Beppo and did some birthday parties for our children together, and over time we became close. Like, really close. I mean family kind of close.

The original plan for the Eleven22 service was going to be a team thing. I was going to teach about 50 percent of it, and then a couple of other teaching pastors at Beach United Methodist Church would cover the other half. So I taught the first seven weeks, and it was going good. And then I was out for four weeks in a row, as we had planned. After those four weeks, Ben and Carrie, mostly Carrie, came to me and said, "You have to run this thing."

I wasn't so sure. "I don't know, man."

But they held their ground. "No, we know. You have to run this."

They also both have some pretty serious charismatic back-grounds, so the idea of God's anointed person is a big deal in their world. Contrast that with the fact that I was coming out of a youth ministry season where I had just decided, because of some of my own struggles with my own ego—because I always feel like I'm the smartest person in the room and I always feel like if you put me in charge it'll go best—I had just decided in some prayer time that I would refuse to advocate for myself in a meeting ever again. I would not push for my own advancement. I just knew it wouldn't be good for my soul. So I said, " I'm not going to bring the idea that I should be in charge," and they said, "Well, we're going to." And I said, "Okay. You do whatever you feel like you need to do." So they went to the leadership of Beach, and I don't know exactly what happened, but within fourteen days I was the pastor of the Eleven22 services. The only reason I share all that is to say that everything that's ever happened at The Church of Eleven22, especially ten-thousand-plus people who have surrendered to Christ, would not have happened without these two in my life. Fact.

The other thing is this. I was thirty-four, thirty-five, and they were either in their late twenties or barely into their thirties, and they came to me and said, "We're following you." There's not a lot of twentysomethings who'll tell a thirtysomething, "We think God has an anointing on your life and we're following you." That was crazy. Soon after, they moved into our neighborhood and we did life together. Halloween, Thanksgiving, Christmas, Easter, all the holidays. Every event. Our children do not know a world without the Williamses. We ate dinner together two or three times a week. We were just together. And then somewhere along the way, we planted what is now The Church of Eleven22. It went awesomely. I wrote in *If the Tomb Is Empty* how Ben pushed us to fast for the seven weeks leading up to Easter one year. That's when the atmosphere changed at Eleven22, and we went from running 300 to 1,500 in one weekend.

Friends is not a strong enough word to describe the bond between the Martins and the Williamses, and not just us four. And it doesn't matter what the combo is—Gretchen served under Ben's ministry for ten years, singing. Our children are tight like that. Carrie and I have the exact same personalities, so we've spent a ton of time together.

Somewhere along the way we started going to DisneyWorld together as families. And we've probably been there twenty times or something like that. And man, we have a routine, okay? I mean, we've got that thing dialed in. Those who turn their nose up to Disney as adults just don't know how to do it right. Everybody's got their mornings on their own, then we start gathering in a pool around lunch-ish. Then we go and hit a park. Gretchen's queen of the fast passes, and she and Carrie get it all worked out and plan the schedule. And then Ben and I just kinda, I don't know, fund it. So last spring, we were at one of our epic Disney trips, and it was just Disney as usual. We went to a park one day, did all the rides and stuff, and then this one particular day, we played a ton of putt-putt at this supersweet semi-golf course where you're not banging it off of clown faces. Way cool. So we played that thing and played that thing.

The following day, which was going to be kind of a lazy day, we walked around Disney Springs, ate some lunch, and went to bed. Pretty chill day.

Carrie tells me, "We were walking around and I remember feeling the nudge of the Holy Spirit so clearly, telling me, 'Hold your husband's hand and don't let go. Just stay close to him.' And I was like, 'Yes, sir. Okay.' "

About midnight, Ben made a noise. Something Carrie had never heard before. She said, "And I just run over to him and I start praying in tongues 'cause that's what I do, and I turned to Kaya and said, 'Call 911.' Then I told Taylor. 'Call Pastor Joby.' "

A few seconds later, Gretchen slapped me on the arm. We were in bed asleep. Her face was worried. Voice too. Now, Gretchen is the lightest sleeper ever. She wakes up every time I exhale. She heard her phone buzz and saw that one of the Williams kids had called us. All Gretchen said was, "Go to the Williamses' room right now. They need you."

I woke from dead sleep, threw on a shirt and some flip-flops, and my first thought was that there was an intruder. I don't know why that would be a thing at Disney, but I thought, *I'm going to fight somebody. Okay. Cowboy up.* Then I got my wits about me and asked Gretchen as I was running out the door, "What's the problem?" And Gretchen said, "Something's wrong with Ben."

So I ran down two flights of stairs, got to their room, and as I got there, paramedics were running behind me and the hotel manager was standing at the door. I turned the corner, burst through the door, and saw that blood was covering the wall, the bed—it was everywhere. Carrie, who is the toughest woman I've ever met in my life, was sort of towering over Ben, jamming her fingers into his mouth, cause he was having a seizure and she didn't want her husband to bite his tongue off. Blood was just squirting on the wall, and she was trying to stop that from happening. I ran through the door and Carrie had enough wits about her to say, "Get the girls." So I pulled them into the hallway, the paramedics moved in, and I took the girls to the stairwell where we sat and just prayed. It was all I knew to do. We prayed.

Months later, Carrie would remember, "I was trying to jam my thumb into his mouth. So much blood. Hardest moment. Worst thing I've ever gone through in my whole life. By far. To this day, if he makes a noise in his sleep...I can't."

Back in the stairwell, I was sitting with the Williams girls. Just huddled. I'd known them since they were born. They were crying, my heart hurt as if they were my own, and so we just prayed. The paramedics asked ten thousand questions, and in the background I could hear Carrie talking to Ben, and Ben was kinda making these groaning noises. Carrie was in fight mode. Talking to the paramedics: "This is what we're gonna do. You're gonna take him to the hospital." She looked at me and she said, "Can you take the girls?" I said, "I got 'em." She nodded. "I'm going with him and I'll call you. I'll be in touch." Carrie was at war. They wheeled Ben out and Ben looked at me, dead in my eyes, but he couldn't talk. He just made a noise like Chewbacca. He looked scared. And that look made me scared.

And then they disappeared into the elevator. We brought the girls into our rooms and nobody slept.

The next morning we got on the phone with Carrie and learned that Ben was having tests to see what happened. Everybody was thinking he was dehydrated. Too much sun. He never eats enough anyway, and doesn't eat real food, so maybe his sugar was off or maybe he didn't drink enough water. We were searching for something to do, anything to feel like we were helping, so we leased a house for a month just in case we had to be there with him. Just anything. But we have service on Thursday night at our church and I was supposed to preach. I don't know how, but we got in the car, and started driving from Orlando to Jacksonville with my kids in the back, when the phone rang. It was Carrie. "It's devastating. This is a nightmare. It's the worst thing I've ever heard in my life." We asked, "What's up? What did the doctors say?" She said, "The doctor says he has a brain tumor and it's cancerous. Category four. He's got three years, maybe eighteen good months. And they are scheduling surgery for tomorrow, right here, in Orlando."

Meanwhile, Ben had returned. Putting the pieces together. He was hearing this. He turned to Carrie and said, "I wanna walk my girls down the aisle."

All of us in the car burst into tears and I was just trying to talk to my friend. Carrie is one of my best friends. I mean, I love this girl so much. Like a sister. And I said, "Well, wait. Hold on." She was choking through the words. "Joby, I need your help. You're the best leader I know. I need your help." I'm crying even now as I write about it.

I would not be in a position of leadership if she hadn't pushed me there. All I could say was, "We got you. I'll call you right back." So we hung up the phone, and one of the good things about being a pastor of a real big church is that although I own nothing, I have access to everything and everybody in Jacksonville. So we started calling all the influencers in Jacksonville and said, "Hey, this is what's happening and this is real time, and what do we do?" Carrie and I got back on the phone together, and we all agree we don't want to do this in Orlando because this could be a long road. Also, we have the Mayo Clinic in Jacksonville, and what an incredible gift that God has given Jacksonville to have the Mayo in town. So, if we could figure out how to do this in town, then all of the follow-up would mean a five-minute drive, not a two-and-a-half-hour drive. It just made life simpler, not to mention that Mayo health care is world-class.

The doctors in Orlando were great to transfer Ben to Mayo in Jacksonville. I showed up to church and I had to preach. And you should know this about Ben—Ben taught me everything I know about worship. I thought worship was merely the three songs you sing before the preaching. Ben changed that. He said, "Look, dude. You're the lead pastor. You are the primary worship leader at our church. Not me. I have the guitar, I have the voice, I have the talent, but you, whatever you do, that's where we go. So, if at any time during my part of the service, if you need to direct us in a way, then you just walk up and I'll move and you do that and then when you get done, I'll just drift back in."

This was a foreign concept to me. "Hold on, man. I've never even heard of this." He taught me all of that. So that Thursday night, obviously he wasn't leading worship; one of our other guys was, and I just told him, "Hey man, at the end of the singing, I need to talk. Before the sermon." So I just got up in front of our church and I said, "Church, we got to pray." It wasn't pretty. This was one of the best friends I've ever had in my whole life, ever. I walked up there and all I could think was *Eighteen months*. The doctor had said, "Eighteen good ones, and then eighteen bad ones, and then it's over." We were talking about Ben. I cannot count the number of times he has strapped on his guitar, opened his mouth, and led me into the worship of the King. And here we were without him.

I stepped up on our stage and tried to speak. "Church, we got to pray. I mean, like for-real pray." And so I choked through it. We've got a praying church and a church that loves some Ben Williams. So we did. The worship team just sang some other stuff, and probably about 80 percent of the room came down to the front of the altar and we just prayed for healing. The entire front of the church was crowded with circles of ten, fifteen people, most didn't know one another, and they were banging on the floor of heaven. It was loud. Ben had led every one of these people in worship over the years, and their hearts hurt too. It was just one of those moments in the life of our church. It was a thing.

So they drugged Ben to get him home, drove him to Jacksonville, and met with the Mayo doctors, who told them they wanted to run some more tests. Get more scans. Do some doctor stuff, then schedule surgery. The Mayo docs didn't seem as hurried as the Orlando docs.

When the scans returned, the doctor looked at everything and said, "Looks like a category two. We can operate. Looks promising." Then he walked us through what a category two is; it's the best possible scenario for an adult. And a completely different report than what we got in the middle of the night from the doctor in Orlando.

I drove to Ben's house on Saturday and we watched the Ryder Cup. Surreal. On the day of his surgery, we all showed up at Mayo. Including all the elders of our church. But COVID is a problem. We couldn't go in, so they brought him to us. We were about to pray over him when this couple shuffled up and the wife gave me that I-think-you're-my-pastor look. It was also the opening day of turkey season, so I was decked out in camo because I was going to the woods after we prayed. We prayed for Ben and then this couple walked up, and the wife explained that her husband was having the same surgery that Ben was having at Mayo. The same doctors were doing the surgery. He was actually the one following Ben's surgery. So we prayed for them also. Afterward, I texted Carrie, "Hey, there's an Eleven22 wife who's gonna be in your waiting room." I also texted a bunch of doctors I knew at Mayo just to go check on Carrie.

Carrie later said, "I was in fight mode. This is my best friend. Not just my husband. He's my best friend in the whole world. So I was ready to burn a hole in the carpet, pacing and praying. And then this sweet couple came in and I was like, 'This is how we're gonna do this, God? Really? Okay.' It was hard. If I'm honest, I just wanted to be alone and just pray and this sweet woman came walking in. I could see it on her face, and I was like, 'Have a seat.' And she began to tell me her story. She was bawling: 'This is the second time they've found a tumor, and the first time we were at a small church and we were friends with the pastor. And you know, kinda the whole church came out for the surgery and I was with them. Now we're at Church of Eleven22, and we don't really know anyone. We definitely don't know the pastor. I knew there was no way to get the pastor to pray for my husband this morning. And we walked up and there he was, with the elders. And they prayed for us.' She was bawling and I was thinking, *Okay, God. All right.* Interestingly, this couple shared the same last name with Carrie and Ben. They were Rebecca and James Williams.

"So James went in after Ben and sat in the waiting room," said Carrie. "And whenever I felt like she needed anything, we'd do it together. And when anybody came in from the church to find me and pray for me, I'd say, 'Can I please introduce you to my friend, Rebecca? She's part of our church family.' And we'd pray for her and James."

Before Ben went into surgery, he sent me this text: "Thanks, Joby, for everything. I know God will get me through this, but if I go home to be with Him, will you promise to help Carrie and the girls through it all? I just need someone who will lead, and you're the best one I know."

How do you respond to that? He's one of my best friends on the planet. I texted back, "I got you, bro. I got your family. You're gonna be fine. That's what I'm praying."

"I know. I'm just covering my bases." Then he said, "With the life insurance, help my girls if the worst happens."

It was getting real now. I said, "Hey, man. We've got it all figured out here. Your family will be whole, no matter what."

"Thanks, bro. See you tomorrow." And then I said, "I'll be forever indebted to you, brother."

If you could see me right then...I was a mess.

So Ben had his surgery. And what was crazy was they woke him up—during surgery—and asked him questions like, "What color is this? How many fingers? What's your favorite song? Can you move your left hand?" Then they cut out a piece of tumor and asked, "Can you still move that finger?" Crazy stuff. While this was happening, Carrie was giving us the play-by-play, which she was getting from the doctor, like, "He's doing great." In the meantime, Carrie was sitting next to this woman we'd just prayed for, who knew no one. She was as alone as alone gets. And yet, her pain mattered to the Lord, so that when she showed up for surgery the elders of her church were standing there, and the toughest warrior woman I've ever met sat with her through surgery. That's the God I worship.

Years prior, Ben had written a song based on the prayer of Saint Patrick. It's become an anthem for our church body. Oddly enough, his surgery was on March 17, Saint Patrick's Day. So, Carrie was circling the waiting room listening to her husband lead her in worship via iTunes. Worshiping her face off. "Ben's voice, that song, 'God Above,' is my lifeline to the Lord while I was waiting to hear how surgery went," she said.

God above me God below
You're beside me never letting go

And if I stumble if I fall
Your love is with me through it all

Ben came out of surgery, and the doctor told Carrie, "I think we got it."

"What do you mean, 'You got it'?"

"I think we got it all. We're gonna need to do some preventative chemo and radiation, but we don't see any bit of it remaining. I really think we got it."

In Orlando, the doctors said, "You have three years."

In Jacksonville, the doctors said, "I think we got it."

The only thing to happen between those two statements was that our church prayed our faces off. I mean, we have never prayed like that. Ben is one of the founding pastors of our church and he matters to the folks at Eleven22, and when I asked them to pray, they emptied their chairs.

Six months later, we were at a deacon commissioning. About eighty-five deacons. We take this stuff seriously. *Deacon* is a word in the Bible. It's an office in the Bible. You don't just throw these things around haphazardly, and we're trying to be a biblically sound, New Testament church. So we were commissioning these deacons. To start the service, we did a worship set, and Ben Williams walked out onstage to lead worship. And everybody was in awe, because of what they had heard. They heard three years with eighteen good months, and now the man was leading worship. His voice bounding off the rafters. First song out of his mouth, and he started singing about the goodness of God, and everybody's half singing. And Ben did the thing that he'd been doing with me for twelve years now. He stopped and rebuked the crowd: "What are y'all doing? Are y'all not paying attention to what we're singing? We're singing about the goodness of God, so if you know He's good, you ought to sing like it."

And then the roof came off the place, man.

When Peter and John were arrested for preaching in the name of Jesus in Acts 4, they were dragged before the religious rulers. Signs and wonders were occurring left and right. The unexplainable had intersected the undeniable. And the only explanation was Jesus. The rulers told them they couldn't preach anymore in that name. Peter responded with, *How can we but speak about what we've seen and heard?* (Acts 4:20). The Joby translation is this—"Bro, kill me if you like, but you do you, I'ma do me." I'm also reminded of John 6, when many people who had been following Jesus left and no longer followed Him. Jesus turned to His disciples and asked, *"Do you want to leave, too?"* Peter responded, *"Where would we go? You have the words of eternal life"* (John 6:67–68).

I don't know how we got from "three years to live" to "we got it all." Same head. One set of scans taken in Orlando. The second set in Jacksonville. The only thing that happened between those two Kodak moments is that we prayed. A lot. Could the first doctors have misdiagnosed it? Sure, but I don't think so. I think they were right given what they had. Then we prayed, God did a thing, and now standing on this side of it, Ben is cancer free. Not a trace. He leads worship a lot. And Carrie is still a warrior.

Looking back over what I've written, from Mimi, to Dr. Asher, to Ike, to Brad, to Ben, I realize we have known and do know suffering and pain. And I don't always understand why God does what He does when He does it, but if I could understand Him and His ways then He wouldn't be God because He could fit inside my fuzzy little head, and the created can't fully understand the creator. It's just not going to happen.

In all of this, we face a choice. Trust Him or not. Bow or bend. Our circumstances do not dictate His goodness. He's Good. Period. This entire book can be boiled down to one question—Do we trust in Him? *Pisteuō* in Him, or not? That's our choice.

I'm a pastor. A shepherd. I care about those God puts under my care. As much as I know my own heart, I hurt when others are hurting, and I want to encourage them and you. I don't know how the next thing will turn out, but on this side, I will trust Him. That is my choice and this is my decision. Where else would we go? He has the words of eternal life. And I won't bend to my enemy. But I will bow to my King.

As for Rebecca and James—get a load of this. As I was literally writing this page, wondering about how they were doing, a text comes in. And no, I didn't make this up. This really just happened. "Hey Joby! It's been a while since we've talked but wanted to update you on James. He finished his last round of chemotherapy last month ending a 6-month chemo schedule. Praise Jesus he tolerated it well and didn't have any serious side effects. We go into mayo today for a brain scan so please pray that they will not see any new tumor growth. We hope you have had a restful sabbatical and family time. We are so appreciative of you, your leadership, and guidance and commitment to the Lord. I'll update you as soon as I get results. Take care! Rebecca Williams"

I thought I'd leave you with some words from Carrie because I think they're worth hearing and I think she's earned the right to speak them: "The worst thing I've ever been through in my life was Ben's seizure. I've seen people have seizures, watched people die. This was the worst. But without the seizure, who knows where we'd be. While it was the worst thing for me, the seizure was probably the best thing for him. Without the seizure they never would have scanned his brain and found the tumor. That led to the surgery that led to his healing. Today, he's here. Doing amazing. And this is what I know—God is who He says He is. I had so many people ask me all kinds of—you know, people ask some weird stuff in the middle of crisis. And I mean, all I could keep saying was, 'Either God is who He says He is or He's not. Period. I believe.' "

* * *

So here we are. Pretty much back where we started. Jerusalem. The empty tomb. So, let's take one more look. Circle the parking lot. Walk around the buses. And walk with me back through the garden. It's quiet in here. Watch out for that hole. That's where they would crush the grapes. This groove is where they would have rolled the stone. And that rusty thing is the remains of the spike that "sealed" the tomb. Step up. Watch your head. Duck slightly. Cross the threshold. Okay, let your eyes adjust. Over there on the left is where the mourners would sit. That was where I prayed with the Nigerian pastor. And over there, on the right, on that shelf cut in the rock that sort of looks like a bed, or cot, that's where they would have laid Him. Go ahead. You can step closer. As you can see, He's not there. And hasn't been for two thousand years. He is risen. So, why would we seek the living among the dead? Because the fact that He's not lying over there in a pile of bones and dust is still the greatest miracle in the history of miracles.

Church, God is who He says He is, or He's not. Let's choose. I'm praying like crazy that you believe, that you *pisteuō* in Him. I know it's hard. And I know you have an enemy who's working really hard to fill you with doubt and fear. But do you really want to live under that tyranny? At the end of the day, do you want to doubt your doubts, or doubt your beliefs? I want to silence the doubts and believe my beliefs. We have a King who is right this second seated on the throne, at the right hand of God the Father, interceding for us. Twenty-four seven. And our undefeated King is no wimp. He defeated death and the grave and paid a debt for our sin that you and I could not pay in ten thousand lifetimes. He did so because He loves us with an indescribable kind of love, and He wants to return us to His and our Father. He is more powerful than anything we can imagine and, though it sounds like Sunday school, He's still got the whole world in His hands. Including you and me. And not only that, but He has sent His very Spirit to help us. To fill us. Live inside us. Empower us.

Church, our King is coming back. Maybe sooner rather than later. This begs the question: How will He find you when He does? Doubting? Or believing? Between here and His return, He has commanded us to ask and to pray. So we will. We will do whatever He tells us to do. And that includes praying for the miraculous. The unexplainable. And the undeniable. Jesus is not a genie, and He doesn't have a magic wand, but He is seated at the right hand of God. He has His ear. And you have His heart. He loves you more than you can fathom. There is no greater power and no greater love, so ask. Just ask.

In the prologue I told you that when someone came to Jesus asking for a miracle, three things were routinely needed: belief, hope, and faith. But, in most cases, they had very little. Like, trace amounts. And notice Jesus never used his X-ray vision to size up their quantity and then send them back until they could muster some minimum threshold on the belief-o-meter. Paul told the Philippians, "For it is God who works in you, both to will and to work for His good pleasure" (Phil. 2:13). If you let that sink in, it'll take the pressure off. "God works in us." With that in mind, I'm praying that you—through the power of the Holy Spirit—believe in, hope that, and have faith for. These three are the stuff that brings people like us pleading to the feet of Jesus.

*   *   *

It is entirely possible that the miracle you're praying for is waiting just on the other side of that small step of faith. Of obedience. Between now and then, I pray you and I live our lives believing in the risen Christ, doing what He tells us to do, and remembering that God raised Him to life and seated Him at His right hand—leaving an empty tomb.

The empty tomb changes everything about everything for everyone who would believe it. Why? Let me remind you of the words of Jesus: "All things are possible for one who believes" (Mark 9:23).

Pray with Me

Our good and gracious heavenly Father, we love You because You have first loved us. God, I thank You that You are still in the miracle business. God, I thank You and praise You that there is no expiration date or term limit on Your wonder-working power. May we never take our eyes off the ultimate miracle, that Jesus walked out of that tomb on the third day and that He is alive and well today. And that whoever would believe in Him would not perish but would have everlasting life. Lord, never allow us to be more focused on the miracle that we need than on You, the miracle worker. Because all that we really need is You. God, I pray for the man or woman who is struggling right now with some set of circumstances that is seemingly out of control. For the person who has lost sight of You because of the size of the mountain that they are confronting. God, I pray that You would give them faith. Faith that You can move mountains. God, I ask that they would cast all their cares upon You because You care for them. I ask that You would give them the words to pray and ask for what they need. I ask that You would guard their hearts and minds in Christ Jesus. I ask that even before circumstances begin to change that hearts would begin to change. God, would You please grant a peace that transcends understanding? And Father, would You answer these prayers? Would You move mountains? Would You heal broken relationships? Would You break chains of addictions that have been there for years? Would You restore families that have been torn apart? Would You heal bodies of sickness and disease? Would You breathe new life into marriages that appear to be lifeless? Would You replace depression and anxiety with hope and joy? Would You bring home prodigal sons and daughters?

Would You restore what the locusts have eaten in the financial lives of your children? Would You save the lost? And God, would You do all of this that others may know that You are the one true God? I thank You for miracles. I thank You that Your super meets our natural and changes everything. I thank You for the greatest miracle of all time. That a holy and perfect and loving God put on flesh and came on a rescue mission for His rebellious children. Father, I thank You for Your Son Jesus Christ, who lived the perfect life, who fulfilled every promise, prophecy, and precept contained in Your word. I thank You that for the joy set before Him, He willingly endured the cross. I thank You that He not only died for us but that He died instead of us. God, I thank You that by the power of the Holy Spirit You breathed new life into His body and brought Him out of the grave. I thank You that the same power that raised Christ dwells in every believer. And because of the miracle of the resurrection we can believe that anything is possible. Lord, I praise that because Jesus put death to death and walked out of that tomb that we too can walk in a manner worthy of the gospel of Jesus. Lord, I thank You for the only eternal miracle available to us today. The miracle of salvation. I thank You that the miracle of salvation is for anyone who would surrender to Jesus. God, I praise You that though You still hear prayers and do miracles and change circumstances, You are greater than all our temporary situations. God, may You never allow us to be a people that seeks the miracle over the giver of the miracle. You are better than life. Now, Father, would You make us aware of the Spirit in us that we may be a generation that fulfills what Jesus said and do even greater works than He did? May we take the gospel to the ends of the earth. May we push back darkness. May we bring Your justice to a crooked and dark world. May we love one another as Christ has loved us. And may we be a people that trust You no matter our circumstances because we know that You have demonstrated Your love for us on the cross. I pray that You orient our hearts to know that because the tomb is empty, You are worthy of all our praise, and all our gratitude, and all our lives. I pray this in the good, strong name of Jesus Christ, our Lord and Savior. And because of Him *we can know that anything is possible for the one who believes. Amen.*

About the Authors

Joby Martin is the founder and lead pastor of The Church of Eleven22 in Jacksonville, Florida. Since launching the church in 2012, he has led a movement for all people to discover and deepen a relationship with Jesus Christ. In addition to providing The Church of Eleven22 with vision and leadership, Pastor Joby is an author and a national and international preacher and teacher. He has been married to his wife, Gretchen, for over twenty years; they have a son, JP, and a daughter, Reagan.

Charles Martin is a *New York Times* bestselling author of seventeen novels, including his most recent, *The Record Keeper.* He has also recently authored three nonfiction works, *What If It's True?, They Turned the World Upside Down,* and *Son of Man.* His work has been translated into more than thirty-five languages.